Sappho to Valéry

Other Books by John Frederick Nims

The Iron Pastoral, 1947
A Fountain in Kentucky, 1950
Knowledge of the Evening, 1960
Of Flesh and Bone, 1967
Selected Poems, 1982
The Kiss: A Jambalaya, 1982
Western Wind: An Introduction to Poetry, 1974, 1983
A Local Habitation: Essays on Poetry, 1985
Translator: *The Poems of St. John of the Cross*, 1959, rev. 1968, 1979
Editor: *Ovid's Metamorphoses.* The Arthur Golding Translation, 1968
Editor: *The Harper Anthology of Poetry*, 1981

Poems in Translation

Sappho to Valéry

John Frederick Nims

Revised and Enlarged Edition

The University of Arkansas Press

Fayetteville   1990   London

Copyright © 1990 by John Frederick Nims

All rights reserved
Manufactured in the United States of America
94 93 92 91 90 5 4 3 2 1

Designer: Chang-hee H. Russell
Typeface: Linotron 202 Times Roman with Zapf Chancery
Typesetter: G & S Typesetters, Inc.
Printer: Braun-Brumfield, Inc.
Binder: Braun-Brumfield, Inc.

The paper used in this publication meets the minimum requirements of the American National Standard for Permanence of Paper for Printed Library Materials Z39.48-1984. ⊗

Library of Congress Cataloging-in-Publication Data

Sappho to Valéry : poems in translation / [compiled] by John Frederick Nims.
    p. cm.
  ISBN 1-55728-141-6 (alk. paper)
  1. Poetry—Collections. I. Nims, John Frederick, 1913– .
PN6099.S34 1990
808.81—dc20   89-38953
                                                      CIP

Originally published 1971 by Rutgers University Press
Princeton University Press Paperback Edition, 1980

For Dudley Fitts
and Robert Fitzgerald
in
grateful and affectionate
memory

Acknowledgments

No man is an island, the translator least of all. I cannot properly thank everyone who has helped me with these ventures. So many people in so many countries over so many years: the person on a train near Granada who used an expression that threw light on a line in García Lorca; the Greek shopkeeper who said something that made a phrase of Sappho come alive. Many I never knew; many I am forgetting. But there are these at least to mention:

For help with Valéry: Ana Maria Brull de Vázquez (whose father Mariano Brull was a friend and himself a translator of Valéry); W. M. Frohock and Jackson Mathews; Allen Tate for choosing among some of my semifinal variants; Andrew Lytle for first publishing the poem. Whatever I know about French poetry owes much to the lectures of W. A. Nitze and Étiemble years ago.

With Ausiàs March: Mercedes Terraza of Barcelona for reading through all of the poems with me; Pere Bohigas (who has done the excellent five-volume edition of March for the "Els Nostrés Clàssics" series) for encouragement and help generously given in person and by letter. It was Gerald Brenan who first brought March to my attention, and whom I must thank too for Rosalía de Castro and Antonio Machado.

With San Juan de la Cruz: again Gerald Brenan. And also Robert Graves, to whose suggestions I am indebted for about a dozen improvements in the English text of "The Spiritual Canticle."

With Goethe: Henry Hatfield for pointing me many years ago toward certain lyrics of Goethe, and Sophie Charlotte Lang Brancaforte of Munich and Urbana for slogging patiently with me through the Rilke I did not translate and

vii

the Goethe I did (while her husband Benito was helpful with Italian and Spanish poetry); Robie Macauley for encouraging my first Goethe translations; Frederick Morgan and John Simon of *The Hudson Review* for encouraging a further audacity: my attempt on what I take to be Goethe's greatest lyric, the "Trilogie der Leidenschaft." I am grateful to Christopher Middleton for suggesting how I might revise some lines when he included the poem, with others, in his *Goethe: Selected Poems.*

With Rosalía de Castro: Maria Carmen Piñeiro de Penasa, herself a Galician poet and native of Rosalía's region.

With modern Spanish poetry: Amado Alonso and many others in Spain, including several friends of García Lorca. I am indebted, too, for everything that concerns Spanish poetry, to the hospitality and knowledge of Dámaso Alonso (who has written the best book on San Juan de la Cruz).

With modern Italian poetry: Aldo Celli of Florence, who in helping me with Dante helped me with all later poetry; Giuseppe Ungaretti and Eugenio Montale for the encouragement of their letters and the meetings that were, alas, too few.

With contemporary Mexican poetry: Jaime Graham-Lujan for his insight into all the poems; Octavio Paz—who is so at ease in English that he could have done his own translations—for his letters that clarified the Spanish text of "Solo a dos voces" and improved the English.

With Greek and Latin poetry: all I know about classical verse owes much to the generosity and learning of Gertrude Smith, who read through all of the Greek tragedies with me at the University of Chicago. I have been continuously grateful, in this field and elsewhere, for the friendship and example of Dudley Fitts and Robert Fitzgerald.

With problems of translation in general: Stanley Burnshaw, whose *The Poem Itself* was in many ways a revelation that gave me the opportunity of researching several of the poems I have here translated; and Harry Levin, both for his writings on translation and for making it possible for me to give a Workshop in the Translation of Poetry for the Department of Comparative Literature at Harvard in 1968–69.

I am grateful to the Fulbright and Smith-Mundt Commissions for the teaching grants that enabled me to spend two years in Italy and later two years in Spain; to the American Council of Learned Societies for a summer grant to work on Catalan poetry, to the National Foundation on the Arts and Humanities for a sabbatical grant for the year during which many of these versions were written, and to the universities that cooperated by making it possible for me to avail myself of these various grants—particularly to the University of Illinois at Urbana and Chicago.

Finally a word of thanks to my favorite translators, William Sloane and Helen Stewart, who for almost twenty-five years translated manuscripts of mine into a language they knew so well: the language of handsome and well-produced volumes. And now I am grateful to Miller Williams, himself one of our finest translators of poetry, for bringing this book of translations back to life.

Some of the translations in this volume have appeared in the following magazines or books. The author and publisher are grateful for permission to reprint them.

Agenda: "The resolute desire that enters" (Arnaut Daniel).

The American Scholar: "I was born at birth of blossoms" (Rosalía de Castro).

Arion: "Odes, I, ix" (Horace).

The Atlantic: "Here," "Pause," "Girl" (Octavio Paz); "Smoke" (Rubén Bonifaz Nuño); "Hecuba's Testament" (Rosario Castellanos); "The Rain Is Falling" ("The Month of June") (Homero Aridjis).

Counter/Measures: "Preciosa and the Wind," "Sleepwalkers' Ballad," "Ballad of Black Grief" (García Lorca); "On your throne, a marvel of art . . ." (Sappho); "I'm the way I am" (Prévert).

Delos: A Journal of Translation: "Poetry: Lost in Translation?"

Delos: "Attis" (Catullus).

The Denver Quarterly: "Parables, I" (Machado).

Evergreen Review: "The Unfaithful Wife" (García Lorca).

Florida Quarterly: "Inventory" (Prévert).

Kentucky Poetry Review: "To waning day, to the wide round of shadow" (Dante).

Mundus Artium: "Epitaph for a Poet" (Aridjis).

Poetry: "Not so with me . . ." (March); "Portrait," *"From Proverbs and Songs, XV"* (Machado); "To Charlotte von Stein," "Song of the Traveler at Evening," "Mignon," "Anacreon's Grave," "Permanence in Change," "Death of a Fly" (Goethe).

Quarterly Review of Literature: "The Eel" (Montale).

Saturday Review: "Men, a word of wisdom . . ." (Bernart de Ventadorn); "Sonnet Right off the Bat" (Lope de Vega).

Sewanee Review: "The Graveyard by the Sea" (Valéry); "Leaving Crete, come visit again . . . ," "There's a man, I really believe . . . ," (Sappho).

Tri-Quarterly (a publication of Northwestern University): "Some for the horsemen . . ." (Sappho).

Virginia Quarterly Review: "When—presto—turf and trees . . . ," "To see the lark . . ." (Bernart de Ventadorn).

Contents

XV

xvi

xvii

Sappho to Valéry
Poems in Translation

Poetry:
Lost in Translation?

Poetry, thought Robert Frost, is what is lost in translation. But surely not so lost as poetry in a language we will never understand? Not quite so lost that there are no techniques of retrieval? It seems to me there are some, and that is the adventure of this volume: a treasure hunt for lost poetry.

I have written these for pleasure. Renato Poggioli, who did an eloquent Italian version of "Le cimetière marin," has analyzed the psychological motives that lead one to translate. Perhaps the translator should not be too aware of his motives; this may be one of the pleasures frustrated by self-consciousness. I am not sure that the enjoyment I had in doing these translations is very different from that of writing "one's own" poetry.

One should translate only poems he cares very much for; poems he has been living with, more often than not, for many years. He translates partly out of dissatisfaction with the versions he has seen—not out of the certainty that he can do them better, but out of a feeling he can at least do them differently, circling in, perhaps, from yet another direction. Thirty years or so of work, off and on, with the lyrics of St. John of the Cross began when, picking up one translation in a bookstore, I saw "En una noche obscura ..." and across from it "Upon a gloomy night . . ." Something, I felt, had to be done about this. We rarely say, in natural English, "Upon a night . . ." (It is *on* a night like this that one wouldn't send a dog out.) *Upon* here is stilted or literary; St. John's poetry is neither. I knew enough too about his passion to realize that whatever kind of darkness his *noche obscura* was, it was not what *gloomy* connotes in English.

Dissatisfaction with existing translations, when there were any, was something I felt more poignantly in the classroom. Such and such a poet, I might find

I

myself saying, wrote sharply, colloquially; his lyrics were simple, sensuous, passionate, as in the poem on the page before us—but the class would already be looking at the page with deepening skepticism. Colloquial? simple? this unnatural word order, these expressions archaic centuries ago? And the limp rhythms? Or no rhythm at all?

Denver Lindley speaks for many of us when he says: "Communication—that is the purpose and the delight of translation. 'This is something I admire so much,' says the translator, 'something I find so profound, so beautiful, so piercing that I must make you understand and admire it too, even though you, through some inadvertence, have neglected to learn the language in which it is written. Let me show you how it goes.'" (A-S 244)*

Let me show you how it goes, I imagine myself saying to the reader curious about Provençal—which he has no intention of learning. He only knows that during the twelfth century some great poetry, it is said, was written in Provence; he would be interested in knowing what it was like. Not just what it said—what it was like. Or he may have heard that Goethe is perhaps the supreme lyrical genius of Europe, and he cannot see why—he has looked at some "plain prose translations of the poetry," at some versions in arthritic verse. Both have left him puzzled: there seems no greatness here. Or he has learned, perhaps from Gerald Brenan's history, that in the fifteenth century there was a poet curiously modern, curiously like Baudelaire. But almost unknown—because he wrote in Catalan. Or that there was a woman in Galicia in the last century (her dates almost the same as Emily Dickinson's) whom some think the greatest woman poet of modern times. But almost unknown—because she wrote in Galician.

If I am to show this reader how the poem goes, I have to show him first of all a poem. The greatest infidelity is to pass off a bad poem in English as representing a good one in another language.

Poets and critics have always been fascinated by the problem of translating poetry, which, they agree, has to be translated—and yet cannot really be translated at all. In our time so much has been written, and written sensibly, about the paradox that we hardly need another discussion of this sort. There are sixteen essays and a bibliography, often with summary, of some two hundred and sixty works from 46 B.C. to 1958 in Reuben A. Brower's *On Translation* (Harvard, 1959; A Galaxy Book, 1966). There are sixteen more in the Arrowsmith-Shattuck collection.* There is George Steiner's Introduction to his *Penguin Book of Modern Verse Translation* (1966); there are Jackson Mathews' studies on Valéry. There are incidental remarks by nearly all of our most distinguished

* William Arrowsmith and Roger Shattuck, *The Craft and Content of Translation.* Anchor Books, 1964.

poets, for those who have translated nothing are few and far between. In the essays of Harry Levin and others there are brilliant asides, and sometimes more, on the translation of poetry: a few pages of Professor Levin's comparative stylistics on how Shakespeare's untranslatability has been translated bring the whole problem into clearer focus ("Shakespeare in the Light of Comparative Literature," *Refractions*. Oxford, 1962).*

When we study a foreign language we work with exercises which—yes—can be translated. They used to consist of sentences like "Have you two round oranges, or is this the umbrella of your grandmother?" (I know of one girl who, coming across such a sentence, dropped her study of the language because she lost so much time trying to imagine just when she might ask *that*.) Absurd as such fancies are, they can be put into another language, probably with little loss of sense. But what is the translator to do with the second of these lines from *Hamlet?*—in which the prince, picking up the cloud imagery from the line before, plays on the words *sun* and *son:* he is sad because of something in his relationship as son.

> *King:* How is it that the clouds still hang on you?
> *Hamlet:* Not so, my lord. I am too much i' the sun.

Here the translator needs a word, one common word, that means both a male offspring and the star that is the central body in our solar system. Chances are that in no language but English does such a word exist. The Italian will look helplessly from *figlio* to *sole*, the Spaniard from *hijo* to *sol*, the German from *der Sohn* to *die Sonne*, which is closer but, especially with the problem of gender, not close enough. The simple word *sun* is untranslatable here.

Or suppose he wants to show Macbeth pondering on his bloodstained hand:

> Will all great Neptune's ocean wash this blood
> Clean from my hand? No, this my hand will rather
> The multitudinous seas incarnadine,
> Making the green, one red.

Not even the plainest of prose translators will hold that this really says the same thing as "What it's going to do is kind of redden the oceans, of which there are many and quite big ones too." Poetry is lost in translation for the same reason that it is lost in paraphrase. In Macbeth's speech the poetry is in such things as the size and sound of *multitudinous* and the way it surges with and against the

*More recent books on translation include George Steiner, *After Babel* (1975), Marilyn Gaddis Rose, ed., *Translation in the Humanities* (1977), and *World of Translation, Papers Delivered at the Conference on Literary Translation* (1970), sponsored by P.E.N. American Center.

There are some fine essays on the translation of poetry in Yves Bonnefoy's *The Act and the Place of Poetry*, University of Chicago Press, 1989.

meter; in the ghost-words that haunt *incarnadine* (carnage, etc.); in the change from the sonorous Latinate words to the simple native ones in the last line. When Macbeth says:

> Duncan is in his grave;
> After life's fitful fever he sleeps well . . .

the poetry is not so much in the idea as in the satiety of the four *f*'s, a too-muchness in the mouth as life itself has come to seem a too-muchness, and in the dreary continuity of the three long *e*'s. The problem is to carry such effects from language to language by some *u*tensil of translation—all leaky pails indeed for such an errand.

It should be unnecessary to remind ourselves yet again that poetry is less a matter of *what* is said than of *how* it is said. The *how* of course can be so powerful that we confuse it with the *what;* it is easy to imagine, in reading Shakespeare, that we are being moved by *what* he is saying. Yet try changing the words, sometimes just a word, and even the *what* seems to vanish. Harry Levin's "The War of Words in English Poetry" (*Contexts of Criticism.* Harvard, 1957), deals specifically with those lexical auras most resistant to translation. I mean to stress below the translator's obligation to sound as well as to sense: Professor Levin has the gist of the matter in his "in practice the sense often seems to echo the sound."

In Paul Valéry's "last testament on poetics" (the reflections he wrote on his version of the *Eclogues* of Virgil), this most analytic of poets is still saying what he had been saying most of his life: "Thought is only an accessory of poetry . . . the chief thing is the *whole,* the power resulting from effects compounded of all the attributes of language. . . ." (DF 306)* attributes which in an earlier essay he had called "the sound, the rhythm, the physical proximity of words . . . their mutual influences. . . ." (DF 157) Thought is only an accessory, and an accessory which the poet may sacrifice to some advantage of the sound: "An intimate alliance of sound and sense, which is the essential characteristic of poetic expression, can be obtained only at the expense of something—that is, thought." (DF 219) If as translator I had need of an *impresa,* it might well be Valéry's "fidelity to meaning alone is a kind of betrayal." (DF 298) One thinks of Emily Dickinson's

> More genuine were Perfidy
> Than such Fidelity.

*Quotations from the prose of Valéry are mostly in the words of Denise Folliot (Paul Valéry, *The Art of Poetry.* Bollingen Series, Princeton University Press, 1958. A book I would highly recommend to translators of poetry).

We can amplify this with a chorus of assent from those who have worked with the problem. Professor Arrowsmith puts it even more strongly: "There are times . . . when the worst possible treachery is the simple-minded faith in 'accuracy' and literal loyalty to the original." (A-S 118) Professor Carne-Ross believes that "a great deal of local distortion, of amplification and even excision, may be necessary if the translator is to follow the curve of his original faithfully." (A-S 8) And Professor Poggioli: "After all, in every artistic pursuit beauty is the highest kind of fidelity, and ugliness is only another name for disloyalty. . . ." (RB 143)* The kind of translation in which the poetry is lost, we might say, is the kind concerned only with meaning or message.

At times the treason of a plain prose translation serves a purpose, especially when the reader who knows something of the other language wants a guide to the thought alone, with the help of which he means to return to the poem itself and retrieve what was lost in form, in sound, in rhythm. This is not the purpose I have in mind; I am trying to show, to readers who may never look at the original, what I think they would find the poem like if they did.

At the opposite end of the spectrum from the plain prose translation is what Dryden, and in our time Robert Lowell, refer to as "imitations," in which the poet does start from an original but writes his own poem on the basis of it, with more regard for the promptings of his own talent than for the intention and tone of the foreign poet. When the talent is as powerful as Mr. Lowell's, remarkable productions may result. Although they show us a great deal of the virtue of the imitator (if one who least imitates can be called an imitator), there may be some disadvantage in the fact that they tell us little about the quality of the original: translations in which the voices of the world's great poets all speak with a single voice, translations in which Sappho and Rilke sound alike, may not satisfy all the possibilities of translation. If the translator is "himself a poet," there will always be a clash of personalities, with the personality of the translator tending to take over. Imitations—which Dryden thinks "the most advantageous way for a translator to show himself, but the greatest wrong which can be done to the memory and reputation of the dead"**—may be brilliant and engaging; they are not what I think I have in mind.

What is, again? To write poems that will show, to some degree, what certain poems in another language are *like*. One cannot translate a poem, but one can try to reconstitute it by taking the thought, the imagery, the rhythm, the sound, the qualities of diction—these and whatever else made up the original—and then attempt to rework as many as possible into a poem in English. Since no

---

*The Brower collection.
**Preface to "Translations from Ovid's *Epistles*."

5

translator can manage equally all such data at the same time, with so many conflicting claims to be reconciled, what he has to do is set up a constantly shifting system of priorities: now the thought has to be flexed into a rhythm, now modulated into another key of sound, now an image has to be refocused, now some clue given to a lost allusion. There is no way—for example—to translate *nostra vita* into English so that the two simplest words for the idea, "our life," preserve the cadence of the Italian. (Unless some wag comes along with a stage Neapolitan accent and suggests "our-a life-a"—a solution probably detrimental to tone.) So something has to give: the translator's fascinating work is made up of decisions, decisions: what to give up in order to gain what? With the all-important *whole* forever in mind: a poem like the original. It may be useful, then, to say that one reconstitutes the poem. Or to think of the process as a kind of exsanguination—the medical procedure in which all blood is removed from an organism, to be replaced by new blood. In the process of translating, certainly the lifeblood of the original is drained away; the poem will survive only if the translator has living blood of his own to supply. We all know translations of poetry that are very pale corpses indeed. Again Valéry, in his essay on a French translation of St. John of the Cross, is with us: "This is really to *translate*, which is to reconstitute as nearly as possible the *effect* of a certain *cause*—here a text in Spanish—by means of *another cause*, a text in French." (DF 286) The right question to ask about a translation of poetry is not "Is it faithful?" but "Does it produce an equivalent effect?" Or perhaps, "a reasonably equivalent effect?" It seems excessive to demand of the poor translator that, since he is working with one of the greatest of lyrics, he must give us, as its equivalent, a lyric that will rank with the greatest in English—and then to condemn the translation as inadequate because it falls short of that demand.

A translation aiming at poetic equivalence has little chance of being literal, or "word for word"—although there are always readers who will compare a translation with its original so that they can "Aha!" triumphantly at any discrepancy. But linguists tell us that word-for-word translation, even at levels far below that of poetry, is often impossible. How does one translate, word for word, expressions like "How do you do" or "So long!" or "jiminy crickets!" Or "What did you put him up to it for?"—in which hardly a word can be translated independently. Frequently indeed, as Eugene A. Nida declares, "reproducing the precise corresponding word may utterly distort the meaning." (RB 12) This has always been realized by poet-translators: Horace might have been speaking for all of them when he warned that a faithful interpreter will not translate *verbum verbo*.

To translate a poem well, as Dryden reminds us more than once, is harder than to write a new poem, in which one is always free to change direction.

Although the thought of the poem may not be its main poetic constituent, the translator has a responsibility to be as faithful to it as the conflicting interests of rhythm and sound permit; certainly he is not free, except in "imitations," to follow his own will. In seeming to belittle content, I only mean that, with poetry, to translate the thought alone is not enough—indeed, is next to nothing.

If the translator is trying to show us how the poetry goes, what he writes has to be first of all a poem. The rhythm must have its élan, diction be in the right register, sound work musically or expressively. Valéry thought sound as important as sense: a poem for him was "cette hésitation prolongée entre le son et le sens" (*Rhumbs*). For Frost, the sound is "the gold in the ore." But should sound duplicate precise effects in the original? In "Le cimetière marin" there are lines composed—as even a foreigner cannot fail to notice—to mimic what they describe: the grating repetitiousness of the cicada that "scratches the dryness," for example:

L'insecte net gratte la sécheresse ...

An "ugly" line, with the three brusque words ending in a *t* and the repeated vowel sound which is hardly mellifluous here. One would think a translator would not ignore the effect; yet it is ignored in English versions. Two of the best-known give us a plain mistranslation, as if the cicada were scratching actual earth, instead of making a scratching sound in the air. (Didn't these translators even glance at Gustave Cohen's famous *Essai d'explication?* How would anyone—though ours is a shoddy age—dare translate a poem like this without reading carefully at least some of the French studies of the stylistics of Valéry's work?)

The poem has been better translated—in a way that saves the poetry—by Rainer Maria Rilke and Jorge Guillén. Both were sensitive to the harshness of the line, and both echoed it in their own, Rilke with

Der harte Käfer ist des Trockenen Säge ...

and Guillén with

Nítido insecto rasca sequedades ...

Another sound-line is about the real gnawer, the irrefutable worm of consciousness:

Le vrai rongeur, le ver irréfutable ...

Five *r*'s, probably the gnawingest of our speech sounds—especially when the *r* is a French one. (The translator might wonder if Valéry, from southern France, had an uvular *r* with its little rasp; he might want to listen to Valéry's own reading of the line, available on records. Just as translators of García Lorca might want to find out if the young man from Granada spoke with a Castilian or an Andalusian accent, since this would affect the sound of certain lines. This kind of information is not—*magari!*—available for all poems; where it is, it should be considered.)

The burring of Valéry's worm has not been brought over into English, as far as I know. But again the poet-translators are concerned with it. Guillén, whose language does not have the same *r*-sound as Valéry's, any more than our own has, makes a discreet but noticeable use of his more emphatic rolled *r:*

El roedor gusano irrefutable ...

Rilke, with a softer sound to call on than the Spanish one, tops even Valéry in his *r*-ishness:

der Wurm, dem keiner widerspricht, der Nager ...

But if Rilke, with his seven *r*'s, seems more expressive here, Guillén does better with the playful alliteration of persistence for the girls' fluttering fingers in

Les derniers dons, les doigts qui les défendent ...

This is caught exactly (partly because the languages are akin) by Guillén's

Últimos dones, dedos defensores ...

It is rather surprising that Rilke does nothing with the line. Could it be that, lacking Valéry's sense of fun, he thought it flamboyant?

Translations must have their own form and rhythm; but must they have the same form and rhythm as the original? We know translators who don't give a thought to the matter, or who would be scornful if they did. "I put down the words as they come," such a one might protest; "to change anything, to add or subtract syllables just to get a rhythm is dishonest!" Not to give us a rhythm may be more dishonest: the poet himself took care to put down no words the meter would not tolerate. Time after time, if the testimony of poets is to be trusted, words are suggested as much by the rhythm as by the argument. Goethe's poems seem to come directly out of lived experiences; and yet he too brooded on technique: "mysterious and great effects," he tells us, "are produced by different poetical forms." Translators indifferent to mysterious and great effects are not likely to give us a faithful translation.

More than one poet has even revealed that the form of his poem existed before the "ideas" did—that he found his mind moving in a rhythm before he knew what it was going to say. No one has put this more clearly than Valéry:

8

As for the *Cimetière marin*, this intention was at first no more than a rhythmic figure, empty, or filled with meaningless syllables, which obsessed me for some time. I noticed that the figure was decasyllabic, and I pondered on the model, which is very little used in modern French poetry. . . . It suggested a stanza of six lines . . . [and other formal considerations suggested the theme of the poem]. My line had to be solid and strongly rhythmical. . . . The type of line chosen, and form adopted for the stanzas, set me conditions that favored certain "movements," permitted changes of tone, called up a certain style. . . . The *Cimetière marin* was *conceived*. A rather long period of gestation followed. (DF 148)

If there is a question of priority, it is clear that the form determined the subject and not the subject the form. I would suggest that the translator's responsibility, then, is at least as much to the form as to the ideas. Form, after all, as paced by line length and rhyme escapement, is the choreography of the poet's spirit.

We tend to think of rhyme today as mere decoration or as a mere mnemonic device. Its worldwide popularity with primitive types—savages, children, folk singers, advertising men—should indicate that something about it goes very deep in the psyche, and not the psyche alone—what is the human body but a system of rhyming parts? (Only the badly crippled move their bodies in free verse.) When there is functional rhyme in a poem, the only reason for a translator to shirk it is that it is "too hard" to make the translation rhyme—too hard to make it rhyme easily and naturally, so that the rhyming words belong as inevitably as all the other words. Slipshod rhyming is easy enough; current translations yield many examples. In my experience it may take a hundred times as long to translate into rhymed lines as it does into unrhymed—to take the constituents of a stanza of St. John of the Cross, say, and work them naturally into the *ababb* of his *lira*. But suppose it does take a hundred times as long? Time, though it is not money in these matters, may be perfection—or as close to it as one is likely to come, and for that almost no cost, in time or effort, is too great.

Yet there are limits to what can be done in transferring effects from language to language—limits in terms of what the new language will bear. When Bernart de Ventadorn carries the very same rhyming sounds of his first stanza through the seven or eight stanzas that follow, or when he composes seventy-two consecutive lines on only two rhyming sounds, the translator should face the reality of English rhyme and decide that although the trick might not be impossible in English, it could probably not be carried off without visible strain.

More important and more complicated than rhyme is the matter of rhythm. Since, even if rhythms could correspond, they would not have the same effect in two languages, is it worthwhile trying to duplicate an exotic form in English? The alexandrine, so fluent in Racine, for us "like a wounded snake, drags its slow length along." Hexameters, so natural and ebullient in Homer, so grave and sonorous in Virgil, seem to come rather pompously from our tongues.

"Even if rhythms could correspond"—but the correspondence is far from perfect. Stress is heavier in some languages than in others. In the eight-syllable *romance* line used by García Lorca, the distribution of accents matters only at the end of the line; in English it makes itself felt throughout. Dante's *endecasillabo* does not have the pattern of expectations that Shakespeare's iambic pentameter does. All transfers of rhythm from language to language are likely to be approximate, analogical. But it may be better to imitate a rhythm even imperfectly than to give no notion at all of its character. Especially inasmuch as, although the rhythms have differed since Babel, their physical basis, the heartbeat and breathing of man, seem to have changed little, if at all.

With Greek and Latin a peculiar vexation arises. These ancient rhythms were made up by patterning syllables according to their musical length—a kind of rhythm our stress-heavy language is not very sensitive to. What we generally settle for, in translating from Greek and Latin, is a transposition of long and short syllables into stressed and unstressed—which may give us as good a notion of the movement of Sappho's verse as we are ever likely to have. A notion of what her rhythm was *like:* certainly it was not like the 1920-ish free verse it is sometimes rendered as. Take a Sapphic line and try *da-dum*-ing its eleven longs and shorts:

$$- \cup - \overset{\cup}{-} - \cup \cup - \cup - \overset{\cup}{-}$$

Is this like any rhythm we have heard in English? Yes, most of us will feel; it is like a very free iambic pentameter with the first three feet reversed or spondaic, and with an extra syllable at the end. As in John Donne's line in the "Epithalamium Made at Lincoln's Inn":

Which when next time you in these sheets will smother . . .

Or as in quite a few lines in Shakespeare's sonnets—if we make the third syllable emphatic, as we might in speech:

Hate of *my* sin, grounded on sinful loving . . . (CXLII)

or

Bearing *thy* heart, which I will keep so chary . . . (XXII)

But these occur in English as variations on a simple meter. An entire poem written in them might be intolerably stiff and mannered, untrue to the cadence of English. The charm and expressiveness of our metrics is that it gives a continual interplay of meter and rhythm, a continual series of variations, whereas to write Sapphics in English is to write the same metrical line over and over.

This is surely why Sapphics and Alcaics sound so artificial to us—like the diversions of a learned dilettante. Hölderlin used them as effectively as possible in German; Goethe, a more spontaneous poet, was probably wise in not going beyond hexameter and elegiacs.

It seemed to me worth the trouble to give most of these translations in something like the form of the original. Yet one cannot insist that stanza forms have to be preserved. Valéry praises a French translation of St. John of the Cross that is paced quite differently from the Spanish.

If one does decide on the original rhythm, or on any rhythm, difficulties immediately crop up—difficulties which translators in a hurry will probably decide are not worth coping with. How is one to say in English "En una noche obscura ..." in the cadence of the Spanish, yet using the simplest and most direct words, as the Spanish are the simplest and most direct for their meaning? "On a dark night" is two or three syllables too short, depending on what one decides to do with the feminine ending, which will have a very different effect in English. The problem: to say "On a dark night" and yet have more syllables. "Aha! padding!" the literalist will exclaim. But not padding—unless what is added is clumsily wadded in. Why not change the metaphor to the one Keats has made famous and say the translator has a rift or two he can load with ore? The trick is to "justify" the line with materials matching so well that no one will notice the reconstruction. Any stanza of a translation starts with gaps to be filled and excesses to be planed away. This is almost the test of a translator of poetry: how deftly, how creatively does he reorganize the debris? Does he work with his materials as the original poet might have worked with his?—for in writing poetry we have the same kind of adjustments to make between what our mind would have us say and what our pulses urge us.

In rendering St. John of the Cross the translator is unusually lucky because the poet himself wrote long explications of some of his poems. The translator may have ten or twenty pages from which to pick a needed phrase or image, from materials which the poet tells us he had in mind when writing the line, and which he himself might have used if the exigencies of his form had suggested it. It is wrong to say that the translator is unfaithful in making such adjustments; there is nothing he can do except bend thought and rhythm toward each other until they touch—and there is a point beyond which the rhythm will not bend. Objections to what some may regard as intrusions, as foreign matter in the English version, generally come from those who do not understand the nature of poetry—those who read the translation and its original on facing pages, line by line, ping-pong fashion, eyes right, eyes left, triumphant when a discrepancy is found. Perhaps it would be better—many have thought so—not even to print the text of a poem together with a translation which itself is meant to be a poem. The original is an experience. The translation, different but analogous, is an experience—but the two experiences cannot well be enjoyed together.

One of the most successful poetic translations of our time is the one Rilke made of "Le cimetière marin." Rilke himself was pleased with what he felt was his success in catching the "equivalences"; yet he is often far from anything like a word-for-word correspondence. In the line about the cicada already quoted, Rilke added an image that made the insect a "saw" of the dryness; there is no saw in Valéry. The objection will come: "*Säge* is lugged in, and only to rhyme with *träge!*" In the fourth line of the poem Valéry's sea is "toujours recommencée"; Rilke adds a different notion and a different image in saying it is "ein immer neues Schenken." Aha! Habitual *aha!*-ers will find about one opportunity per line in Rilke's version, which aims primarily at showing German readers what the poem is like. (That at least is its effect; Rilke may have done the work purely for his own pleasure.) A. Grosser, in a study which translators of Valéry will have come across in *Études germaniques* (October-December, 1949), stresses Rilke's primary concern: "ce qui fait sans doute l'excellence de la traduction de Rilke: le rythme, les sonorités, en un mot la poésie...." If, with all translators of poetry, I have sometimes been forced to add or omit for the sake of a higher fidelity, it is reassuring to feel behind me the shadow of Rilke. There are lovers of Goethe's "Wandrers Nachtlied" who will feel that I have profaned it by adding "to the west" in

> Birds are through
> That sang in their wood to the west . . .

It is true it was added for the cadence. But it seems to me the kind of thing Goethe might have said if he had needed it for *his* cadence. It goes with the sound; it makes sense enough: birds would sing last in woods to the west, where the light would fade last; and *west* has suggestions appropriate to the poem. It seems closer to Goethe's thought than the addition which Werner Winter tells us Lermontov made in his Russian version: a line meaning "no dust rises from the road." I mention the phrase I have added to Goethe's poem; it is typical of what has happened many times in the poems translated here.

Everywhere in the translation of poetry one struggles with this problem: how to "justify"—the printer's term seems more apt than the upholsterer's—a line of so many syllables when a natural translation of the words does not yield that number. Just as everywhere one struggles with this: how can the words be changed, yet kept right and natural, when their sounds are discordant or inept in the second language? One of the most resistant lines I have come across is the opening of St. John's poem:

¿Adónde te escondiste ...?

Spanish readers have professed to hear, in the sonorous *dond-cond* echo, hollow reverberations of the dungeon in which the poem was written. But nothing reverberates in "Where did you hide. . . ?"

While we are thinking of equivalences, we might wonder if translations from Italian and related languages should be done in an English line shorter than the original. Many common words, which have two or three syllables in Italian, turn into our basic English monosyllables: love, death; day, night; land, sea; boy, girl; dog, cat—so that many Italian lines, translated with the simplicity they deserve, fall into shorter lines in English. What if Dante were done in eight-syllable lines, perhaps like these (which lack, however, the full drive of his rhyming)?—

The middle of life's journey: I
   came conscious in a darkening wood;
   lost, the right road to travel by.
Grim chore, to make its nature clear,
   that wildwood, thick and thorny—such
   even the memory's full of fear.
So bitter, death is barely more . . .

Perhaps more of Dante's crispness would come through in the shorter line? But would it be at too great a cost in dignity and amplitude?—qualities which, together with a racy vigor, come through so resonantly in the translation by John Ciardi.

I began to wonder about this years ago, during what was probably the closest and most rewarding study I ever made of a poet. Under probably the most stirring circumstances. The poet was Dante, the city Florence, with the Tuscan countryside, panoramic beyond our windows, changing from fall to winter to the spring. Here, two or three afternoons a week, before a fire on the colder days, and with wine or Campari on the table, I read through most of the *Commedia* with a young Florentine who knew English well enough to discuss the complexities of his own language. Sometimes—an additional pleasure—Robert Fitzgerald came down from Fiesole to join us. Aldo Celli would read a line, or, as the weeks went by, perhaps a dozen lines; his student would repeat them, not for the pronunciation alone, but perhaps in the hope there was some magic in the Florentine cadence. Then the questions came—searching out, line by line, the kind of information the dictionaries are chary of. They were about words mostly, about their tone, their status in the language. This word, Professor Celli would say, was still the common Tuscan word; another he had never heard, although it "sounded Florentine." One had become proverbial; another was used only as a Dante allusion. One word survived in Tuscany, but he thought not elsewhere; another sounded Sienese. One was poetic today; another suggested nineteenth-century rhetoric. One was used only by old folks in the country; another was a child's word—though he thought parents would discourage its use if they heard it. One was used in writing, but not in speech; another used only ironically, as in the funny papers or by students joking. One survived only as the name of a street in Florence.

I learned also that to an Italian ear such and such a line would sound flat, or clumsy, or overrich in music. All of this is treasure for the translator, treasure hard to come by in any other way. The translator, with poetry especially, gives us not only words but the tone of words: their tone determines the kind of English he writes. Surely among the commonest faults of translation are faults of tone: the easy and colloquial perhaps lost in the stiff and literary, or perhaps overtranslated into a slang which is born ephemeral, or into the distractingly personal idiom of an E. E. Cummings, which is not really for export.

This kind of close reading reveals other effects a foreigner would be likely to miss: what excitement, for example, there can be in displacements of emphasis, as in the second of these famous lines, in which the expected stress on the eighth syllable is shifted plangently to the seventh:

Per me si va ne la città dolente,
   per me si va ne l'eterno dolore,
   per me si va tra la perduta gente....

so that *eterno* resonates with strange effect, the deepest note in the passage.

Though a modern Florentine devoted to literature may be closer to Dante than anyone alive, he is still centuries away. The reading I have described has to be supplemented by the scholarly notes of five or six editions. Achilles Fang insists that "a translator must comprehend not only his text but also its numerous glosses . . . it would be nothing short of folly to translate a passage before he is perfectly satisfied with the text and can explain every word of it." Nothing is more helpful for a translator than to be able to discuss his poem with someone who has known from childhood the language in which it is written. It seems to me there is no substitute for such discussion, when it is possible; I have been lucky enough to be able to search and research in this way most of the poems here translated. One is not likely to turn up an ancient Greek around here any more, but one can read Catalan with a native of Barcelona who speaks it in preference to Spanish; one can read Galician with someone from the northwestern corner of Spain who learned it at his mother's knee. With most languages that might concern us, help is even closer at hand. No one, even after living for years in a country, knows the language well enough to catch all the nuances of poetry: many words have for us the suggestions they have because of what they meant to us in childhood. As late learners we are always likely to blunder. I remember how pleased I was, even after two years in Spain, to find a Spanish poet referring to a round mirror as *la luna*—until an amused Spaniard informed me that this was not the poet's metaphor at all, but only the usual term for a mirror of that shape. Almost nowhere is hybris more conspicuous than in translating poetry: everyone thinks he knows more than he knows. Conceit, indolence, carelessness, haste, these are the vices of the translator; and where they thrive, the boners blossom. If these boners sometimes provide as much delight as the poetry transferred, that is probably no part of the writer's intention. There was the Spanish translator of Emily Dickinson who thought the moor she had never seen was the kind of Moor that figured in Spanish history; he had some trouble making sense of the poem. Or the translator who enlivened his text by having a lady "ride naked" through a town, when the original only meant she "rode bareback." Or the Italian who missed the idiom in "Come up and see me tonight. I've got nothing on." Boners, though they may be funny, are always a kind of ugliness, because ignorance and carelessness are ugly. Even Ezra Pound, who has given us some marvelous poems in the guise of translations, sometimes reads with too hasty an eye. When for the Provençal

Tout m'a mo cor, e tout m'a me,
e se mezeis e tot lo mon ...

he gives us

She hath all my heart from me, and she hath from me all my wit
And myself and all that is mine . . .

it certainly looks as if he thought *tout* was like the French word and meant *all*. But *tout* in Provençal is the past participle of *tolre* (the Latin *tollere*). He also seems to have confused "m'a me" and "lo mon" with other words. This is a trifle, but it rather shakes our confidence in a translator's sensitivity to, and respect for, his text. Of course one takes liberties in the interests of any poetic effect, but one should know what liberties he is taking, and with what—and above all should approach a great original with that respect and care which is a kind of humility.

Discussing the poem with a native speaker should be in addition to and not in place of some experience with the language. When the language is unknown, no amount of discussion will help very much. Recently it was my good fortune to have as my dinner companion a Japanese lady; we talked—I asking, she explaining—for perhaps an hour about Bashō's famous haiku:

Furu ike ya
kawazu tobikomu
mizu no oto.

She told me it "meant":

An old pond—
frog jumped in:
water's-sound.

Then she tried to show me why this is the most celebrated of all haiku. I understood every word she said, yet had almost no idea what she was getting at. "But you'd have to live in Japan!" she laughed finally. Later, consulting Professor Henderson's introduction to haiku, I was only more puzzled by his remarks on the poem, which he says Bashō thought the most important turning point in his poetic life: "Many competent critics have found in this a deep and esoteric meaning; others have considered it too darkly mysterious to understand at all." Obviously I am not ready to translate this poem, and probably never will be—although it has become the fashion for poets nowadays, sometimes encouraged by institutions, to "translate" from languages which they do not know, on the basis of literal versions, explications, and perhaps conferences with someone who does know the language. This seems to me a bit shabby. I know that others do not share my prejudice; certainly handsome poems have been produced in this secondhand fashion.

One element of poetry hardly touched on in this discussion is imagery. If a poet says something is like a compass or a glowworm golden or a red, red rose, this might seem as easy to translate as those "two brown pencils" or that "pen of my aunt." And one might feel, with Vladimir Nabokov (*New York Review of Books,* December 4, 1969), that "a poet's imagery is a sacred, unassailable thing." Yet difficulties can arise: images too are expressed in words, and words have qualities. Suppose the word for something in the source language is a long lovely word, all *l*'s and *m*'s, somehow like its meaning: Nabokov gives us an example when he says "The Russian word, with its fluffy and dreamy syllables, suits admirably this beautiful tree. . . ." (RB 104) Suppose the corresponding English word is short and ugly; suppose we called the tree a scab-bark or a snotch. Images sound different in different languages; Jean Paris thinks that "sauvage vent d'ouest" is no real equivalent for "wild west wind." Or suppose the image evokes an object well known to speakers of the first language but totally unfamiliar to those of the second. Two perhaps overfamiliar examples: for the Eskimos "lamb of God" turns to "seal of God"; and for some tribesmen of hot regions "white as snow" becomes "white as egret's feathers." Under such conditions, are lamb and snow indeed sacred and unassailable? Connotation too must be reckoned with: Sidney Monas, translating from Russian into English, changes a "mourning cuckoo" to a "mourning dove," since cuckoo has the wrong connotations in English. Such considerations led me to change a "weasel" to a "mink" in a poem of Antonio Machado. "The reader who takes this sort of alteration of figure to be a mistranslation," says Jackson Mathews, "has much to learn about translating poetry." Again, certain images that conveyed specific information to members of one culture may mean nothing to those of another: the sparrows, for example, that drew the chariot of Aphrodite in Sappho's poem. They sound rather silly to us. We can save the image by thinking of a cloud of sparrows, as Tiepolo might have painted them; but even so we have to know that sparrows—if that is the ornithologically correct term—were thought of as sexy birds, so sacred to Aphrodite that their flesh was used as an aphrodisiac. Maybe the translator should insert a clarifying word, just to safeguard the sanctity of the image? (Perhaps this is a step I should have taken with Valéry's "filles chatouillées." W. M. Frohock, from his wide experience with the backgrounds of French poetry, informs me that the proper way to tickle girls in southern France is with fistfuls of hay.)

Another difficulty to deal with is that frequency of image varies in different languages. Shakespeare is more concrete, invokes the senses more, than Racine: the difference is not only in individual talent but in the very languages they use. The concreteness of English is one of its glories; perhaps when a line from a less concrete language is fully translated into English it tends to settle into images "not in" the original. "The English [version]," wrote Dudley Fitts of one translation, "demands a harder, more urgent kind of particularity." (RB 38) All very well for Valéry to have his cicada scratching the dryness; in English we are more likely to have it scratching a dry thing, if only the air or the atmosphere. (Not, I think, the earth.) We have seen that Rilke, in translating into German, provided the insect with a saw; we might want to do something of that sort in English. Such modifications of imagery may be necessary in view of differing linguistic habits: what we want in the translation of poetry is equivalent effect, which we hardly get by writing English as if it were a foreign language. Here the translator is operating at a depth far below linguistic peculiarity, below the surface of diction and the layers of imagery,

> Auprès d'un coeur, aux sources du poème,
> Entre le vide et l'évenément pur …

trying to discover the urgencies that expressed themselves in *these* words and *these* images in one language, but which might have surfaced differently in another. One cannot say too often that it is not correspondence of detail that matters; it is correspondence of feeling and movement and tonality. Poems have, we know, not only meaning but being; it is this very being of the poem that a translator is trying to give us.

But poems are more important than talk about poetry. Here are some poems. I have tried to show you, at least remotely, how they go.

AFTERTHOUGHT

The last word, like the first, is Valéry's. A poem—he has been paraphrased as saying—is never finished; it is abandoned in despair. This is even more true of translations of poetry.

I

Paul Valéry

(1871–1945)

Πρὸς χάριν. A favorite motto of Valéry's. I put his poem first "for the pleasure of it." And because it seems an emblem for what I am undertaking here. Translations of poetry—what are they, next to the original, but graveyards by the life-giving sea? "Tant de marbre . . . sur tant d'ombres." I put him first too because he said, in the introductory remarks to his own verse translation of Virgil's *Eclogues,* that when one is dealing with poetry "fidelity to meaning alone is a kind of betrayal." A poem is not a poem by virtue of its paraphrasable, or translatable, meaning—as we know very well when speaking of poetry in our own language. But we sometimes forget that a translation does not give us the poem at all if it merely gives us the "meaning"—the thought which, Valéry reminds us, a good poet is always ready to sacrifice to some seduction of the form: to a temptation to do better in sound, or in rhythm, or in the physical interplay of words.

If the translator wants to give us something of the heartbeat of the poem, if he aims at more than a plain prose translation, he has a responsibility not only to thought but also to sound, to rhythm, to diction—and to so much more. He has to take into account such matters as the sound-effect in Valéry's line about the cicada in the twelfth stanza, and the fact that *vaste* in the same stanza has not only its common French meaning but also (as many words have in Valéry's work) its Latin resonance—*devastated*. He cannot disdain the very deliberate and functional alliteration in stanzas sixteen and nineteen, or, in the very last line of the poem, overlook the unusual rhythm or the pun (permitted to pass if not indeed calculated) which French ears have found disconcerting. Above all, he cannot ignore the rhythm of the poem or the rhyme escapement of its stanzas—these are matters that Valéry himself tells us he meditated on and was moved by even before he knew what the poem was to be about—in a way they lie deeper in the creative psyche than the "thought" itself. Fidelity to meaning alone is a kind of betrayal—a denial, in fact, of the very nature of poetry.

Valéry has written a good deal about the composition of his most famous poem. In *Inspirations mediterranéennes* he tells us how, all of his life, he liked to gaze out over the Mediterranean, his hours of apparent dreaminess consecrated to "the three or four undeniable gods, the Sea, the Sky, the Sun." The poem, as the title shows, is about life and death. The sea surface, its infinite momentary sparkles like the infinite lives of men, also hints at the hidden depths of the soul; and the sun, precisely at high noon, is like the impersonal All in the universe, the Absolute of the philosophers. Zeno, brought in by the poet "just to borrow a little color" from philosophy, denied motion and change—which for Valéry make up the beauty and excitement of human existence.

The poem—surely one of the best of our time—has been often translated. Probably the most successful poetic version is Rainer Maria Rilke's "Der Friedhof am Meer." Rilke, who translated in the form of the original, worked along lines Valéry would have approved of, and was himself happy with the result: he told Lou Andreas-Salomé, in a letter of December 29, 1921, that he thought his version done "with a perfection in the equivalence" he would not have thought possible in the two languages.

The text is from Paul Valéry, *Œuvres*. Edited by J. Hytier. 2 volumes. (Bibliothèque de la Pléiade). Librairie Gallimard, Paris. 1957 and 1960.

The Graveyard
by
the Sea

LE CIMETIÈRE MARIN

Μή, φίλα ψυχά, βίον ἀθάνατον
σπεῦδε, τὰν δ' ἔμπρακταν ἄντλει μαχανάν.

Pindare, *Pythiques*, III.

Ce toit tranquille, où marchent des colombes,
Entre les pins palpite, entre les tombes;
Midi le juste y compose de feux
La mer, la mer, toujours recommencée!
O récompense après une pensée
Qu'un long regard sur le calme des dieux!

Quel pur travail de fins éclairs consume
Maint diamant d'imperceptible écume,
Et quelle paix semble se concevoir!
Quand sur l'abîme un soleil se repose,
Ouvrages purs d'une éternelle cause,
Le Temps scintille et le Songe est savoir.

Stable trésor, temple simple à Minerve,
Masse de calme, et visible réserve,
Eau sourcilleuse, Œil qui gardes en toi
Tant de sommeil sous un voile de flamme,
O mon silence!... Édifice dans l'âme,
Mais comble d'or aux mille tuiles, Toit!

Temple du Temps, qu'un seul soupir résume,
A ce point pur je monte et m'accoutume,
Tout entouré de mon regard marin;
Et comme aux dieux mon offrande suprême,
La scintillation sereine sème
Sur l'altitude un dédain souverain.

Comme le fruit se fond en jouissance,
Comme en délice il change son absence

THE GRAVEYARD BY THE SEA

*Do not be anxious, dear soul, for eternal
life, but make what you can of the possible.*
Pindar, *Pythian* III.

This quiet roof, bestirred with pigeon plumes,
Seen through the pine is pulsing, through the tombs.
Here Noon the just composes, all a blaze,
The sea, the sea, the recommencing yet!
O recompense, for brows in effort set,
Over the gods' own calm to gaze and gaze.

Fine lightnings work the diamond, crush it quite
To many a gem in seafoam out of sight.
And what a peace we fancy here below!
Over a blue abyss the noon at pause
—Pure products, then, of an eternal cause,
Time's all a shimmer, and to dream's to know.

Minerva's simple shrine, firm treasury,
A power of calm, all affluence to see,
Waves' ruffling brow, Eye hooded and aloof
Over deep slumber on the blazing shoal,
O silence, mine! . . . and structure in the soul
With domes of gold, tile over tile—you, Roof!

Temple of Time, its very gist a sigh,
I scale pure heights and grow at home here, I;
Vision of sea enfolds me, turn by turn.
And like my own last gift to gods supreme,
This dazzle, grander on the ocean-stream,
Sows the immense with languorous unconcern.

Fruit foundering in its juice to other's joy
Is crushed itself in pleasuring girl or boy,

23

Dans une bouche où sa forme se meurt,
Je hume ici ma future fumée,
Et le ciel chante à l'âme consumée
Le changement des rives en rumeur.

Beau ciel, vrai ciel, regarde-moi qui change!
Après tant d'orgueil, après tant d'étrange
Oisiveté, mais pleine de pouvoir,
Je m'abandonne à ce brillant espace,
Sur les maisons des morts mon ombre passe
Qui m'apprivoise à son frêle mouvoir.

L'âme exposée aux torches du solstice,
Je te soutiens, admirable justice
De la lumière aux armes sans pitié!
Je te rends pure à ta place première :
Regarde-toi!... Mais rendre la lumière
Suppose d'ombre une morne moitié.

O pour moi seul, à moi seul, en moi-même,
Auprès d'un cœur, aux sources du poème,
Entre le vide et l'événement pur,
J'attends l'écho de ma grandeur interne,
Amère, sombre et sonore citerne,
Sonnant dans l'âme un creux toujours futur!

Sais-tu, fausse captive des feuillages,
Golfe mangeur de ces maigres grillages,
Sur mes yeux clos, secrets éblouissants,
Quel corps me traîne à sa fin paresseuse,
Quel front l'attire à cette terre osseuse?
Une étincelle y pense à mes absents.

Fermé, sacré, plein d'un feu sans matière,
Fragment terrestre offert à la lumière,
Ce lieu me plaît, dominé de flambeaux,

Soon in the mouth an absence, fruit no more.
I sniff in this my drift—to ash in air.
Soul's worn away; the chanting heavens declare
Change of the surf to rumor on the shore.

Fine sky, true sky, consider me: I change.
After a fit of pride, a fit of strange
Laziness—lazy yes, but full of strength—
I yield to this; the brilliant space prevails;
On mansions of the dead my shadow trails
With many a lesson in its meager length.

My soul exposed to noon-fires of the sky,
I bear the brunt of your inspection, high
Courts of the angry light, that bristle doom.
Study yourself: immaculate as before
I set you where you were. But mirrors wore
Always a dusky underside of gloom.

Oh by myself, in me, for me alone,
Close to a heart where poems stir from stone,
Between the nothing and the pure event,
I on the edge of grandeur hang and hark:
The reservoir reverberant, surly, dark
—Threats of erosion in the echo sent.

You'd know—by hoax of foliage prisoned here,
Gulf in whose glare thin spindles disappear,
On my closed eye, old secrets brilliant red—
What body draws me to the dawdling zone,
What forehead presses to a mulch of bone?
A spark, there, flickers for my absent dead.

Sworn holy, fenced away, all fuelless fire,
Fragment of earth to light exposed, entire—
I like the place: with torch of cypress crowned;

Composé d'or, de pierre et d'arbres sombres,
Où tant de marbre est tremblant sur tant d'ombres;
La mer fidèle y dort sur mes tombeaux!

Chienne splendide, écarte l'idolâtre!
Quand solitaire au sourire de pâtre,
Je pais longtemps, moutons mystérieux,
Le blanc troupeau de mes tranquilles tombes,
Éloignes-en les prudentes colombes,
Les songes vains, les anges curieux!

Ici venu, l'avenir est paresse.
L'insecte net gratte la sécheresse;
Tout est brûlé, défait, reçu dans l'air
A je ne sais quelle sévère essence...
La vie est vaste, étant ivre d'absence,
Et l'amertume est douce, et l'esprit clair.

Les morts cachés sont bien dans cette terre
Qui les réchauffe et sèche leur mystère.
Midi là-haut, Midi sans mouvement
En soi se pense et convient à soi-même...
Tête complète et parfait diadème,
Je suis en toi le secret changement.

Tu n'as que moi pour contenir tes craintes!
Mes repentirs, mes doutes, mes contraintes
Sont le défaut de ton grand diamant...
Mais dans leur nuit toute lourde de marbres,
Un peuple vague aux racines des arbres
A pris déjà ton parti lentement.

Ils ont fondu dans une absence épaisse,
L'argile rouge a bu la blanche espèce,
Le don de vivre a passé dans les fleurs!
Où sont des morts les phrases familières,

Of stone, of gold, of somber foliage made,
Houses of marble on the homes of shade,
Tombs that the faithful sea can doze around.

Keep, fiery bitch, the idolater away!
Alone, my shepherd-smile in place, I stray
At leisure, with mysterious sheep about,
My feeding troop of many a placid slab.
The doves that cluck of prudence, fat and drab,
Vain dreams and curious angels—cast them out!

Once here, the future yawns, an empty stare.
The curt cicada grates the bone-dry air.
All's burnt away, undone, in sky refined
To some astringent essence. Wide debris—
Life, with its wild addiction *not* to be!
Here bitterness is sweet, and clear the mind.

The hidden dead are well in earth interred;
Their mystery incinerated, cured.
Up there the Noon, the Noon unmoving too
Broods on its self-concern, itself the law . . .
Impeccable head, tiara without flaw,
See, I'm the secret change astir in you.

The fears you move—I hold them, I alone.
Repentance, doubt, compulsion, moods I've known
Show as your noble diamond's only blur.
Still, in that dark the ponderous marble chokes,
A slow folk gathering at the root of oaks
Lend to your cause their many a signature.

These in a massive absence melted quite.
The redder clay has drunk away the white.
The gift of life gone wandering: flower and grass.
The dead are where? Their favorite turn of phrase,

27

L'art personnel, les âmes singulières?
La larve file où se formaient des pleurs.

Les cris aigus des filles chatouillées,
Les yeux, les dents, les paupières mouillées,
Le sein charmant qui joue avec le feu,
Le sang qui brille aux lèvres qui se rendent,
Les derniers dons, les doigts qui les défendent,
Tout va sous terre et rentre dans le jeu!

Et vous, grande âme, espérez-vous un songe
Qui n'aura plus ces couleurs de mensonge
Qu'aux yeux de chair l'onde et l'or font ici?
Chanterez-vous quand serez vaporeuse?
Allez! Tout fuit! Ma présence est poreuse,
La sainte impatience meurt aussi!

Maigre immortalité noire et dorée,
Consolatrice affreusement laurée,
Qui de la mort fais un sein maternel,
Le beau mensonge et la pieuse ruse!
Qui ne connaît, et qui ne les refuse,
Ce crâne vide et ce rire éternel!

Pères profonds, têtes inhabitées,
Qui sous le poids de tant de pelletées,
Êtes la terre et confondez nos pas,
Le vrai rongeur, le ver irréfutable
N'est point pour vous qui dormez sous la table,
Il vit de vie, il ne me quitte pas!

Amour, peut-être, ou de moi-même haine?
Sa dent secrète est de moi si prochaine
Que tous les noms lui peuvent convenir!
Qu'importe! Il voit, il veut, il songe, il touche!

Souls all their own, their own especial ways?
There, where a tear would tremble, larvae pass.

Keen glee of girls the fingers stir and tease;
The eyes, the teeth, the moistening eyelid—these!
The breasts, so pretty flirting with the flame;
Blood brilliant in the lips about to dare;
The final gift; defending fingers there
—All reabsorbed in earth. The eternal game.

And you, grand soul, conceive a heaven designed
Free of that fond mirage our lashes find
There in the long shore's glory, gold or blue?
When you're a mist, your singing lips can live?
Away! The world's in flight. My flesh a sieve.
Days of the holy hankering finish too.

Lean immortality, black, ormolu,
Horrid with laurel looped—you'd soothe us, you!
A mother's breast, the pit they pitch us in!
Here's a fine fib, a fine religious trick!
Who doesn't know, who wouldn't turn half-sick
From skulls eternal only in their grin?

Fathers profound at last, unlived-in heads
Shovels of earth sent packing to your beds,
How you confuse our footfall, earthy things!
The grinding worm, grim vermin none deny,
Spurns you, beneath the table where you lie.
It likes the live flesh better. Clings and clings.

Love, maybe? Hate of self? Who'd give a straw!
The secret tooth, within me, turns to gnaw
So near the bone that—take a name: it's true!
A name! It sees, it dreams; would touch, would keep.

Ma chair lui plaît, et jusque sur ma couche,
A ce vivant je vis d'appartenir!

Zénon! Cruel Zénon! Zénon d'Élée!
M'as-tu percé de cette flèche ailée
Qui vibre, vole, et qui ne vole pas!
Le son m'enfante et la flèche me tue!
Ah! le soleil... Quelle ombre de tortue
Pour l'âme, Achille immobile à grands pas!

Non, non!... Debout! Dans l'ère successive!
Brisez, mon corps, cette forme pensive!
Buvez, mon sein, la naissance du vent!
Une fraîcheur, de la mer exhalée,
Me rend mon âme... O puissance salée!
Courons à l'onde en rejaillir vivant!

Oui! Grande mer de délires douée,
Peau de panthère et chlamyde trouée
De mille et mille idoles du soleil,
Hydre absolue, ivre de ta chair bleue,
Qui te remords l'étincelante queue
Dans un tumulte au silence pareil,

Le vent se lève!... il faut tenter de vivre!
L'air immense ouvre et referme mon livre,
La vague en poudre ose jaillir des rocs!
Envolez-vous, pages tout éblouies!
Rompez, vagues! Rompez d'eaux réjouies
Ce toit tranquille où picoraient des focs!

It likes my flesh, my flesh awake, asleep.
It lives, and I'm its creature through and through.

O Zeno, cruel! Cruel Zeno Elea bore!
Your feathered arrow streaking me with gore!
It thrills, it flies—it flies, not changing place.
The twang began me and the arrow kills.
But ah the sun! a tortoise-shade that wills—
What but Achilles stockstill in the race?

No! To the fleeting era, *once* by *once!*
Off with those poses of a thoughtful dunce!
Revel in wind; it quickens! Drink and thrive!
A coolness breathing from the open sea
Restores—O vigor of salt!—my soul for me!
Plunge in the surf! Come springing out, alive!

Yes, the great ocean given to trance, that drags
Panther-pelt fringe or classic robe in rags,
Torn by a thousand splinters, sun on sea,
Dotes on its own blue body, roaring drunk
—Hydra released, with shimmering tail, teeth sunk
Deep in itself. Carousing soundlessly.

The freshening wind! Let's live, or try to! Look,
The vast air ruffles and claps shut my book;
Reckless, the surf goes geysering on the rocks.
Sun-spangled pages, dazzled, blow away!
Waves, shatter! Shatter in a jubilant spray
This quiet roof where jabbed the fo'c'sle flocks.

II

Bernart de Ventadorn

(Twelfth Century)

Had Bernart de Ventadorn (or Ventadour) written in a language more widely read than Provençal, he would have taken his place centuries ago, says Jeanroy, among "les grands classiques d'amour." About his life we know very little; most biographies simply romanticize what his own forty-odd poems tell us. He must have been alive from about 1140 to 1180, but how long before or after we have no certainty. He seems to have wandered about southern France, which he never left except to visit England in 1154 for the coronation of Henry II and Eleanor of Aquitaine, for whom some of his poems were written and with whom he may have been in love—romantic hearts are happy to think that the greatest of the troubadours may have had an affair with the glamorous mother of Richard the Lion-Hearted.

What a typical Provençal poet was supposed to be we know from such descriptions as Professor Bowra's ("Medieval Love-Song," in *In General and Particular*): he "falls in love at first sight but remains faithful to his beloved through all his days. She is for him the embodiment of perfection, physical, intellectual, and moral, and his dominating desire is to be worthy of her . . . he must be the embodiment of chivalrous manhood, courteous, modest, gentle, and brave. . . ." His love was chiefly platonic, of soul for soul, although "physical relations are spoken of with restraint and caution. . . ." This "rarefied, exacting conception of love" reached its height, thinks Bowra, in Bernart and two or three others.

And yet the passionate Bernart does not fit comfortably among these well-behaved singers. His keener honesty, sometimes like Donne's, is one of the qualities that make him the greatest of the Provençal poets. He tells his lady

33

quite frankly that if she keeps him waiting he can find other girls elsewhere; he points out that charming as she is, she by no means embodies perfection; indeed he becomes so enraged at her that, as Ernest Hoepffner says, he comes close to blasphemy. Far from being always courteous and gentle, he calls one girl "a low-down lying traitress—from a bad family too!" What he desires he expresses with no particular restraint or caution: he says that he wants to kiss another so passionately that people can tell a month afterward just by looking at her face; he says rather often that what he wants most of all is to be snugly in bed with his love—some of his passages were rather a problem for nineteenth-century textual scholars, who couldn't believe a certified troubadour really meant that.

Nor did he seem particularly modest: his own poems are better than anyone else's, he says, because they originate in his deeper love—it is his conviction that love alone can write good poetry. This "Racine of the troubadours" was passionately sincere, and because of his sincerity ran the gamut, sometimes in the course of a single poem, from exultation to despair. At times he can be the most joyful of poets, and joy is a theme hard to handle convincingly. For all the complexity of his feelings, the poems are simple—very far from the hermetic *trobar clus* of the more gnarled Provençal poets. The musical simplicity of his style is all the more surprising since Bernart used some of the most demanding stanza forms and rhyme schemes a poet has ever set himself. Generally the rhyming sounds of the first stanza are carried all through the poem—one poem of seventy-seven lines employs only two rhyming sounds, an effect these translations have not attempted to duplicate. Rhyme is not merely ornamental in Bernart's songs; good rhyme never is. In Bernart's work the sound tended to stress the key ideas and feelings; rhyming words were like the focal points at which these could shine out with special brilliance. It may be of some interest that he was the first to introduce the ten-syllable line into Provençal poetry— and with that we are on the way to Dante's ten-plus-one and to Chaucer and to at least three-fourths of English poetry ever since.

Bernart's poems are songs, for some of which the music still exists. The translations, however, seem to me more in the manner of a speaking voice than of a singing one.

The text is from *Bernart de Ventadour, Troubadour du XIIe Siècle: Chansons d'Amour.* Edited by Moshé Lazar. Librairie C. Klincksieck, Paris. 1966. (In XXV, I have omitted four lines which seem to have been added later to the end of the poem, and admitted a variant reading [in brackets] toward the end of XVII.)

IV

IV

Tant ai mo cor ple de joya,
tot me desnatura.
Flor blancha, vermelh' e groya
me par la frejura,
c'ab lo ven et ab la ploya
me creis l'aventura,
per que mos chans mont' e poya
e mos pretz melhura.
Tan ai al cor d'amor,
de joi e de doussor,
per que·l gels me sembla flor
e la neus verdura.

Anar posc ses vestidura,
nutz en ma chamisa,
car fin' amors m'asegura
de la freja biza.
Mas es fols qui·s desmezura
e no·s te de guiza.
Per qu'eu ai pres de me cura,
deis c'agui enquiza
la plus bela d'amor,
don aten tan d'onor,
car en loc de sa ricor
no volh aver Piza.

De s'amistat me reciza!
Mas be n'ai fiansa,
que sivals eu n'ai conquiza
la bela semblansa.

IV

Joy! a heart so overflowing,
look, the world's enchanted!
Red, blue, yellow!—winter's sowing
flowers around? Though granted
snows are deep and northers blowing
and the hail comes slanted,
lucky me! what gusto showing!
and what chanteys chanted!
I'm wild with love for you,
sweetness and fever too!
Drifts are yellow, red, and blue.
Snow?—or June transplanted?

In my heart what ardors glowing!
Though the north wind rake it,
I could walk the snowfield, throwing
clothes away! go naked!
Could, but—foolish way of going!
I should undertake it?
Best-behavior's what I'm showing
lately—why forsake it?
When I set out to woo
your loveliness, I knew
could I have, instead of you,
Pisa—hell could take it!

If I think her friendship's cooling,
I allow: but clearly
here's a girl delights in fooling
one she loves sincerely.

Et ai ne a ma deviza
tan de benanansa,
que ja·l jorn que l'aurai viza,
non aurai pezansa.
Mo cor ai pres d'Amor,
que l'esperitz lai cor,
mas lo cors es sai, alhor,
lonh de leis, en Fransa.

Eu n'ai la bon' esperansa.
Mas petit m'aonda,
c'atressi·m ten en balansa
com la naus en l'onda.
Del mal pes que·m desenansa,
no sai on m'esconda.
Tota noih me vir' e·m lansa
desobre l'esponda.
Plus trac pena d'amor
de Tristan l'amador,
que·n sofri manhta dolor
per Izeut la blonda.

Ai Deus! car no sui ironda,
que voles per l'aire
e vengues de noih prionda
lai dins so repaire?
Bona domna jauzionda,
mor se·l vostr' amaire!
Paor ai que·l cors me fonda,
s'aissi·m dura gaire.
Domna, per vostr' amor
jonh las mas et ador!
Gens cors ab frescha color,
gran mal me faitz traire!

Oh I'm lucky in love's schooling,
lucky me! I merely
catch her eye, and all that grueling
day's rewarded dearly.
My heart's gone off with you;
my soul's away there too;
body drags in France, a blue
bleak cadaver, nearly.

Hope's the only hope remaining.
She, for my devotion,
worries me like timbers straining
in an angry ocean.
Harbor from such wind-and-raining?
Where—I've not a notion.
All the night I toss, complaining,
lord! that bed's commotion!
I suffer more for you
than Tristram dared to do
for his blond Iseult—those two
and their magic potion.

God! to be a swallow skimming
under heaven's cover,
settled, as the west is dimming,
on the bed above her.
Gentle breast, with laughter brimming,
under clay and clover
stow me—such a trouble's coming
as I won't get over.
O lady, look! my two
palms pressed adoring you;
blond and rose thing, eyes of blue,
how you vex your lover!

Qu'el mon non a nul afaire
don eu tan cossire,
can de leis au re retraire,
que mo cor no i vire
e mo semblan no·m n'esclaire.
Que que·m n'aujatz dire,
si c'ades vos er veyaire
c'ai talan de rire.
Tan l'am de bon' amor
que manhtas vetz en plor
per o que melhor sabor
m'en an li sospire.

Messatgers, vai e cor,
e di·m a la gensor
la pena e la dolor
que·n trac, e·l martire.

Nothing else is worth the knowing
for a single minute.
When they stand there *Ah!*ing, *Oh!*ing
over her, caught in it
I feel such elation growing,
who's to discipline it?
Let them guess, from cheeks so glowing,
I've a thing to grin at.
My love's so right and true,
these lashes, damp for you,
prove, for all that grief can do,
there's a rapture in it.

Messenger, paint me true,
flame-colored through and through;
tell our You-Know-Who
fire can burn what's in it.

XVII

Lo gens tems de pascor
ab la frescha verdor
nos adui folh' e flor
de diversa color,
per que tuih amador
son gai e chantador
mas eu, que planh e plor,
c'us jois no m'a sabor.

A totz me clam, senhor,
de midons e d'Amor,
c'aicist dui traïdor,
car me fiav'en lor,
me fan viur' a dolor
per ben e per onor
c'ai faih a la gensor,
que no·m val ni·m acor.

Pen' e dolor e dan
n'ai agut, e n'ai gran,
mas sofert o ai tan.
No m'o tenh ad afan;
c'anc no vitz nulh aman,
melhs ames ses enjan,
qu'eu no·m vau ges chamjan
si com las domnas fan.

Pois fom amdui efan,
l'am ades e la blan;
e·s vai m'amors doblan

XVII

The good time of the year
when sweeter fields appear.
Leaves, flowers, and all. The sheer
silk greenery, dark or clear.
Then love's exultant men
take singing up again.
Not I. I'm mournful when
I think of joy that's been.

I'm all complaints: You know
love and this girl? They go
urging my overthrow
—stab in the back—although
I swore my faith to these,
tried with my soul to please
the best girl heaven sees,
who rates me at—two peas?

Snubs, suffering, loss, regret—
I've known them, know them yet;
chewed on "Forgive, forget";
learned to endure. Will bet
you'll never see the day
I promise, then betray.
I'm different. Girls now, they
fall often by the way.

From childhood on, my true
and one great passion: you.
All weathers, grey or blue,

a chascu jorn del an.
E si no·m fai enan
amor e bel semblan,
cant er velha, ·m deman
que l'aya bo talan.

Las! e viure que·m val,
s'eu no vei a jornal
mo fi joi natural
en leih, sotz fenestral,
cors blanc tot atretal
com la neus a nadal,
si c'amdui cominal
mesurem s'em egal?

Anc no vitz drut leyal,
sordeis o aya sal,
qu'eu l'am d'amor coral,
ela·m ditz: "no m'en chal."
enans ditz que per al
no m'a ira mortal.
E si d'aisso·m vol mal,
pechat n'a criminal.

Be for'oimais sazos,
bela domna e pros,
que·m fos datz a rescos
en baizan guizardos,
si ja per als no fos,
mas car sui enveyos,
c'us bes val d'autres dos,
can per fors' es faihz dos.

Can vei vostras faissos
e·ls bels olhs amoros,

my ardor grew and grew.
Unless, though, you outpour
favors of love before
old age leans on the door—!
Try coaxing then for more.

Life gives—? well nothing quite
like having day and night
the one joy mine by right:
in bed, by window-light
yourself undressed, a glow
merry as Christmas snow,
where we lie fitted so
we're snug from head to toe.

None ever loved so well
or with worse news to tell.
As my pure longings swell
she'll stretch—a yawning spell!—
and then a shrug, "Well I
really don't care, is why."
If true, or if some lie,
that damns her by and by.

I plead: "But who's to miss
(well, some day, if not this)
one tiny sip of bliss,
a quick dark-stairway kiss?"
You'll kiss me, no? Encore?
And never ask what for.
Forced charity's a chore.
Give freely is give more.

Seeing your face among
the crowd, with all eyes hung

be · m meravilh de vos
com etz de mal respos.
E sembla · m trassios,
can om par francs e bos
e pois es orgolhos
lai on es poderos.

Bel Vezer, si no fos
mos [Denan-totz e] vos,
laissat agra chansos
per mal dels enoyos.

on you, so warm, so young,
I think: her terrible tongue!
It's treason, plain to see,
when "flowers of courtesy"
go frozen, at the plea
of one poor bended knee.

Now Blue-Eyes, but for you
(and sweet Miss Other too)
I'd play it mum, lip curled,
in so morose a world.

XX

Can l'erba fresch' e·lh folha par
e la flors boton' el verjan,
e·l rossinhols autet e clar
leva sa votz e mou so chan,
joi ai de lui, e joi ai de la flor
e joi de me e de midons major;
daus totas partz sui de joi claus e sens,
mas sel es jois que totz autres jois vens.

Ai las! com mor de cossirar!
Que manhtas vetz en cossir tan:
lairo m'en poirian portar,
que re no sabria que·s fan.
Per Deu, Amors! be·m trobas vensedor:
ab paucs d'amics e ses autre senhor.
Car una vetz tan midons no destrens
abans qu'eu fos del dezirer estens?

Meravilh me com posc durar
que no·lh demostre mo talan.
Can eu vei midons ni l'esgar,
li seu bel olh tan be l'estan:
per pauc me tenh car eu vas leis no cor.
Si feira eu, si no fos per paor,
c'anc no vi cors melhs talhatz ni depens
ad ops d'amar sia tan greus ni lens.

Tan am midons e la tenh car,
e tan la dopt' e la reblan
c'anc de me no·lh auzei parlar,
ni re no·lh quer ni re no·lh man.

XX

When—presto—turf and trees are green
and blossoms cocked where they belong,
and the wild singer tweedles keen
and chuckles gruff to try the song,
it's joy the bird! and joy, the wood astir!
joy, me myself! and double joy in her!
On all sides joy assailing me—too much!
But joy in her's the joy no joy can touch.

Only, confusion of desire!
Time and again I want her so
I'm in a daze—if baled in wire
and carted off, I'd never know.
For God's sake, Love! I'm hardly fit to fight
world conquerers such as you, no friend in sight.
Persuade the girl, for once, to be my own
before I'm dates and curlicues in stone.

Miraculous, how I survive
and never let the fever show.
I hover, watch the girl arrive,
follow her eyes and where they go—
stockstill. I'd break away, and nearly do,
in her direction but—no courage to.
Her honey-blond neat body rounded so
for making love, and yet—so round a *No?*

I think my lady such a dear
I wouldn't vex her; still I stay,
hush-hush all talk of love, for fear
one murmur and she's off away.

Pero elh sap mo mal e ma dolor,
e can li plai, mi fai ben et onor,
e can li plai, eu m'en sofert ab mens,
per so c'a leis no·n avenha blastens.

S'eu saubes la gen enchantar,
mei enemic foran efan,
que ja us no saubra triar
ni dir re que·ns tornes a dan.
Adoncs sai eu que vira la gensor
e sos bels olhs e sa frescha color,
e baizera·lh la bocha en totz sens,
si que d'un mes i paregra lo sens.

Be la volgra sola trobar,
que dormis, o·n fezes semblan,
per qu'e·lh embles un doutz baizar,
pus no valh tan qu'eu lo·lh deman.
Per Deu, domna, pauc esplecham d'amor;
vai s'en lo tems, e perdem lo melhor!
Parlar degram ab cubertz entresens,
e, pus no·ns val arditz, valgues nos gens!

Be deuri'om domna blasmar,
can trop vai son amic tarzan,
que lonja paraula d'amar
es grans enois e par d'enjan,
c'amar pot om e far semblan alhor,
e gen mentir lai on non a autor.
Bona domna, ab sol c'amar mi dens,
ja per mentir eu no serai atens.

Messatger, vai, e no m'en prezes mens,
s'eu del anar vas midons sui temens.

She guesses, though, my wound and all its cause;
brings, when she will, right medicine and gauze.
And, when she won't, I'm quiet; live on less.
Suppose I grumble, and the gapers guess—

Had I the science of a witch
I'd blast them!—little wits so blurred
they'd never know a who from which
nor snigger one malicious word.
And then I'd be all eyes, myself alone,
for her fine face, fine body's flesh and bone;
I'd kiss her mouth some hundred ways, so well
weeks after, just by looking, you could tell.

Only to stumble on her where
she lies alone! Pretending sleep?
I'd have the lips I never dare
ask for as yet. Will roses keep?
God, girl, we're getting nowhere fast in love!
Time's running out, a stuff we've little of.
Let's deal in codes and hidden winks; we could
work by finesse, if being brave's no good.

A lover's in the right to blame
a lady who excuses, balks;
makes love a conversation game
and talks and talks. And talks and talks.
You can love here, and elsewhere say you do;
tell a fine lie when none's to check on you.
Lady, receive your lover! Then you'll learn
how I can lie and lie to serve your turn.

Messenger, here's the message. Let her know
how—with this pounding pulse—I'd quake to go.

XXV

Era · m cosselhatz, senhor,
vos c'avetz saber e sen:
una domna · m det s'amor,
c'ai amada lonjamen;
mas eras sai de vertat
qu'ilh a autr' amic privat,
ni anc de nul companho
companha tan greus no · m fo.

D'una re sui en error
e · n estau en pensamen:
que m'alonje ma dolor,
s'eu aquest plaih li cossen,
e s'aissi · l dic mon pessat,
vei mo damnatge doblat.
Cal que · n fassa o cal que no,
re no posc far de mo pro.

E s'eu l'am a dezonor,
esquerns er a tota gen;
e tenran m'en li pluzor
per cornut e per soften.
E s'aissi pert s'amistat,
be · m tenh per dezeretat
d'amor, e ja Deus no · m do
mais faire vers ni chanso.

Pois voutz sui en la folor,
be serai fols, s'eu no pren
d'aquestz dos mals lo menor;
que mais val, mon essien,

XXV

Men, a word of wisdom. Give,
you that know a thing or two.
One for whom alone I live
said she loved me. Very true;
yet it's true the rumor's out
there's a secret friend about.
Nothing I've gone halves in yet
would I share with such regret.

Head a whirl of worries, I
sit and puzzle: what to do?
Let her practice on the sly
and assume I never knew?
Or would humoring hurt more
than it would to rant and roar?
Should or shouldn't? shouldn't? should?
What's the best of nothing good?

Say I'm mum: they nudge and wink
and I'm everybody's fool.
Just an easy mark, they think;
too adjustable a tool.
If I lose my love, to boot,
I'm forever destitute.
Nothing to inspire me then;
little cause to write again.

Close to bedlam as I live,
I'd be in the place for good
if I brooded "Won't forgive!"
Play it smarter's what I should.

qu'eu ay' en leis la meitat
que·l tot perda per foldat,
car anc a nul drut felo
d'amor no vi far son pro.

Pois vol autre amador
ma domn', eu no lo·lh defen;
e lais m'en mais per paor
que per autre chauzimen;
e s'anc om dec aver grat
de nul servizi forsat,
be dei aver guizerdo
eu, que tan gran tort perdo.

Li seu belh olh traïdor,
que m'esgardavon tan gen,
s'atressi gardon alhor,
mout i fan gran falhimen;
mas d'aitan m'an mout onrat
que, s'eron mil ajostat,
plus gardon lai on eu so,
c'a totz aicels d'eviro.

De l'aiga que dels olhs plor,
escriu salutz mais de cen,
que tramet a la gensor
et a la plus avinen.
Manhtas vetz m'es pois membrat
de so que·m fetz al comjat:
que·lh vi cobrir sa faisso,
c'anc no·m poc dir oc ni no.

Domna, a prezen amat
autrui, e me a celat,
si qu'eu n'aya tot lo pro
et el la bela razo.

Seeing how the chances run,
better half a girl than none.
Lovers loud about their "right"
pace the empty rooms at night.

Since my lady rides her heart
tandem, should I make a scene?
No, I'd stutter at the start;
couldn't tell her what I mean.
And, if any heard "Thank *you!*"
for a thing he's made to do,
then she owes me thanks—and more.
Things I've made allowance for!

Beautiful deceiving eyes
once upon my own would play
in a flicker of surmise.
Though they've turned another way,
there's a fact I can't forget:
how, when gala crowds are met,
though her eyes go hither, yon,
mostly mine they linger on.

Tears are in the ink I fling
harum-scarum: greetings to
the world's most attractive thing,
madly most delicious you!
With a thought no years erase:
how you covered up your face
at good-by—were sobbing so
couldn't breathe a yes or no.

Lady, in the eyes of men
play at love and play again.
Love me where there's none to see:
words for others; lips for me.

Can vei la lauzeta mover
de joi sas alas contral rai,
que s'oblid' e·s laissa chazer
per la doussor c'al cor li vai,
ai! tan grans enveya m'en ve
de cui qu'eu veya jauzion,
meravilhas ai, car desse
lo cor de dezirer no·m fon.

Ai, las! tan cuidava saber
d'amor, e tan petit en sai,
car eu d'amar no·m posc tener
celeis don ja pro non aurai.
Tout m'a mo cor, e tout m'a me,
e se mezeis e tot lo mon;
e can se·m tolc, no·m laisset re
mas dezirer e cor volon.

Anc non agui de me poder
ni no fui meus de l'or' en sai
que·m laisset en sos olhs vezer
en un miralh que mout me plai.
Miralhs, pus me mirei en te,
m'an mort li sospir de preon,
c'aissi·m perdei com perdet se
lo bels Narcisus en la fon.

De las domnas me dezesper;
ja mais en lor no·m fiarai;
c'aissi com las solh chaptener,
enaissi las deschaptenrai.

XXXI

To see the lark, delighted, dare
its wings in joy against the sun,
and reckless, somersault in air,
half tumbling, that exultant one—
such envy flares within me when
I see pure happiness at play,
I marvel at my own heart then:
not, with its yearning, burnt away?

This love! that once I thought I knew
so thoroughly! and know nothing of,
nothing. A fool in being true,
in reaching for the moon in love:
for one that took my heart, and me,
and took herself, and took the rest.
Leaving, left what for memory?
Passion and havoc in the breast.

I couldn't do a thing with me,
wasn't my own a single day
since in her eyes she let me see
the brightest of all mirrors play.
I looked, O mirror, deep in you
and read what only grief can tell;
ruined as he was ruined too—
Narcissus spellbound at the well.

These girls! no trusting any more
in these, no certainty again.
I championed one and all before.
That's over. That's for other men.

Pois vei c'una pro no m'en te
vas leis que·m destrui e·m cofon,
totas las dopt' e las mescre,
car be sai c'atretals se son.

D'aisso's fa be femna parer
ma domna, per qu'e·lh o retrai,
car no vol so c'om deu voler,
e so c'om li deveda, fai.
Chazutz sui en mala merce,
et ai be faih co·l fols en pon;
e no sai per que m'esdeve,
mas car trop puyei contra mon.

Merces es perduda, per ver,
et eu non o saubi anc mai,
car cilh qui plus en degr'aver,
no·n a ges, et on la querrai?
A! can mal sembla, qui la ve,
qued aquest chaitiu deziron
que ja ses leis non aura be,
laisse morrir, que no·l aon!

Pus ab midons no·m pot valer
precs ni merces ni·l dreihz qu'eu ai,
ni a leis no ven a plazer
qu'eu l'am, ja mais no·lh o dirai.
Aissi·m part de leis e·m recre;
mort m'a, e per mort li respon,
e vau m'en, pus ilh no·m rete,
chaitius, en issilh, no sai on.

Tristans, ges no·n auretz de me,
qu'eu m'en vau, chaitius, no sai on.
De chantar me gic e·m recre,
e de joi e d'amor m'escon.

58

Not one made efforts to reprieve
me with that bitter lady—none!
And now I'm wary, disbelieve.
You know the saying: Six of one . . .

My love's a woman through and through;
it seems I'm blaming her for that.
She's fond of what she shouldn't do;
what's proper, she makes faces at.
I've fallen out of favor, yes—
"Fool on a bridge," as people say.
Why fallen? I can only guess:
attempting too uphill a way?

No chance of favor; gone for good.
I never knew a kindness yet!
And if she does none, she who should
be mercy's self, then where's it met?
Who'd watch so sweet a girl and think
she'd let this dismal lover crawl
off in his trouble toward the brink
—well knowing she's my all in all?

My merit's nothing now to her,
nothing, her natural sympathy.
I touch on love, she doesn't stir
a finger. And that's that, from me.
I'll pack my heart up, pack and go
among the tombstones—track me there.
I'm off now, since she wants it so,
lonely, in exile, who knows where?

Lady, you'll get no more from me.
I'm off now, lonely, who knows where?
Regions remote from poetry;
no pleasure in the loveless air.

59

III

The First Sestinas

Arnaut Daniel (fl. 1180–1200)
Dante Alighieri (1265–1321)

In the *Divine Comedy*, Dante has Guido Guinizelli, founder of the "sweet new style" in which Dante too came to write, refer to Arnaut Daniel as the "miglior fabbro del parlar materno," the better craftsman of the mother tongue. Arnaut, who wrote in Provençal, was indeed a craftsman, the deviser of elaborate stanzaic forms, intricate rhyme schemes, and other feats of technique. Among the inventions with which he is credited is the sestina, now familiar to every poet who has been in a workshop. Arnaut did not create it from nothing; earlier poets had experimented with the repetition and patterning of line endings, but it was Arnaut, it seems, who gave us the form we know today, perfectly regular and symmetrical (except that the first line of each of his stanzas has eight syllables instead of the eleven of the other lines). Some think his structuring in sixes has its origin in symbolic numerology, in such correspondences as Jehovah's creating the world in six days. However the sestina may have originated, it has had a long history, though with many lapses, and still seems vigorous.

About a century after Arnaut, Dante wrote the best known of the early sestinas. Many would say no better one has been written since. One of his *rime petrose*, or "stony poems," it is addressed to the lady he calls Petra, whose heart, at least in his regard, seemed hard as stone.

About the history of the sestina in western literature through the centuries, there is a good deal more to say. Some of it has been said in my essay on that history in *A Local Habitation: Essays on Poetry* (University of Michigan Press, 1985).

The text of Arnaut Daniel's poem is from his *Canzoni*. Edited by Gianluigi Toja. Sansoni, Firenze. 1960. The text of Dante's is that of the Società Dantesca Italiana, second edition. 1960.

Arnaut Daniel

LO FERM VOLER Q' EL COR M' INTRA

Lo ferm voler q'el cor m' intra
no · m pot ies becs escoissendre ni ongla
de lausengier, qui pert per mal dir s'arma;
e car non l'aus batr'ab ram ni ab verga,
sivals a frau, lai on non aurai oncle,
iauzirai ioi, en vergier o dinz cambra.

Qan mi soven de la cambra
on a mon dan sai que nuills hom non intra
anz me son tuich plus que fraire ni oncle,
non ai membre no · m fremisca, neis l'ongla,
aissi cum fai l'enfas denant la verga:
tal paor ai no · l sia trop de l'arma.

Del cors li fos, non de l'arma,
e cossentis m'a celat dinz sa cambra!
Que plus mi nafra · l cor que colps de verga
car lo sieus sers lai on ill es non intra;
totz temps serai ab lieis cum carns et ongla,
e non creirai chastic d'amic ni d'oncle.

Anc la seror de mon oncle
non amei plus ni tant, per aqest'arma!
C'aitant vezis cum es lo detz de l'ongla,
s'a liei plagues, volgr'esser de sa cambra;
de mi pot far l'amors q'inz el cor m'intra
mieills a son vol c'om fortz de frevol verga.

Pois flori la seca verga
ni d'en Adam mogron nebot ni oncle,
tant fin' amors cum cella q'el cor m'intra

Arnaut Daniel

THE RESOLUTE DESIRE THAT ENTERS

The resolute desire that enters
My heart, won't give for prying fingernail,
For liar with black tongue—that damns his soul!
Since such I dare not thrash with birch or rod,
Secret at least, none near in shape of uncle,
Joy I'll enjoy, in orchard or . . . her own room.

When memory turns to that, her own room
Where no man—to my grief I say—can enter
(They're worse, the pack of them, than brother, uncle!)
No part of me's not quivering, not a fingernail;
I'm like a truant when he sees the rod,
For fear I've given her less than all my soul.

My wish is body, not just soul!
I wish she'd ease me, secret, in her own room.
My heart's sick, feels it worse than pain of rod,
That where she is her loyal man can't enter.
I'm with her always, snug as skin to fingernail;
Care nothing for rough tongue of friend or uncle.

Not even the sister of my uncle
Did I love more, as much even, by my soul!
Familiar as a finger with its fingernail
Is what I'd be (she willing) with her own room.
Love bends me to its might, when once it enters,
Easy as strong men bend a feeble rod.

Since burst in flower the barren rod,
Since from Sir Adam down came nephew, uncle,
So pure a love as in my own heart enters

non cuig fos anc en cors, ni eis en arma;
on q'ill estei, fors en plaz', o dins cambra,
mos cors no · is part de lieis tant cum ten l'ongla.

C'aissi s'enpren e s'enongla
mos cors en lei cum l'escorss' en la verga;
q' ill m'es de ioi tors e palaitz e cambra,
e non am tant fraire, paren ni oncle:
q'en paradis n'aura doble ioi m'arma,
si ia nuills hom per ben amar lai intra.

Arnautz tramet sa chansson d'ongl'e d'oncle,
a grat de lieis que de sa verg'a l'arma,
son Desirat, cui pretz en cambra intra.

I can't believe there was, in body or soul.
Wherever she is—in public, in her own room—
My heart won't stir from her the width of a fingernail.

My heart holds, clings like fingernail,
As fast to her as bark does to its rod.
For me she's pleasure's palace, tower—its own room.
I've no such love for brother, parent, uncle.
In heaven a bliss on bliss will flood my soul,
If loving well's what qualifies to enter.

So Arnaut sends his song of "nail" and "uncle"
To pleasure her whose rod rules all his soul,
His one Desired, whose own room splendour enters.

Dante Alighieri

AL POCO GIORNO E AL GRAN CERCHIO D'OMBRA

Al poco giorno e al gran cerchio d'ombra
son giunto, lasso! ed al bianchir de' colli,
quando si perde lo color ne l'erba;
e 'l mio disio però non cangia il verde,
sì è barbato ne la dura petra
che parla e sente come fosse donna.

Similemente questa nova donna
si sta gelata come neve a l'ombra;
che non la move, se non come petra,
il dolce tempo che riscalda i colli
e che li fa tornar di bianco in verde
perché li copre di fioretti e d'erba.

Quand'ella ha in testa una ghirlanda d'erba,
trae de la mente nostra ogn'altra donna;
perché si mischia il crespo giallo e 'l verde
sì bel ch'Amor li viene a stare a l'ombra,
che m'ha serrato intra piccioli colli
più forte assai che la calcina petra.

La sua bellezza ha più vertù che petra,
e 'l colpo suo non può sanar per erba;
ch'io son fuggito per piani e per colli
per potere scampar da cotal donna;
e dal suo lume non mi può far ombra
poggio né muro mai né fronda verde.

Dante Alighieri

TO WANING DAY, TO THE WIDE
ROUND OF SHADOW

To waning day, to the wide round of shadow
I've come, alas, and come to whitening hills
Now when all color dwindles from the grasses.
Not so with my desire: no change of green,
So sunk its roots are in the ruthless stone
That listens, talks—you'd think a very woman.

But like the season, this incredible woman
Stands frozen there, a bank of snow in shadow.
The heart within her no more melts, than stone
When softer weather mellows all the hills,
Changing them back from chilly white to green,
The time it nestles them in flowers and grasses.

When round her head's a garland of sweet grasses,
Out of my thought goes every other woman!
So trim they mingle, curly gold and green,
That love comes down to linger in their shadow
—Love that enfolds me in those gentle hills
Tighter by far than mortar holds a stone.

More magic power than any fabulous stone
Her beauty has; its pain no herb, no grasses
Have skill to heal. Across wide plains, through hills
I've fled to escape the glamor of this woman.
In vain: from sun so bright no hope of shadow,
No hill, no wall, no wood's deep leafy green.

Io l'ho veduta già vestita a verde
sì fatta ch'ella avrebbe messo in petra
l'amor ch'io porto pur a la sua ombra;
ond' io l'ho chesta in un bel prato d'erba
innamorata, com'anco fu donna,
e chiuso intorno d'altissimi colli.

Ma ben ritorneranno i fiumi a' colli
prima che questo legno molle e verde
s'infiammi, come suol far bella donna,
di me; che mi torrei dormire in petra
tutto il mio tempo e gir pascendo l'erba,
sol per veder do' suoi panni fanno ombra.

Quandunque i colli fanno più nera ombra,
sotto un bel verde la giovane donna
la fa sparer, com'uom petra sott'erba.

There was a day I saw her dressed in green,
And such, she would have driven the very stone
Wild with the love I feel for her least shadow.
How I'd have wished her then, in pleasant grasses,
As deep in love as ever man knew woman
—And wished our field were snug among high hills.

But sooner the low rivers ride high hills
Than this young plant, so succulent and green,
Bursts into flame for me, as lovely woman
So often does for man. I'd couch on stone
My whole life long, feed like a beast on grasses,
Only to see her skirt in swirls of shadow.

Whenever now the hills throw blackest shadow,
With her delicious green the one young woman
Hides all that dark, as summer grass a stone.

IV

Dante Alighieri

(1265–1321)

In the introductory essay, "Poetry: Lost in Translation," I have described (pp. 13–14) how I read Dante during a year spent in Florence, and how I wondered if one difference between Italian and English ought to be taken into account in translating the *Commedia*. In Italian, many common words have two or more syllables: *amore, morte, giorno, notte, terra, mare, ragazzo, ragazza, cane, gatto,* etc. In English the corresponding words are monosyllables: *love, death, day, night, land, sea, boy, girl, dog, cat,* etc. If one translates Dante's *endecasillabo* (eleven-syllable line) into our iambic pentameter, as is generally done, do we find that the English lines often have to be padded to bring them to the required length? Would a shorter line, say an eight-syllable line, give a better sense of the compactness of his writing? That is what I was trying to find out in this version of his first canto.

The Italian text is that of the Società Dantesca Italiana, as given in the edition of Carlo Grabher, 14th edition, Casa Editrice Giuseppe Principato, Milan, 1953—one of several editions I made use of in the translation.

INFERNO, CANTO I

Nel mezzo del cammin di nostra vita
   mi ritrovai per una selva oscura,
   ché la diritta via era smarrita.
Ah quanto a dir qual era è cosa dura
   esta selva selvaggia e aspra e forte
   che nel pensier rinova la paura!
Tant'è amara che poco è piú morte;
   ma per trattar del ben ch'io vi trovai,
   dirò de l'altre cose ch'io v'ho scorte.
Io non so ben ridir com'io v'entrai,
   tant'era pieno di sonno a quel punto
   che la verace via abbandonai.
Ma poi ch'i' fui al piè d'un colle giunto,
   là dove terminava quella valle
   che m'avea di paura il cor compunto,
guardai in alto, e vidi le sue spalle
   vestite già de' raggi del pianeta
   che mena dritto altrui per ogni calle.
Allor fu la paura un poco queta
   che nel lago del cor m'era durata
   la notte ch'io passai con tanta pièta.
E come quei che con lena affannata
   uscito fuor del pelago a la riva,
   si volge a l'acqua perigliosa e guata,
cosí l'animo mio, ch'ancor fuggiva,
   si volse a retro a rimirar lo passo
   che non lasciò già mai persona viva.
Poi ch'èi posato un poco il corpo lasso,
   ripresi via per la piaggia diserta,
   sí che 'l piè fermo sempre era 'l piú basso.

INFERNO, CANTO I

The middle of life's journey: I
    came conscious in a darkening wood;
    lost, the right road to travel by.
Grim chore, to make its nature clear,
    that wildwood, thick and thorny—such
    even the memory's full of fear.
So bitter, death is barely more;
    but, for the good I got, suppose
    I tell of other things I bore.
How I had strayed there, hard to say,
    so drugged with slumber at the time
    I must have stumbled from the way.
But coming just beneath a hill
    at the far end of that ravine
    where fear's a penetrating chill,
I looked above: the shoulders shone
    gold in the glory of that sun
    that everywhere guides everyone.
That for a moment dulled the dread
    that over my heart's tarn had hung
    all the long night I spent half dead.
As some survivor gasps for air
    and struggling beyond surf to sand
    turns on the perilous sea his stare,
my soul, in trepidation still,
    paused to look backward on the pass
    none ever trod and lived to tell.
A moment there to breathe, and straight
    I headed for the lonesome rise,
    letting my set foot take the weight.

Ed ecco, quasi al cominciar de l'erta,
una lonza leggiera e presta molto,
che di pel maculato era coverta;
e non mi si partía dinanzi al vólto,
anzi impediva tanto il mio cammino,
ch'i' fui per ritornar piú volte vòlto.
Temp'era dal principio del mattino,
e 'l sol montava 'n su con quelle stelle
ch'eran con lui quando l'amor divino
mosse di prima quelle cose belle;
sí ch'a bene sperar m'era cagione
di quella fera a la gaetta pelle
l'ora del tempo e la dolce stagione;
ma non sí che paura non mi desse
la vista che m'apparve d'un leone.
Questi parea che contra me venesse
con la test'alta e con rabbiosa fame,
sí che parea che l'aere ne temesse.
Ed una lupa, che di tutte brame
sembiava carca ne la sua magrezza,
e molte genti fe' già viver grame,
questa mi porse tanto di gravezza
con la paura ch'uscía di sua vista,
ch'io perdei la speranza de l'altezza.
E qual è quei che volontieri acquista,
e giugne 'l tempo che perder lo face,
che 'n tutt'i suoi pensier piange e s'attrista;
tal mi fece la bestia sanza pace,
che, venendomi incontro, a poco a poco
mi ripigneva là dove 'l sol tace.
Mentre ch'i' ruinava in basso loco,
dinanzi a li occhi mi si fu offerto
chi per lungo silenzio parea fioco.
Quando vidi costui nel gran diserto,
«Miserere di me» gridai a lui,
«qual che tu sii, od ombra od omo certo!»

Till there! at bottom of the trail
   a lynx came flickering, slim and quick,
   satiny, dappled head to tail.
It slunk in front, obstructed so
   it made impossible that path.
   Time and again I turned to go.
Freshness of morning blew above,
   the sun arising with those stars
   that followed him when divine love
impelled such loveliness afloat:
   some reason to hope wonders of
   that creature with the glamorous coat
on a spring morning soft and bright
   —not that I wasn't shaken when
   a lion erupted on my sight,
making as if to charge, a sheer
   frenzy of hunger, head on high,
   such, that the very air took fear.
And then a she-wolf, gaunt with greed;
   for all her gorging, skin and bone;
   thousands she'd pinched to direst need.
Such dismal apprehensions fill
   my thought on seeing her, I lost
   all hope of making it uphill.
As speculators, cornering all,
   rake in the take, complacent—then
   luck changes, and their spirits fall,
so I, to see that creature come
   with sinews twitching—inch by inch
   she drove me where the sun fell dumb.
As I went stumbling back below,
   vague in my vision floated one
   silent, it seemed, from long ago.
There in that godforsaken land
   "Have pity upon me," I cried,
   "whichever, ghost or mortal man."

Rispuosemi: «Non omo, omo già fui,
   e li parenti miei furon lombardi,
   mantovani per patrïa ambedui.
Nacqui sub Iulio, ancor che fosse tardi,
   e vissi a Roma sotto 'l buono Augusto
   al tempo de li dèi falsi e bugiardi.
Poeta fui, e cantai di quel giusto
   figliuol d'Anchise che venne da Troia,
   poi che 'l superbo Ilïòn fu combusto.
Ma tu perché ritorni a tanta noia?
   perché non sali il dilettoso monte
   ch'è principio e cagion di tutta gioia?»
«Or se' tu quel Virgilio e quella fonte
   che spandi di parlar sí largo fiume?»
   rispuos'io lui con vergognosa fronte.
«O de li altri poeti onore e lume,
   vagliami il lungo studio e 'l grande amore
   che m'ha fatto cercar lo tuo volume.
Tu se' lo mio maestro e 'l mio autore;
   tu se' solo colui da cu' io tolsi
   lo bello stilo che m'ha fatto onore.
Vedi la bestia per cu' io mi volsi:
   aiutami da lei, famoso saggio,
   ch'ella mi fa tremar le vene e i polsi».
«A te convien tenere altro vïaggio»
   rispuose poi che lagrimar mi vide,
   «se vuo' campar d'esto loco selvaggio:
ché questa bestia, per la qual tu gride,
   non lascia altrui passar per la sua via,
   ma tanto lo 'mpedisce che l'uccide;
e ha natura sí malvagia e ria,
   che mai non empie la bramosa voglia,
   e dopo il pasto ha piú fame che pria.
Molti son li animali a cui s'ammoglia,
   e piú saranno ancora, infin che 'l Veltro
   verrà, che la farà morir con doglia.

"No man;" he answered, "man I was.
　　Latin, of Lombardy my stock.
　　Both of my parents, Mantua's.
Born under Julius—late, it's true—
　　I under good Augustus lived,
　　when gods were bogus, bugaboo.
I was a poet, sang the just
　　son of Anchises, who fled Troy
　　when the proud city burned to dust.
But you, back to such grief?—who might
　　ascend there the enchanting hill
　　offering all manner of delight?"
"Then you're that Virgil, you're the spring
　　outspreading to so vast a flood
　　of song!" I faltered, coloring.
"O of all poets crown and light,
　　may they avail, the study and
　　love that I lavished day and night.
My master and sole model too,
　　for, if I wore the laurel, still
　　the handsome style I took from you.
But look, the thing there! If I swerve,
　　no wonder why. O famous sage,
　　help, for I'm slack in every nerve."
"You a far other way awaits,"
　　he answered, seeing me despond,
　　"out of these melancholy straits.
The beast you clamor at, they say
　　lets none go by alive; her mind
　　fixes on nothing but *slay, slay!*
Her temper's all on evil set—
　　fangs and a maw that nothing crams;
　　glutted, she goes gluttonous yet;
huddles with many a mate in lust;
　　will hunch with more, until the Hound
　　stretches her whining in the dust.

77

Questi non ciberà terra né peltro,
   ma sapïenza, amore e virtute,
   e sua nazion sarà tra feltro e feltro.
Di quella umile Italia fia salute
   per cui morí la vergine Cammilla,
   Eurialo e Turno e Niso di ferute.
Questi la caccerà per ogni villa,
   fin che l'avrà rimessa ne lo 'nferno,
   là onde invidia prima dipartilla.
Ond'io per lo tuo me' penso e discerno
   che tu mi segui, e io sarò tua guida,
   e trarrotti di qui per luogo eterno,
ov'udirai le disperate strida,
   vedrai li antichi spiriti dolenti,
   che la seconda morte ciascun grida;
e vederai color che son contenti
   nel foco, perché speran di venire
   quando che sia a le beate genti.
A le qua' poi se tu vorrai salire,
   anima fia a ciò piú di me degna:
   con lei ti lascerò nel mio partire;
ché quello imperador che là su regna,
   perch'io fu' ribellante a la sua legge,
   non vuol che 'n sua città per me si vegna.
In tutte parti impera e quivi regge;
   quivi è la sua città e l'alto seggio:
   oh felice colui cu' ivi elegge!»
E io a lui: «Poeta, io ti richeggio
   per quello Dio che tu non conoscesti,
   acciò ch'io fugga questo male e peggio,
che tu mi meni là dov'or dicesti,
   sí ch'io veggia la porta di san Pietro
   e color cui tu fai cotanto mesti».
Allor si mosse, e io li tenni retro.

No gold, no acres puff *his* pelt:
   his food is wisdom, justice, love;
   His birthplace?—think of *felt* and *felt*.
He'll make low-lying Italy well
   for which the girl Camilla died,
   Eurylus, Nisus, Turnus fell.
He'll hunt the she-wolf far and wide
   until he drags her back to hell,
   roping what ancient spite untied.
Now, for my counsel in your case:
   follow with me; I'll be your guide
   from here through our eternal place.
You'll hear how desperation wails,
   see spirits in their ancient pain
   there, where a death on death prevails.
You'll ponder on the souls at rest
   even in fire, who soon or late
   count on rejoicing with the blest.
Heaven if you've a mind to try,
   not mine to guide, but when we part
   there comes a worthier soul than I,
because that sovereign of the height,
   seeing me alien to his law,
   bans me forever from his sight.
True, his dominion's everywhere,
   but heaven his city-state and throne.
   Imagine the rapture, welcomed there!"
And I, "My poet, I implore
   by the great God you never knew,
   if I'm to avoid this grief and more,
oh show me to the place you said:
   show me where Peter keeps the gate,
   show the most dismal of the dead."
He started. And I followed straight.

V

Ausiàs March

(1397?–1459)

"One of the strangest and finest poems which any man has ever written," says the Catalan anthologist Joan Triadú of the body of work left us by Ausiàs March. But what was said above about Bernart's relatively unfamiliar language is even truer here. Ezra Pound remarks that he has interested only about half a dozen people in Provençal poetry, but who except Gerald Brenan tries to interest us in Catalan?—which is not Spanish nor even a dialect of Spanish. It is much closer to Provençal, although less close in March's time than it had been two centuries earlier, when troubadours wandered back and forth across the Pyrenees. Brenan, whose history of Spanish literature considers the Catalan poets because they are geographically Spanish, makes March appear the fascinating figure he indeed turns out to be: a "really great poet" who should appeal to us today, "a psychological poet whose subject is *Angst* . . . introspective, perversely tormented—so that one finds it hard to believe [his work] was written in the Middle Ages"—more like Baudelaire, thinks Brenan, than like any other poet. And sometimes like Donne—certainly closer to Donne in his darker moods than Bernart is.

Ausiàs March (pronounced *mark*) was born near Valencia probably in 1397. He was trained as a warrior-knight; when young he fought under Alfonso the Magnanimous in Sardinia, Corsica, Naples, Sicily, and Africa. Rewarded for his military service, he settled down as a tough and efficient feudal lord in the kingdom of Valencia. His interests were hawking, women, philosophy, and poetry—though not necessarily in that order nor in any order. If he had been able to set his various lives, inner and outer, in order, he might not have been what the literary historian Ruiz I Calonja calls him: "a feudal lord with a problem of conscience." And he might not have been the great poet he became.

March's two marriages were childless, but he had at least five children of other provenance. His greatest love poems were written to a certain Dona Teresa, who was married but not to him—a lady he worshiped in a tormented platonic way. One can see from these facts why March lived in a state of tension about love in its sexual and spiritual aspects, and why love was the source of nearly all of his poetry. If one can imagine an impolite Petrarch, unmusical, abrupt, infuriated, one can imagine what March was like.

Jagged, concentrated, violent stuff his poetry is, all storm clouds and lightning—such poetry as hardly comes from a soul at peace with itself. His deeply divided mind, which could look on one woman with spiritual worship while he was getting another, his own slave-girl, with child, which could return from the savagery of medieval warfare to the toughly intellectual contemplation of Aristotle, Aquinas, and Dante—this mind gave us a kind of poetry like itself. Here springtime brings nothing good. Nature is stormy and ominous; it seems to belong more to northern skies than to Valencia's blue and gold. The sea boils furiously—like "a casserole in the oven," he says, in a typical image. Everywhere in his work, images burst from his own inner turbulence. His style is difficult, his syntax violent, with so many ellipses that we are sometimes puzzled as to what *is* meant. Unlike Bernart, he disdained the musicality of poetry, was deliberately harsh, with many proverbial and popular expressions, and with sudden "thingy" metaphors that recall those of Dante, though they tend to be developed at more length. He knew Provençal well and was influenced by it, yet broke abruptly with its conventions and its diction—the first to write poetry in his native Catalan instead of the more literary language glamorized by tradition.

The Catalan text is from Ausiàs March, *Poesies*. Edited by Pere Bohigas. 5 volumes. Editorial Barcino, Barcelona. 1952–59.

1

.

I

Axí com cell   qui·n lo somni·s delita
e son delit   de foll pensament ve,
ne pren a mi,   que·l temps passat me té
l'imaginar,   qu·altre bé no·y habita,
sentint estar   en aguayt ma dolor,
sabent de cert   qu·en ses mans he de jaure.
Temps de · venir   en negun bé · m pot caure;
aquell passat   en mi és lo millor.

Del temps present   no·m trobe amador,
mas del passat,   qu·és no-res e finit;
d'aquest pensar   me sojorn e·m delit,
mas quan lo pert,   s'esforça ma dolor
sí com aquell   qui és jutgat a mort
he de lonch temps   la sab e s'aconorta,
e creure·l fan   que li serà estorta
e·l fan morir   sens un punt de recort.

Plagués a Déu   que mon pensar fos mort,
e que passàs   ma vida en durment!
Malament viu   qui té lo pensament
per enamich,   fent-li d'enuyts report;
e com lo vol   d'algun plaer servir
li'n pren así   com dona · b son infant,
que si verí   li demana plorant
ha ten poch seny   que no·l sab contradir.

Ffóra millor   ma dolor sofferir
que no mesclar   pocha part de plaher
entre · quells mals,   qui·m giten de saber
com del passat   plaher me cové · xir.

84

I

Much as a man who takes delight in dreaming
—all his delight a fantasy: thin air—
even so with me: upon the past my fancies
fasten and dote. No other joy but there.
I sniff ahead disaster in the offing;
reckon for sure I'm numbered with her prey.
The days to come add nothing whatsoever.
All that was best went off with yesterday.

I find myself no lover of time present.
I'm for the past: all nothingness, all done.
There in the long ago my comfort beckons,
only it's harsh awakening, come the sun.
Much as—imagine someone under sentence
of death so long he's blunted, couldn't care;
only suppose his jailers joke, "You're pardoned!"
dragging him off to the scaffold then and there.

I wish to God my thoughts were like a dead man's!
Wish I could snore and slumber out my day!
My life's no life—at daggers drawn with reason,
all my emotions bogging in dismay.
If, for a change, a break in sorrow offers,
think of a mother when her pride and joy,
spying a flask of poison, howls to have it.
She'd be a fool to gratify the boy.

I'd rather drink my bitters undiluted
than try to blend a sugary syrup too
among those dregs that plunge the brain in fever,
seeing I've lost old happiness I knew.

Las! Mon delit   dolor se converteix;
doble's l'affany   aprés d'un poch repòs,
sí co·l malalt   qui per un plasent mos
tot son menjar   en dolor se nodreix;

com l'ermità,   qui·nyorament no·l creix
d'aquells amichs   que tení·en lo món,
essent lonch temps   qu·en lo poblat no fon,
per fortuyt cars   hun d'ells li apareix,
qui los passats   plahers li renovella,
sí que·l passat   present li fa tornar;
mas com se'n part,   l'és forçat congoxar:
lo bé com fuig,   ab grans crits mal apella.

Plena de seny,   quant amor és molt vella,
absença és   lo verme que la guasta,
si fermetat   durament no contrasta,
e creura poch,   si l'envejós consella.

Now my enjoyment souring into sorrow
doubles the torment after scant relief,
like someone sick who bolts too rich a morsel—
thereupon all his supper turns to grief.

Also it's like some hermit: never lonely
for cronies in the world, he doesn't pine
after the days of long forgotten folly.
Only suppose a friend of auld lang syne
happening by, recalls the old occasions;
back to a gala day the decades spin.
But, left alone, the hermit humphs and grumbles.
Joy at the door tells Sorrow: This way in.

O Soul-Of-Thought: when love is long in blossom
Being-away's the devastating worm.
Unless one turn a stony ear to slander;
unless one keep the affectionate spirit firm.

II

Pren-m· enaxí   com al patró qu·en platga
té sa gran nau   e pens· aver castell;
vehent lo cel   ésser molt clar e bell,
creu fermament   c'un· àncor· assats haja.
E sent venir   soptós hun temporal
de tempestat   e temps incomportable;
leva son juhi: que si molt és durable,
cerquar los ports   més qu· aturar li val.

Moltes veus és   que·l vent és fortunal,
tant que no pot   surtir sens lo contrari,
e cella clau   qui·us tanqua dins l'armari
no pot obrir   aquell matex portal.
Así m'à pres,   trobant-m· anamorat,
per sobres-alt   qui·m ve de vós, m· aymia:
del no amar   desalt ne té la via,
mas hun sol pas   meu no·y serà trobat.

Menys que lo peix   és en lo bosch trobat
e los lleons   dins l'aygu· an lur sojorn,
la mi· amor   per null temps pendrà torn,
sol conexent   que de mi·us doneu grat;
e fiu de vós   que·m sabreu bé conèxer,
e, conegut,   no·m serà mal grahida
tota dolor   havent per vós sentida;
ladonchs veureu   les flames d'amor créxer.

Si mon voler   he dat mal a parèxer,
creheu de cert   que ver· amor no·m luny;
pus que lo sol   és calt al mes de juny,
ard mon cor flach   sens algun grat merèxer.

88

II

Know what I'm like? Some captain moors his ship
safe alongshore, and gloating, "There's my castle!"
nods satisfied the skies are fine and clear,
one anchor more than answering for the vessel.
Soon he's surprised by unexpected heaven
splintering into hail and hurricane.
He reckons, if the heavy seas continue,
better to scud for harbor than remain.

Often the gusts are such, no likely headway
for any craft until the wind's about,
just as the latch that lets us in the closet
won't necessarily lift to let us out.
I fell in love like this: such tides of pleasure
out of your nature to my nature flowed.
Displeasure works the other way: to un-love.
Never expect to see me on that road.

More chance you'll find a mackerel in the greenwood,
lions that snort and frolic far at sea,
than for this love, come rain or shine, to falter,
only assured of this: you're pleased with me.
I know you know the knowing ways to know me,
and, known for what I am, no labor's lost
of all that grief and heartbreak in your service.
Love, taken note of, flares. A holocaust.

If I've been undemonstrative in loving,
don't for a moment think I'm low on love.
Come well of it, come ill, my heart's a furnace
burning as hot as bluest June above.

Altre sens mi   d'açò merex la colpa;
vullau-li mal,   com tan humil servent
vos té secret   per son defaliment;
cert, és Amor   que mi, amant, encolpa.

Ma volentat   ab la rahó s'envolpa
e fan acort,   la qualitat seguint,
tals actes fent   que·l cors és defallint
en poch de temps   una gran part de polpa.
Lo poch dormir   magres· al cors m'acosta,
dobla'm l'engýn   per contemplar Amor;
lo cors molt gras,   trobant-se dormidor,
no pot dar pas   en aquest· aspra costa.

Plena de seny,   donau-me una crosta
del vostra pa,   qui·m leve l'amargor;
de tot mengar   m'à pres gran desabor,
si no d'aquell   qui molt· amor me costa.

In this I'm not at fault. Call love the culprit;
tangle with him, who schemes to keep me hid
(shy servant that I am) for my destruction.
Love on the lover blames what loving did.

My will and reason, hand in glove together,
conclude a pact: integrity of soul
is what they covet, unconcerned if body
sink pale and meager overnight. Such toll
in flesh the lack of sleep demands—in turn though
doubles the wit to meditate on love.
The blubber-paunch all logy with his pudding
gets nowhere on the athletic heights above.

O Soul-Of-Thought: bestow a loaf's-end only
of that sweet bread takes bitterness away.
I've nausea now for all food else—excepting
what's bought with love. That currency I'll pay.

XI

¿Quins tan segurs   consells vas encerquant,
cor malastruch,   enfastijat de viure?
Amich de plor   e desamich de riure,
com soferràs   los mals qui·t són davant?
Acuyta't, donchs,   a la mort qui·t espera,
e per tos mals   te allongues los jorns;
aytant és luny   ton delitós sojorns
com vols fugir   a la mort falaguera.

Braços uberts   és exid·a carrera,
plorant sos ulls   per sobres de gran goig;
melodiós   cantar de sa veu hoig,
dient: "Amich,   hix de casa strangera.
En delit prench   donar-te ma favor,
que per null temps   home nat l'à sentida,
car yo defuig   a tot home que·m crida,
prenent aquell   qui fuig de ma rigor."

Ab hulls plorant   e carra de terror,
cabells rompent   ab grans hudulaments,
la vida·m vol   donar heretaments
e d'aquests dons   vol que sia senyor,
cridant ab veu   orrible y dolorosa,
tal com la mort   crida·l benauyrat;
car si l'om és   a mals aparellat,
la veu de mort   li és melodiosa.

Bé·m maravell   com és tan ergullosa
la voluntat   de cascun amador;
no demanant   a mi qui és Amor,
en mi sabran   sa força dolorossa.

XI

Out scouting for sound counsels? How to prosper?
heart grim with grief and tedium of existence,
old bosom friend of tears, no friend of laughter,
how cope with troubles gathering in the distance?
No time to lose. Be off for death; she's waiting.
Linger in life? That's adding sigh to sigh.
Unfriendly with affectionate death?—forgetting
close to her throne the ecstatic countries lie?

Arms open wide, she's on the road to meet you.
Tears on her cheek—the happiness they're from!
Listen, her words are mellower than music:
"Up from the house of strangers, friend, and come.
I'm longing to confer a special favor
no mother's son, time out of mind, has known.
I only take to lonely folk who shun me;
those who would nudge and wheedle, leave alone."

Tears in her eyes—she also!—face of panic,
tearing her tresses, caterwauling woe,
life offers this and that of her possessions:
"Enjoy them all! Yours! Yours!" she urges, though
all in a tone as querulous and dour as
death's would appear to favorites riding high.
For any wretch bent double with his burdens,
no merrier song to hear than: Time to die.

I wonder much in studying these lovers
—talk of hauteur! the lovers hereabout!—
those with the nerve to mock, "Is love so mighty?"
My ruined heart's the exhibit quashing doubt.

Tots, maldient,   sagramentegaran
que may Amor   los tendrà · n son poder,
e si · ls recont   l'acolorat plaer,
lo temps perdut,   sospirant, maldiran.

Null hom conech   o don · a mon senblan,
que dolorit   per Amor faça plànyer;
yo són aquell   de qui · s deu hom complànyer,
car de mon cor   la sanch se'n va lonyan.
Per gran tristor   que li és acostada,
sequa's tot jorn   l'umit qui · m sosté vida,
e la tristor   contra mi és ardida,
e · n mon socors   mà no s'i trob · armada.

Liir entre carts,   l'ora sent acostada
que civilment   és ma vida finida;
puys que del tot   ma sperança · s fugida,
m · arma roman   en aquest món dampnada.

94

And yet they brag—such perjury in the pompous!—
"Me in love's clutches? Never! Not a chance!"
Suppose though I rehearse her touted pleasures—
then, for love lost, the curses, groans, and rants.

There's not a man I've heard of, not a woman,
whose suffering at love's hand should wring a sigh.
Only myself. I've rights to *Miserere,*
blood draining from a heart eroded dry.
Such desolation gaping there, it parches
rivers on which the roots of life are fed.
So savagely it swells, fanatical sorrow,
none raise a hand to help me, out of dread.

Lily-Among-The-Thistles: so it's ending,
life, or what's reckoned such by settled men.
Long, long ago hope showed her heels and bolted.
Damned in this world, can I be damned again?

XIII

Colguen les gents   ab alegria festes,
loant a Déu,   entremesclant deports;
places, carrers   e delitables orts
sien cerquats   ab recont de grans gestes;
e vaja yo   los sepulcres cerquant,
interrogant   ànimes infernades,
e respondran,   car no són companyades
d'altre que mi   en son contínuu plant.

Cascú requer   e vol a son senblant;
per ço no·m plau   la pràtica dels vius.
D'imaginar   mon estat són esquius;
sí com d'om mort,   de mi prenen espant.
Lo rey xipré,   presoner d'un heretge,
en mon esguart   no és malauyrat,
car ço que vull   no serà may finat,
de mon desig   no·m porà guarir metge.

Cell Texion   qui·l buytre·l menga·l fetge
e per tots temps   brota la carn de nou,
en son menjar   aquell ocell may clou;
pus fort dolor   d'aquesta·m té lo setge,
car és hun verm   qui romp la mia pensa,
altre lo cor,   qui may cessen de rompre,
e llur treball   no·s porà enterrompre
sinó ab ço   que d'aver se defensa.

E si la mort   no·m dugués tal offensa
—ffer mi absent   d'una tan plasent vista—,
no li graesch   que de tera no vista
lo meu cors nuu,   qui de plaer no pensa

XIII

Let others hail the holidays with laughter,
with pomp in church, and parties here and there;
traipsing from park to plaza round a city
gala with rich old ballads in the air.
That's not for me. I'm trudging off for tombstones,
bursting with topics for the infernal folk.
We'll have a word or two. What other crony
could the long moan, the terrible tears evoke?

Each to his own; it's so. Birds of a feather—
I answer, all men living are my foes.
Refusing to allow for my condition,
they stare aghast, as if a dead man rose.
The King of Cyprus in a pagan dungeon,
you'd call his dawdlings genuine miseries,
weighed against mine? I want what's not for having;
medical men despair of my disease.

Old Tityus, with the vulture at his stomach,
gobble by gobble sees the gashes heal,
and still the feast goes on, the great fowl jabbing—
grimmer than this, the settled grief I feel.
For there's a worm that gnaws the brain's sweet tissue;
another gnaws the heart. Remorselessly.
Nothing to interrupt their devastation;
nothing, except the one thing closed to me.

And were not death so savage an extorter
as snatch me from what's loveliest to see,
he'd never have my thanks for not a-bundling
this pulp away in earth, bereaving me

de perdre pus   que lo ymaginar
los meus desigs   no poder-se complir;
e si · m cové   mon derrer jorn finir,
seran donats   térmens a ben amar.

E si · n lo cel   Déu me vol allogar,
part veura Ell,   per complir mon delit
serà mester   que · m sia dellay dit
que d'esta mort   vos ha plagut plorar,
penedint-vos   com per poqua mercè
mor l'ignoscent   e per amar-vos martre:
cell qui lo cors   de l'arma vol departre,
si ferm cregués   que · us dolrríeu de se.

Lir entre carts,   vós sabeu e yo sé
que · s pot bè fer   hom morir per amor;
creure de mi,   que só en tal dolor,
no fareu molt   que · y doneu plena fe.

of nothing much as pleasure goes: some fancies,
certain desires, varieties of dearth.
Also because: the day I die means finish
for truest of all true love on this earth.

If God saw fit to lodge me in his heaven,
for actual bliss (apart from seeing him)
I'd have to know, and know on good assurance,
that hearing of my death, your eyes went dim;
hear you repented, grieving: Such and such a
favor had saved this innocent, that dies
a martyr to your love and would have sped his
death, had he thought you'd gasp, with stricken eyes.

Lily-Among-The-Thistles: you know, I know,
a muscular man may sicken to a wraith
and die for love. As I do now, believe me.
Only believe your eyes. No need of faith.

Lo jorn ha por   de perdre sa claror
quant ve la nit   qu· espandeix ses tenebres;
pochs animals   no cloen les palpebres,
e los malalts   crexen de llur dolor.
Los malfactors   volgren tot l'any duràs
perquè llurs mals   haguessen cobriment,
mas yo qui visch   menys de par, en turment
e sens mal fer,   volgra que tost passàs.

E d'altra part   faç pus que si matàs
mil hòmens justs,   menys d'alguna mercè,
car tots mos ginys   yo solt per trahir-me;
e no cuydeu   que·l jorn me'n escusàs,
ans en la nit   treball rompent ma penssa
perquè·n lo jorn   lo trahiment cometa;
por de morir   ne de fer vida streta
no·m toll esforç   per donar-me offensa.

Plena de seny,   mon enteniment pensa
com abtament   lo laç d'Amor se meta;
sens aturar,   pas tenint via dreta;
vaig a la fi   si mercè no·m deffensa.

XXVIII

The day's in dread of losing her bright features
when night arrives, unloosener of gloom.
Few living things but shut the eye in slumber;
patients at midnight ebbing, sniff the tomb.
But burglars urge that night to last the year out,
having, with her, security in crime.
I pitch and toss, no other so tormented;
working no wrong, I long for dawn to climb.

No wrong. And yet do worse than if I murdered
a thousand innocent men—no reason why.
Traps that I set at night recoil against me;
little relief with morning in the sky.
No, in the night I rack my brain devising
ways of betrayal set for all day long.
No dread of death nor fear of a lean future
softens my rage to do myself a wrong.

O Soul-Of-Thought: here's theme for meditation:
how snugly love adjusts the hangman's noose.
See how I march, eyes straight, to my destruction.
No hope, unless your mercy work me loose.

LXVIII

No · m pren axí   com al petit vaylet
qui va cerquant   senyor qui festa · l faça,
tenint-lo calt   en lo temps de la glaça
e fresch, d'estiu,   com la calor se met;
preant molt poch   la valor del senyor
e concebent   desalt de sa manera,
vehent molt clar   que té mala carrera
de cambiar   son estat en major.

¿Com se farà   que visca sens dolor
tenint perdut   lo bé que posseÿa?
Clar e molt bé   ho veu, si no ha follia,
que may porà   tenir estat millor.
¿Donchs què farà,   puix altre bé no · l resta,
sinó plorar   le bé del temps perdut?
Vehent molt clar   per si ser decebut,
may trobarà   qui · l faça millor festa.

Yo són aquell   qui · n lo temps de tempesta,
quant les més gents   festegen prop los fochs
e pusch haver   ab ells los propris jochs,
vaig sobre neu,   descalç, ab nua testa,
servint senyor   qui jamés fon vassall
ne · l vench esment   de fer may homenatge,
en tot leig fet   hagué lo cor salvatge,
solament diu   que bon guardó no · m fall.

Plena de seny,   leigs desigs de mi tall;
erbes no · s fan   males en mon ribatge;
sia entès   com dins en mon coratge
los penssaments   no · m devallen avall.

LXVIII

Not so with me as with the little page
hunts up and down a more obliging sire,
to keep him warm when violent winters rage,
see that he's cool when summer sky's afire.
His present lord he mocks: not worth a bubble;
groans at his ways; annoyance grows to hate.
Knows in his heart, along the road there's trouble
in jockeying so to better his estate.

How learn to live indifferent to disaster,
burning that bridge, the once familiar role?
No rainbow's end ahead, no finer master—
now the boy knows it, if his wits are whole.
What's to be done but sit, and sit a-weeping
(as doors are shut) the rejected bed and board?
Sees in a flash that all he's sowed he's reaping.
No chance to find a more considerate lord.

Quite otherwise with me. I'm one, come winter
when good folk, snug in firelight, mull the rum
and call me in to celebrate, won't enter,
but wade the drifts, bareheaded, barefoot, numb
page for a lord pays reverence to no one
—reverence? what's remoter from his mind?
His joy in any meanness he can show one;
mocking with, "Lucky you! A lord so kind!"

Discerning girl: low lust I shear away;
no ragged weed in meadows I patrol.
Then know me well: in all my heart and soul
no thought but lifts, none furrowing the clay.

LXXXIII

Si co·l malalt,   qui lonch temps ha que jau
e vol hun jorn   esforçar-se llevar,
e sa virtut   no li pot molt aydar,
ans, llevat dret,   soptament, plegat, cau,
ne pren a mi,   que·m esforç contr· Amor
e vull sequir   tot ço que mon seny vol;
complir no·u pusch,   perquè la força ·m tol
un mal estrem   atraçat per Amor.

LXXXIII

As someone on his back for months of illness
would leave the bed one morning; tries and tries
with little help from bone or muscle; striving
upward, he doubles over, cannot rise;
just so with me: I struggle against loving;
wish to believe what thought assures me of,
only cannót, cannót—no strength remaining
after the long infirmity of love.

VI

François Villon

(1431–1463?)
Translating the Dead Ladies

Villon's famous ballade, to which a later editor gave the title "Ballade des Dames du Temps Jadis," became familiar to readers of English through Rossetti's nineteenth-century translation, whose refrain, as the OED confirms, gave to our vocabulary the word "yesteryear," now dear even to sportswriters. Ever since, the poem has seemed to most readers a mournful reverie on beauties of the past and their inevitable fate.

A different way of reading it was advocated about twenty years ago by David Kuhn in his *La Poétique de François Villon*. Kuhn begins by reminding us that the context in which the ballade occurs in "Le Testament" is "sardonic and mocking"; he believes that the question with which it opens is itself derisive, since no answer is possible. (Objection: abrupt changes of tone are not unusual in Villon's poetry.)

To us today, the names that Villon chooses to mention may be vaguely suggestive of old romance. But to fifteenth-century readers they would have been familiar from literature and the oral tradition—as familiar as names in the headlines are to us today. Villon's strangely assorted list contains not the names of beautiful ladies, Kuhn believes, but of "femmes fatales": outnumbering the two or three innocent characters are prostitutes, political schemers, ladies who were deformed, lascivious, incestuous, given to murder. Villon spelled none of this out for his readers; the names alone said it all.

In the figures which are named, Kuhn detects patterns of ambivalence: Flora, for example, is the Roman goddess of flowers but also a notorious prostitute mentioned by Juvenal; Echo, with her echoes, may be lovely, but her dying curse condemned Narcissus to death. Is Kuhn straining when he also finds there images of death and transfiguration?—Buridan, victim of a woman, is reborn in water, Joanne of Arc in fire, etc.

He would also like us to recall that snow was not thought beautiful by the inhabitants of a largely rural France: it was a hardship, to be endured only because, like fertilizer, it would revitalize the fields in spring. Nor did snow add to the pleasure of city life. Villon's "Le Lais" begins with a description of Christmas time as the

> morte saison
> Que les loups se vivent de vent
> Et qu'on se tient en sa maison
> Pour le frimas, près de tison ...

No paeans here to "The snow, the snow, the beautiful snow!" Kuhn quotes Panofsky's observation that "the first snow landscape in all painting" is the February scene in the "Très Riches Heures du Duc de Berry," painted about twenty years before Villon's own birth in 1431. It is true that the living creatures in the Limbourgs' painting do not seem very happy in their snowy environment: there is no rollicking in the drifts or après-ski conviviality there. (Objection: one need not feel that snow is beautiful to be struck by the fact that it is indeed ephemeral—even more ephemeral in most places than the grass to which all flesh is likened in *Isaiah* and the *Psalms*.)

As a matter of fact, there had been earlier associations, in literature, of the snow with beauty. One is in the poetry of the Provençal Bernart de Ventadorn, three centuries before Villon, who described the body of the woman he loved as

> ... blanc tot atretal
> com la neus a nadal ...

"white just like the snow at Christmas."

But for readers of Villon's time, Kuhn is convinced, the famous refrain would have had different resonances than it has for us. Where would the snow have really gone? Into fertilizing and enriching the fields. For Kuhn, the refrain has a redemptive value, in that it implies a transformation. He finds this notion supported by a complex hierarchical structure in the listing of the names, which culminates with that of the Virgin, revered throughout the Middle Ages as "une fontaine" of animating power. And so he sees the dead ladies named in the poem as the vitalizing force by which nature sustains itself: "Dans le sein de la femme, dit le poème de Villon, est l'essence de la fertilité."

Whether or not we agree with much of this (and not all scholars of the period do agree), it does seem that Villon's ballade is more than the simple-minded threnody it is popularly taken to be. We can never, of course, hope to read the poem with the eyes and minds of Villon's contemporaries. How many of us know, for one thing, that some of its apparently innocent words (*blanche* is one such) had obscene meanings in the vulgar speech of the fifteenth century?— meanings which Villon and his associates were by no means above relishing.

Such matters as we have been discussing raise a problem for the translator. Should he simply list the names without comment, as Villon does, or should he hint at connotations once intended but now lost to us? In my translation I have chosen at least to hint, or sometimes more. Most readers will still prefer the tone of Rossetti's

> Tell me now in what hidden way is
> Lady Flora the lovely Roman?

But perhaps in doing so they are not reading anything like the poem that Villon wrote, which may well be at the same time both coarser and more aspiring than modern readers have found it.

The French text is from Villon's *Oeuvres*. Edited by Auguste Longnon. Librairie Ancienne Honoré Champion, Paris. 1932.

BALLADE

Dictes moy ou, n'en quel pays
Est Flora la belle Rommaine,
Archipiades, ne Thaïs
Qui fut sa cousine germaine,
Echo parlant quant bruyt on maine
Dessus riviere ou sus estan
Qui beaulté ot trop plus qu'humaine,
Mais ou sont les neiges d'antan?

Ou est la tres sage Helloïs
Pour qui chastré fut et puis moyne
Pierre Esbaillart a Saint Denis?
Pour son amour ot ceste essoyne;
Semblablement, ou est la royne
Qui commanda que Buridan
Fust geté en ung sac en Saine?
Mais ou sont les neiges d'antan?

La royne Blanche comme lis
Qui chantoit a voix de seraine,
Berte au grant pié, Bietris, Alis,
Haremburgis qui tint le Maine,
Et Jehanne la bonne Lorraine
Qu'Englois brulerent a Rouan;
Ou sont ilz, ou, Vierge souveraine?
Mais ou sont les neiges d'antan?

Prince, n'enquerez de sepmaine
Ou elles sont, ne de cest an,
Qu'a ce reffrain ne vous remaine:
Mais ou sont les neiges d'antan?

BALLADE

Tell me where, in what country, where
Is bounteous Flora, Roman belle?
Archipiade? Thaïs? a pair
Cousins in beauty, stories tell.
Does Echo's musical answer swell
—Then where?—by what mirrored brook or mere?
Her charm more binding than mortal spell
—But where are snows of a bygone year?

Where's Héloise? wise as debonaire,
Whom, unstrung and made monk as well,
Abélard loved so; poor Pierre,
Love's reward was a eunuch's cell.
Where is that dawdling dowsabel,
Queen who had bagged and flung, we fear,
Buridan into the Seine pêle-mêle?
—But where are snows of a bygone year?

Where is Queen Lily White who'd snare
Men with her siren song? Or Swell-
Foot Bertha? or Beatrice? quick to flare,
Maine's Erambour? Or that nonpareil,
Good Joanne of Arc, her fiery knell
Rung at Rouen, as the English jeer?
Where now, Virgin and Queen, pray tell?
—But where are snows of a bygone year?

Prince, though for weeks now you compel
Reply, or the whole year long, you'll hear
One and the same refrain, note well:
—But where are snows of a bygone year?

VII

San Juan de la Cruz
(1542–1591)

Dámaso Alonso tells us that it is the unanimous opinion of discerning Spaniards that St. John of the Cross is their greatest poet. For Pedro Salinas, his best works, with their "incomparable sensual power," are "charged with poetic potency like no other work in this world." For Jorge Guillén, the three best poems—two are included here—"form a series which is perhaps the highest culmination of Spanish poetry." García Lorca is no less admiring: "The Muse of Góngora and the Angel of Garcilaso must yield up the laurel wreath when the *Duende* of St. John of the Cross passes by. . . ."

Though brought up in great poverty in Old Castile, the young Juan de Yepes cared about art, about popular music, about poetry in Latin and Spanish, and especially about the beauty of nature and mankind—all of this as reflecting dimly a kind of super-being beyond it. During his life as a Carmelite friar, he was frequently in serious trouble with his order because of his efforts to reform it in the direction of greater integrity and simplicity. The poems included here were written, apparently, in prison.

St. John's subject was mystical love; he knew that for such experience we have no words in our vocabularies, no frame of reference in our minds: matter cannot relate to non-matter any more than a piece of clockwork can appreciate music. This is why St. John felt that poetry was a better vehicle than prose for what he had to say: poetry, through its images, metaphors, comparisons (and, he might have added, its sound and rhythm) can suggest, hint, allude to, can let us feel a meaning that could never be put rationally—it would be ignorance, he says, to think it could. What can be explained, or paraphrased, in his poems is "ordinarily the least part of what they contain."

Poetry for St. John is not statement; it is more like a system of suggestions. There is hardly any question here of "literal" meaning; I stress this because some have felt that since St. John meant everything literally he should be translated literally. He himself said his poetry was *not* meant literally; though he wrote long explications, he is not authoritative: "There is no reason why anyone should be bound to this exposition." In allowing readers to find their own meaning, as much meaning as they are capable of finding, he anticipates Valéry's "My poems have the meaning one gives them."

García Lorca calls the poet a professor of the five senses. St. John could have agreed: he thinks statement less important to poetry than the symbolic use we make of sense impressions from the universe around us. The good poet more often than not has a grasp of this reality; Guillén says that St. John, in this most unworldly, otherworldly of poetry, "never breaks with the laws of this world."

St. John was not only an intuitive poet; he was, and knew he had to be, a deliberate craftsman as well. He cares about stanza form and the symbiosis of metaphor; he works to make sound dramatize sense, perhaps most spectacularly in the last line of the seventh stanza of the "Cántico" ("Canciones . . ."). Anyone trying to translate this poetry, particularly anyone who remembers what St. John thought poetry was, should also care about things like these. And he should care about the kind of language the poet uses. No dictionary will easily give us this information; few of us know any foreign language well enough to be sure of nuances of tone. We have to rely on such expert judgment as that of Dámaso Alonso, who tells us that St. John liked simple everyday expressions, popular, colloquial words that occur in folk song and might be used by country people. Literary words almost never. Then what is one to make of translators who have him say, "Whither hast vanishèd, Belovèd?" or "Oh who my grief can mend?" or "O happy-hapless plight!"? Among what kind of speakers can such translators have been living?

The English versions that follow seem to be works in progress. The longer one was first published in *Poetry* in 1952. It was considerably revised for *The Poems of St. John of the Cross* (Grove Press, 1958). About three-fourths was again rewritten for the edition of 1968. Since then about a third of the stanzas have been done over yet again—all this bearing—or so I hope—in the direction of greater simplicity. One often works hardest—as Yeats thought—so it will seem he has not worked at all.

The Spanish text—in the spelling of his time, from a manuscript which it seems the poet proofread—is from *Cántico espiritual y poesías de San Juan de la Cruz, según el códice de Sanlúcar de Barrameda.* Edited by P. Silverio de Santa Teresa, C.D. 2 volumes. Tipografia El Monte Carmelo, Burgos. 1928.

114

The English versions are (basically) those in *The Poems of St. John of the Cross*. Third Edition, University of Chicago Press, 1979. Some of the above remarks are also quoted or adapted from the longer discussions in that book.

CANCIONES ENTRE

el alma y el esposo

Esposa

Adonde te escondiste
amado y me dexaste con gemido?
como el cieruo huiste
auiendome herido
sali tras ti clamando, y eras ydo.

Pastores los que fuerdes
alla por las majadas al otero
si por uentura vierdes
aquel que yo mas quiero
Dezilde que adolesco, peno, y muero.

Buscando mis amores
yre por esos montes y riberas
ni cogere las flores
ni temere las fieras
y passare los fuertes y fronteras.

pregunta a las criaturas

O bosques, y espesuras:
Plantadas por la mano del amado
ô prado de verduras
de flores esmaltado
Dezid si por uosotros ha passado.

respuesta de las criaturas

Mil gracias deramando
Passo por estos sotos con presura
e yendolos mirando
con sola su figura
Vestidos los dexo de hermosura.

116

THE SPIRITUAL CANTICLE

Songs between the soul and the bridegroom

The bride

Where have you hidden away,
lover, and left me grieving, care on care?
Hurt me and wouldn't stay
but off like a deer from there?
I hurried forth imploring the empty air.

You shepherds, you that rove
over the range where mountains touch the sky,
if you should meet my love
—my one love—tell him why
I'm faint, and in a fever, and may die.

I'll wander high and low
after the one I worship; never fear
the wild things where I go;
not gather flowers; get clear
of all the mighty and over the frontier.

A question to the creatures

O fields and woods between,
foliage planted by a lover's hand,
O bluegrass, evergreen,
with marigolds japanned,
tell me: has he been lately in your land?

Their reply

Lavishing left and right
a world of wonders he went streaming by
the woodland, quick as light.
And where it touched, his eye
left a new glory on the earth and sky.

Esposa

Ay quien podra sanarme
acaba de entregarte ya de vero
no quieras embiarme
de oy mas ya mensagero
que no saben dezirme lo que quiero.

I todos quantos vagan
de ti me van mil gracias refiriendo
y todos mas me llagan
y dexame muriendo
un no se que que quedan balbuciendo.

Mas como perseueras
o vida no viuiendo donde viues
y haziendo porque mueras
las flechas que reciues
de lo que del amado en ti concibes.

Porque pues has llagado
aqueste coraçon, no le sanaste?
y pues me le has robado
por que assi le dexaste,
y no tomas el robo que robaste?

Apaga mis enojos
pues que ninguno basta a deshazellos
y veante mis ojos
pues eres lumbre dellos
y solo para ti quiero tenellos.

O christalina fuente
si en essos tus semblantes plateados
formases de repente
los ojos desseados
que tengo en mis entrañas dibuxados.

The bride

Left me new suffering too!
Once and for all be really mine, and cure it.
  Yourself! no making do
  with couriers—who'd endure it?
I want your living voice, and these obscure it.

  All that come and go
tell of a thousand wonders, to your credit.
  New rumors—each a blow!
  Like death I dread it.
Something—the telltale tongue, a-stumble, said it.

  How manage breath on breath
so long, my soul, not living where life is?
  Brought low and close to death
  by those arrows of his?
Love was the bow. I know. I've witnesses.

  And wounds to show. You'd cleave
clean to the heart, and never think of healing?
  Steal it, and when you leave
  leave it? What sort of dealing,
to steal and never keep, and yet keep stealing?

  O shorten the long days
of burning thirst—no other love allays them.
  Let my eyes see your face,
  treasure to daze them.
Except for love, it's labor lost to raise them.

  If only, crystal well,
clear in your silver mirror could arise
  suddenly by some spell
  the long-awaited eyes
sketched in my heart of hearts, but cloudy-wise.

Apartalos amado
que voy de buelo:

el esposo

bueluete paloma
que el cieruo vulnerado
por el otero asoma
al ayre de tu buelo: y fresco toma.

la esposa

Mi amado las montañas
los valles solitarios nemorosos
las insulas estrañas
los rios sonorosos
el siluo de los ayres amorosos.

La noche sosegada
En par de los levantes de la aurora
la musica callada
la soledad sonora
la cena que recrea y enamora.

Nuestro lecho florido
de cueuas de leones enlaçado
en purpura tendido
de paz edificado
de mil escudos de oro coronado.

A zaga de tu huella
las jouenes discurren al camino
al toque de centella
al adobado vino
emissiones de balsamo diuino.

Love, cover those bright eyes!
I'm lifted! off on air!

The bridegroom

Come settle, dove.
The deer—look yonder—lies
hurt on the hill above,
drawn by your wing he loves the coolness of.

The bride

My love: the mountains' height,
forest ravines—their far-away recesses;
torrents' sonorous weight;
isles no explorer guesses;
the affectionate air, all whisper and caresses;

night sunk in a profound
hush, with the stir of dawn about the skies,
music without a sound,
a solitude of cries,
a supper of light hearts and lovelit eyes.

Our bed, a couch of roses,
guarded by lions sunning with their young;
our room which peace encloses,
her purple curtains swung;
our wall, with a thousand gold escutcheons hung.

Seeing your sandal-mark,
girls whirl to the four winds; their faces shine
stung by a sudden spark,
flushed with the glorious wine.
Their breath a very heaven—the air's divine!

En la interior bodega
de mi amado beui; y quando salia
por toda aquesta vega
ya cosa no sabia
y el ganado perdi que antes seguia.

Alli me dio su pecho
alli me enseño sciencia muy sabrosa
y yo le di de hecho
a mi sin dexar cosa:
alli le prometi de ser su esposa.

Mi alma se ha empleado
y todo mi caudal en su seruicio
ya no guardo ganado
ni ya tengo otro officio
que ya solo en amar es mi exercicio.

pues ya si en el exido
de oy mas no fuere vista ni hallada
direis que me he perdido
que andando enamorada
me hize perdidiza, y fui ganada.

De flores y esmeraldas
en las frescas mañanas escogidas
haremos las guirnaldas
en tu amor florecidas
y en un cabello mio entretexidas.

En solo aquel cabello
que en mi cuello bolar consideraste
mirastele en mi cuello
y en el presso quedaste
y en uno de mis ojos te llagaste.

Shown deeper than before
in cellars of my love I drank; from there
went wandering on the moor;
knew nothing, felt no care;
the sheep I tended once are who knows where?

There he made gently free;
had honey of revelation to confide.
There I gave all of me;
hid nothing, had no pride;
there I promised to become his bride.

Forever at his door
I gave my heart and soul. My fortune too.
I've no flock any more,
no other work in view.
My occupation: love. It's all I do.

If I'm not seen again
in the old places, on the village ground,
say of me: lost to men.
Say I'm adventure-bound
for love's sake. Lost on purpose to be found.

In the cool morning hours
we'll go about for blossoms, sweet to wear;
match emeralds and weave flowers
sprung in love's summer air;
I'll give for their entwining the very hair

curling upon my shoulder.
You loved to see it lifted on the air.
You loved it, fond beholder
caught fascinated there;
caught fast by an eye that wounds you, unaware.

Quando tu me mirauas
tu gracia en mi tus ojos imprimian
por esso me adamauas
y en eso merecian
los mios adorar lo que en ti vian.

No quieras despreciarme
que si color moreno en mi hallaste
ya bien puedes mirarme
despues que me miraste
que gracia y hermosura en mi dexaste.

Cogednos las raposas
que esta ya florecida nuestra viña,
entanto que de rosas
hazemos vna piña
y no paresca nadie en la montiña.

Detente Cierço muerto
ven austro que recuerdas los amores
aspira por mi huerto
y corran sus olores
y pacera el amado entre las flores.

Esposo

Entrado se ha la esposa
en el ameno huerto desseado
y a su sabor reposa
el cuello reclinado
sobre los dulces braços de el amado.

Debaxo de el mançano
alli comigo fuiste desposada
alli te di la mano
y fuiste reparada
donde tu madre fuera violada.

Your eyes in mine aglow
printed their living image in my own.
   No wonder, marveling so,
   you loved me, thought me grown
worthier to return the fervor shown.

   But thought me, cheek and brow,
a shade too Moorish, and were slow to praise.
   Only look this way now
   as once before: your gaze
leaves me with lovelier features where it plays.

   Now that the bloom uncloses
catch us the little foxes by the vine,
   as we knit cones of roses
   clever as those of pine.
No trespassing about this hill of mine.

   Keep north, you winds of death.
Come, southern wind, for lovers. Come and stir
   the garden with your breath.
   Shake fragrance on the air.
My love will feed among the lilies there.

The bridegroom

   She enters, the bride! closes
the charming garden that all dreams foretold her;
   in comfort she reposes
   close to my shoulder.
Arms of the lover that she loves enfold her.

   Under the apple tree,
hands joined, we spoke a promise, broke the spell.
   I took you tenderly,
   hurt virgin, made you well
where all the scandal on your mother fell.

A las aues ligeras,
leones, cieruos, gamos saltadores,
   montes, valles, riberas,
   aguas, ayres, ardores,
y miedos de las noches veladores.

   Por las amenas liras,
y canto de serenas os conjuro
   que cesen vuestras iras,
   y no toqueis al muro
porque la esposa duerma mas seguro.

Esposa

   O nymphas de Judea
entanto que en las flores, y rosales
   el ambar perfumea
   morâ en los arabales
y no querais tocar nuestros humbrales.

   Escondete Carillo
y mira con tu haz a las montañas
   y no quieras dezillo
   mas mira las compañas
De la que ua por insulas estrañas.

Esposo

   La blanca palomica
al arca con el ramo se a tornado
   y ya la tortolica
   al socio desseado
en las riberas verdes a hallado.

   En soledad biuia
y en soledad a puesto ya su nido
   y en soledad la guia

Wings flickering here and there,
lion and gamboling antler, shy gazelle,
peak, precipice, and shore,
flame, air, and flooding well,
night-watchman terror, with no good to tell,

by many a pleasant lyre
and song of sirens I command you, so:
Down with that angry choir!
All sweet and low
and let the bride sleep deeper. Off you go!

The bride

Girls of Jerusalem,
now that the breath of roses more and more
swirls over leaf and stem,
keep further than before.
Be strangers. And no darkening our door.

Stay hidden close with me,
darling. Look to the mountain; turn your face.
Finger at lips. But see
what pretty mates embrace
the passer of fabulous islands in her chase.

The bridegroom

The little pearl-white dove
with frond of olive to the Ark returns.
Wedded, the bird of love
no longer yearns,
settled above still water, among ferns.

Hers were the lonely days;
in loneliest of solitudes her nest.
Her guide on lonesome ways

a solas, su querido
tambien en soledad de amor herido.

Esposa

Gozemonos amado
y vamonos a uer en tu hermosura
al monte u al collado
do mana el agua pura
entremos mas adentro en la espesura.

y luego a las subidas
cauernas de la piedra, nos iremos
que estan bien escondidas
y alli nos entraremos
y el mosto de granadas gustaremos.

Alli me mostrarias
aquello que mi alma pretendia
y luego me darias
alli, tu uida mia,
aquello que me diste el otro dia.

El aspirar de el ayre
el canto de la dulce Philomena
el soto y su donayre
en la noche serena
con llama que consume y no da pena.

Que nadie lo miraua
Aminadab tan poco parecia
y el cerco sosegaua
y la caualleria
a uista de las aguas decendia.

her love—ah, loneliest,
that arrow from the desert in his breast.

The bride

A celebration, love!
Let's see us in *your* beauty! Jubilees
   on the hill and heights above!
   Cool waters playing! Please
on with me deep and deeper in the trees!

   And on to our eyrie then,
in grots of the rock, high, high! Old rumor placed it
   far beyond wit of men.
   Ah but we've traced it,
and wine of the red pomegranate, there we'll taste it.

   There finally you'll show
the very thing my soul was yearning for;
   and the same moment, O
   my dearest life, restore
something you gave the other day: once more

   the breathing of the air,
the nightingale in her affectionate vein,
   woods and the pleasure there
   in night's unruffled reign—
these, and the flames embracing without pain.

   With none around to see.
Aminadab the demon fled offended.
   Above, the cavalry,
   their long siege ended,
sighted the shining waters and descended.

129

CANCIONES DE EL ALMA,
QUE SE GOZA DE AUER LLEGADO

Canciones de al alma, que se goza de auer llegado al alto estado de la
perfeccion, que es la union con Dios por el camino de la negacion
espiritual

En una noche obscura
Con ansias en amores inflamada
   o dichosa uentura
   sali sin ser notada
Estando ya mi casa sosegada

A escuras, y segura
Por la secreta escala disfraçada
   o dichosa uentura
   a escuras y ençelada
Estando ya mi casa sosegada

En la noche dichosa
En secreto que nadie me ueya.
   Ni yo miraua cosa
   Sin otra luz y guia
Sino la que en el coraçon ardia

Aquesta me guiaua
Mas cierto que la luz del medio dia
   adonde me esperaua
   quien yo bien me sabia
En parte donde nadie parecia

O noche que guiaste
o noche amable mas que el aluorada
   o noche que juntaste

THE DARK NIGHT

Songs of the soul, which rejoices at having reached that lofty state of perfection: union with God by the way of spiritual negation

Once in the dark of night
when love burned bright with yearning, I arose
   (O windfall of delight!)
   and how I left none knows—
dead to the world my house in deep repose.

In the dark, where all goes right,
thanks to a secret ladder, other clothes,
   (O windfall of delight!)
   in the dark, and wrapped in those—
dead to the world my house in deep repose.

There in the lucky dark,
none to observe me; darkness far and wide;
   no sign for me to mark,
   no other light, no guide
except for my heart—the fire, the fire inside!

That led me on
true as the very noon is—truer too!—
   to where there waited one
   I knew—how well I knew!—
in a place where no one was in view.

O dark of night, my guide!
night dearer than anything all your dawns discover!
   O night drawing side to side

        amado con amada
Amada en el amado transformada

        En mi pecho florido
que entero para el solo se guardaua
        alli quedó dormido,
        y yo le regalaua
y el ventalle de cedros ayre daua

        El ayre de la almena
quando yo sus cabellos esparzia
        con su mano serena
        en mi cuello heria
y todos mis sentidos suspendia.

        Quedeme y oluideme
El rostro recline sobre el amado
        cesò todo, y dexeme
        dexando mi cuidado
Entre las açucenas oluidado.

the loved and lover—
she that the lover loves, lost in the lover!

Upon my flowering breast,
kept for his pleasure garden, his alone,
the lover was sunk in rest;
I cherished him—my own!—
there in air from plumes of the cedar blown.

In air from the castle wall,
as my hand in his hair moved lovingly at play,
he let cool fingers fall
—and the fire there where they lay!—
all senses in oblivion drift away.

I stayed, not minding me;
my forehead on the lover I reclined.
Earth ends. And I went free,
left all my care behind
among the lilies falling and out of mind.

Ya que era llegado el tiempo
en que de nacer auia
assi como desposado
de su thalamo salia
abraçado con su esposa
que en sus braços la traia
al qual la graciosa madre
en un pesebre ponia
entre unos animales
que a la sazon alli auia
los hombres dezian cantares
los angeles melodia
festejando el desposorio
que entre tales dos auia
Pero Dios en el pesebre
alli lloraua y gemia
que heran joyas: que la esposa
al desposorio traya
y la madre estaua en pazmo
el que tal trueque veia
el llanto de el hombre en dios
y en el hombre la alegria
lo qual de el uno y de el otro
tan ageno ser solia.

CHRISTMAS BALLAD

In time it came round, the time
ripe for the birth of a boy.
Much as a bridegroom steps
fresh from the chamber of joy,

arm in arm he arrived
entwining the sweetheart he chose.
Both in a byre at hand
the pleasant mother reposed

among oxen and burros and such
as the winter sky drove in.
How they struck up a tune, those folk!
Sweeter the angels sang!

There was a bridal to chant!
There was a pair well wed!
But why did he sob and sob,
God in his rough-hewn bed?

Such a dazzle of tears!—this gift
all that the bride could bring?
How the mother was struck at so
topsy-turvy a thing:

distress of the flesh, in God!
in man, the pitch of delight!
Pairs never coupled so;
different as day and night.

VIII

Goethe

(1749–1832)

"Translators are like matchmakers who praise the charms of some half-veiled beauty," said Goethe. "They arouse an irresistible longing for the original." But for some reason very little irresistible longing has yet been aroused here for the works of a poet we are assured again and again is probably the supreme lyrical genius of Europe—Goethe himself. It seems that his lyrics do not travel well into English, even though it has been said of him that he writes more like an Englishman than a German. Henry Hatfield, in his *Goethe: A Critical Introduction,* can even regret that "it is almost impossible to find adequate translations of Goethe's poetry." Good poets come to grief in the attempt to translate him, with lines like

Know you the land where bloom the lemon trees . . . ?
But there, but there
Our way being bound, O Father, let us fare!

What stiff unnatural inversions, which this poet would never have permitted himself in his own work! We often remember Pound's saying that poetry ought to be at least as well written as prose, but less often realize that a translation into English ought to be into good English, into the natural and colloquial English of our speech if the original is colloquial. The poet of "where bloom the lemon trees" has left us somewhere on the frontiers of our language instead of taking us into the heartlands. He has given us a sort of English, yes; but not the sort we would be likely to use ourselves. Surely the first requirement of good English is the native speech pattern: natural words in the natural order. Unless colloquially used, inversion who needs?

The life of Johann Wolfgang Goethe—the "von" was an honorific conferred by a patron—is too well known to need summary. What matters is that he was a natural poet if ever a poet was; his poems came immediately from experiences he lived—so much so that he had little interest in the imagination as a source of poetry. He was also what Roethke calls a "thingy spirit": his poems come from the thinginess of experience and express themselves in the thinginess of images. He saw himself as a friend of tangible things—"als Freund fasslicher Gestalten"—uncomfortable without them. Even in his eighties, says Barker Fairley (*A Study of Goethe*), "Again and again he had to insist to one person or another that unless he could see and touch things, he was helpless and lost. 'I must have things in front of me. . . .'"

His ideas and feelings turned immediately into images, as they must for a poet. In "Mondlied," for example, the moonlight and the restless river are not just aspects of nature but are also psychic events: his own hard-won calm, his own past confusions. "Das Veilchen" (no doubt a trifle, but Mozart liked it enough to make a song of it), "Heidenröslein," and "Gefunden" are not about flowers, but about passionate human relationships. This aspect of Goethe's poetry a translator should be able to handle: images—there are exceptions—should be as easy to translate as "two brown pencils" or "the pen of my aunt." *Should* be; but images in poetry do not exist apart from sound and rhythm.

Goethe's very ease makes him anything but easy to translate. As Professor Fairley says in his selection of Goethe's lyrics: "The truth is . . . Goethe's originality is so effortless that it escapes us continually. . . . So unartificially does he write that we forget he is writing. It is like the miracle of living, which is there all the time and we take it for granted. . . . In late life Goethe writes with a nonchalance that few poets have reached, and none perhaps at this level." His poetry sprang forth in language for the most part fresh and simple, almost new to poetry, in strong physical rhythms that we think of as old-fashioned today because they go back to the dawn of human consciousness— rich in those half-mysterious correspondences between sound and sense difficult to discuss and almost impossible to realize in translation—the kind of essentially poetic effect that led Robert Frost to say that poetry is what is lost in translation. This indeed is probably why, while lesser poets have caught the eye and ear of the Nobel committees, Frost himself has been underrated in Europe. His poetry is so much a matter of cadence and sound that it goes flat in another language. What is the translator to make of a line like the one about the woman who liked to sleep with a night light: "Good gloom on her was thrown away"? Sound is mysteriously right like this in line after line of Goethe's poetry. The strange poem to Charlotte von Stein opens with "Warum gabst du uns die tiefen Blicke . . . ?"—the dark vowels of the first five syllables (so unlike "Why did you give . . .") as if heavy with the fatality which the poem addresses, and then the suddenly sharper *ee-ee* of "die tiefen"! How meaningful, yet how close to nonsense a comment like this is. But yet, the gloomy sound of "Das Auge starrt auf düstrem Pfad verdrossen" in the great "Trilogy"! Or the deep-drawn breaths of "Über allen Gipfeln . . ."

These marvelously sophisticated effects, effects that the most conscious art often works in vain to achieve, seem to come naturally to Goethe, as do the inevitabilities of the long logically structured sentences. Sound effects are an endless delight and source of study to readers as sensitive as Ezra Pound, who, in urging the young poet to "fill his mind with the finest cadences he can discover" tells him to "dissect the lyrics of Goethe coldly into their component sound values, syllables long and short, stressed and unstressed, into vowels and consonants." (*A Retrospect*)

The selection of Goethe lyrics here is not representative, since, coming to them chronologically, I have done more early poems than late. A better balanced selection would include some of the *Roman Elegies* and more of the later poems—more, especially, from the *West-Östlicher Divan*.

In the *Conversations with Eckermann* (under the date of February 25, 1824) there are some interesting remarks on "Das Tagebuch": "Today, Goethe showed me two remarkable poems; both highly moral in their tendency, but in their several *motifs* so unreservedly natural and true, that they are of the kind which the world styles immoral. On this account, he keeps them to himself, and does not intend to publish them." Of the two poems, Eckermann thought one (undoubtedly "Das Tagebuch") "far more hazardous. It relates an event of our day in the language of our day; and, as it thus comes quite unveiled into our presence, the particular features seem far more audacious." "You are right," Goethe agreed, "mysterious and great effects are produced by different poetical forms. If the import of my Roman elegies were put into the measure and style of Byron's *Don Juan* [as "Das Tagebuch" was], the whole would be found infamous."

Only a few months before, Goethe had shown Eckermann his far greater "Trilogie der Leidenschaft." "I thought that the feelings were more strongly expressed than we are accustomed to find in Goethe's other poems, and imputed this to the influence of Byron—which Goethe did not deny." (Goethe indeed thought Byron "undoubtedly . . . the greatest genius of our century.") The background of the "Trilogy" is well known: in 1824, fifty years after he had published "Die Leiden des jungen Werther," Goethe evoked, in the first part of the "Trilogy," the ghost of the sentimental young man who had killed himself for love. Goethe himself had recently had a Werther-experience of his own: at the age of seventy-four he had fallen wildly in love with the pretty teen-ager

Ulrike von Levetzow at Marienbad. The second part of the "Trilogy," sometimes called the "Marienbad Elegy," is about their last day together and its memories. His sense of loss and despair is resolved, in the third part, by the power of music, through which he feels we may guess at the splendor of some ultimate unity beyond the broken notes of earth.

The German text is from *Sämtliche Gedichte*. Edited by Emil Staiger. 2 volumes, 1950–53; and (for "Selige Sehnsucht") from *West-Östlicher Divan*. Edited by Hellmuth Freiherrn von Maltzahn. 1948. Both published by Artemis Verlag, Zürich and Stuttgart.

The Meeting,
the Departure

WILLKOMMEN UND ABSCHIED

Es schlug mein Herz, geschwind zu Pferde!
Es war getan fast eh gedacht.
Der Abend wiegte schon die Erde,
Und an den Bergen hing die Nacht;
Schon stand im Nebelkleid die Eiche,
Ein aufgetürmter Riese, da,
Wo Finsternis aus dem Gesträuche
Mit hundert schwarzen Augen sah.

Der Mond von einem Wolkenhügel
Sah kläglich aus dem Duft hervor,
Die Winde schwangen leise Flügel,
Umsausten schauerlich mein Ohr;
Die Nacht schuf tausend Ungeheuer,
Doch frisch und fröhlich war mein Mut:
In meinen Adern welches Feuer!
In meinem Herzen welche Glut!

Dich sah ich, und die milde Freude
Floß von dem süßen Blick auf mich;
Ganz war mein Herz an deiner Seite
Und jeder Atemzug für dich.
Ein rosenfarbnes Frühlingswetter
Umgab das liebliche Gesicht,
Und Zärtlichkeit für mich—ihr Götter!
Ich hofft es, ich verdient es nicht!

Doch ach, schon mit der Morgensonne
Verengt der Abschied mir das Herz:
In deinen Küssen welche Wonne!

THE MEETING, THE DEPARTURE

My pulses rushed, and, quick, to saddle!
No sooner thought about than—done!
With evening easy in her cradle
And dark hills covering the sun.
In wraiths of vapor hooded, towering,
The oak tree—what a giant!—there.
In shrubs a hundred eyes were glowering,
The dark—observant everywhere.

The moon already peaked with grieving
Through cloudy cover leaned to peer.
The nightwind stirred its feathers, leaving
A wail and shudder at my ear.
The darkness crawled with *things,* surrounding
The cruppers—I was buoyant though!
What ardor in the blood abounding!
Along the pulses what a glow!

I saw you, in your eye the greeting
That floods me—sweetness through and through.
For you alone my heart was beating;
For you alone the breath I drew.
Your face a glory: May and roses
Its native weather! Such concern
For me as every look discloses
I hoped for; never hoped to earn.

Damnation, dawn already! This is
Our darkest moment, parting so.
The world of rapture in your kisses!

In deinem Auge welcher Schmerz!
Ich ging, du standst und sahst zur Erden,
Und sahst mir nach mit nassem Blick:
Und doch, welch Glück, geliebt zu werden!
Und lieben, Götter, welch ein Glück!

But in your eye, the worlds of woe!
I left—your look, though lowered, stealing
Its tearful glances by the gate.
Yet being loved! It's great, the feeling!
And loving—! God above, it's great!

MAILIED

Wie herrlich leuchtet
Mir die Natur!
Wie glänzt die Sonne!
Wie lacht die Flur!

Es dringen Blüten
Aus jedem Zweig
Und tausend Stimmen
Aus dem Gesträuch

Und Freud und Wonne
Aus jeder Brust.
O Erd, o Sonne!
O Glück, o Lust!

O Lieb, o Liebe!
So golden schön,
Wie Morgenwolken
Auf jenen Höhn!

Du segnest herrlich
Das frische Feld,
Im Blütendampfe
Die volle Welt.

O Mädchen, Mädchen,
Wie lieb ich dich!
Wie blickt dein Auge!
Wie liebst du mich!

MAY SONG

How fine a light on
Nature today!
The sun's in glory!
The fields at play!

What feats of blossom
A twig achieves!
A thousand voices
Delight the leaves!

And every pleasure
For girl, for boy!
The sun-warm country
Of joy on joy!

O love! O lovely!
My golden girl!
Like clouds at morning
Your rose and pearl!

You lean in blessing
On earth's cool bloom,
The world a richness of
Dense perfume!

O darling, darling!
I'm wild for you!
Your lashes dazzle:
You love me too!

So liebt die Lerche
Gesang und Luft,
Und Morgenblumen
Den Himmelsduft,

Wie ich dich liebe
Mit warmem Blut,
Die du mir Jugend
Und Freud und Mut

Zu neuen Liedern
Und Tänzen gibst.
Sei ewig glücklich,
Wie du mich liebst!

The lark loves singing
Away up there;
The flowers at morning
Delight in air,

As I adore you, with
Blood a-thrill!
It's youth you give me,
Ecstatic will

For newer music
And dancing! Be
In bliss forever,
As you love me!

HEIDENRÖSLEIN

Sah ein Knab ein Röslein stehn,
Röslein auf der Heiden,
War so jung und morgenschön,
Lief er schnell, es nah zu sehn,
Sahs mit vielen Freuden.
Röslein, Röslein, Röslein rot,
Röslein auf der Heiden.

Knabe sprach: Ich breche dich,
Röslein auf der Heiden!
Röslein sprach: Ich steche dich,
Daß du ewig denkst an mich,
Und ich wills nicht leiden.
Röslein, Röslein, Röslein rot,
Röslein auf der Heiden.

Und der wilde Knabe brach
's Röslein auf der Heiden;
Röslein wehrte sich und stach,
Half ihm doch kein Weh und Ach,
Mußt es eben leiden.
Röslein, Röslein, Röslein rot,
Röslein auf der Heiden.

ROSEBUD IN THE HEATHER

Urchin saw a rose—a dear
Rosebud in the heather.
Fresh as dawn and morning-clear;
Ran up quick and stooped to peer,
Took his fill of pleasure.
Rosebud, rosebud, rosebud red,
Rosebud in the heather.

Urchin blurts: "I'll pick you, though,
Rosebud in the heather!"
Rosebud: "Then I'll stick you so
That there's no forgetting, no!
I'll not stand it, ever!"
Rosebud, rosebud, rosebud red,
Rosebud in the heather.

But the wild young fellow's torn
Rosebud from the heather.
Rose, she pricks him with her thorn;
Should she plead, or cry forlorn?
Makes no difference whether.
Rosebud, rosebud, rosebud red,
Rosebud in the heather.

DAS VEILCHEN

Ein Veilchen auf der Wiese stand
Gebückt in sich und unbekannt;
Es war ein herzigs Veilchen.
Da kam eine junge Schäferin
Mit leichtem Schritt und munterm Sinn
Daher, daher,
Die Wiese her, und sang.

Ach! denkt das Veilchen, wär ich nur
Die schönste Blume der Natur,
Ach, nur ein kleines Weilchen,
Bis mich das Liebchen abgepflückt
Und an dem Busen matt gedrückt!
Ach nur, ach nur
Ein Viertelstündchen lang!

Ach! aber ach! das Mädchen kam
Und nicht in acht das Veilchen nahm,
Ertrat das arme Veilchen.
Es sank und starb und freut' sich noch:
Und sterb ich denn, so sterb ich doch
Durch sie, durch sie,
Zu ihren Füßen doch.

THE VIOLET

A violet in the deepest green
Of meadows, curling up unseen—
A precious little violet!
A glowing shepherdess came by,
Elate her step, her spirits high,
And all along
The meadow, sang her song.

Ah, thought the violet, were I just
Of all these blossoms loveliest
A little moment only!
Until she'd pluck me, where I lie
And hold me to her heart to die,
Oh just, oh just
A quarter-hour with her!

The lady came on soft footfall,
But thought of violets not at all.
Poor little bud—she crushed it!
It sank, its ecstasy complete:
I die, it thought, but death is sweet,
For her, for her!
Beneath her very feet.

DER KÖNIG IN THULE

Es war ein König in Thule
Gar treu bis an das Grab,
Dem sterbend seine Buhle
Einen goldnen Becher gab.

Es ging ihm nichts darüber,
Er leert' ihn jeden Schmaus;
Die Augen gingen ihm über,
Sooft er trank daraus.

Und als er kam zu sterben,
Zählt' er seine Städt' im Reich,
Gönnt' alles seinen Erben,
Den Becher nicht zugleich.

Er saß beim Königsmahle,
Die Ritter um ihn her,
Auf hohem Vätersaale,
Dort auf dem Schloß am Meer.

Dort stand der alte Zecher,
Trank letzte Lebensglut,
Und warf den heilgen Becher
Hinunter in die Flut.

Er sah ihn stürzen, trinken
Und sinken tief ins Meer.
Die Augen täten ihm sinken;
Trank nie einen Tropfen mehr.

THE KING IN THULE

There lived a king in Thule,
Right faithful, to the grave.
He loved a golden goblet
His dying sweetheart gave.

He loved it: nothing dearer.
Would not a-feasting go
But soon the cup was lifted
And soon the tears would flow.

His time of death approaching,
He counts his towns out, so.
Wills all away, and gladly.
But not the goblet, no.

The scene: a royal banquet,
His knights around his knee;
The lofty hall, ancestral,
High-castled by the sea.

Then rose the snowy toper;
A toast! to life's last glow!
His sainted cup he catches,
Flings to the foam below.

He watched it falling, filling;
He saw it settle, sink.
His eyelids ebb; then never
Another drop to drink.

HYPOCHONDER

Der Teufel hol das Menschengeschlecht!
Man möchte rasend werden!
Da nehm ich mir so eifrig vor:
Will niemand weiter sehen,
Will all das Volk Gott und sich selbst
Und dem Teufel überlassen!
Und kaum seh ich ein Menschengesicht,
So hab ichs wieder lieb.

ILL HUMOR

The devil take the human race!
Enough to drive you crazy!
Time and again I swear to God
I'm finished! through! with people.
They're God's affair. Their own affair.
Especially the devil's.
But then I see a human face
And—back in love with people.

AN BELINDEN

Warum ziehst du mich unwiderstehlich,
Ach, in jene Pracht?
War ich guter Junge nicht so selig
In der öden Nacht?

Heimlich in mein Zimmerchen verschlossen,
Lag im Mondenschein,
Ganz von seinem Schauerlicht umflossen,
Und ich dämmert ein;

Träumte da von vollen goldnen Stunden
Ungemischter Lust,
Hatte schon dein liebes Bild empfunden
Tief in meiner Brust.

Bin ichs noch den du bei so viel Lichtern
An dem Spieltisch hältst?
Oft so unerträglichen Gesichtern
Gegenüber stellst?

Reizender ist mir des Frühlings Blüte
Nun nicht auf der Flur;
Wo du, Engel, bist, ist Lieb und Güte,
Wo du bist, Natur.

TO BELINDA

Let you drag me here, without demurring,
Where it's all so bright?
Wasn't I, good simple soul, as happy
In my lonely night?

In my room and snug, with none to see me
As the moonlight lay
Sweet and eerie in a mist around me
Till I'd drift away,

Deep in dreams, and what delirious spells of
Unabated bliss!
Nuzzled to your image warm within me,
Dreaming dreams of this.

I'm myself? Among the candelabra
Planted! Made to play
Cards!—with those insufferable faces
A nose-length away!

Why? You draw me more than any meadow's
Fragrance in the spring.
Angel, where you are is warmth and loving,
Every natural thing.

JÄGERS ABENDLIED

Im Felde schleich ich still und wild,
Gespannt mein Feuerrohr.
Da schwebt so licht dein liebes Bild,
Dein süßes Bild mir vor.

Du wandelst jetzt wohl still und mild
Durch Feld und liebes Tal,
Und ach, mein schnell verrauschend Bild,
Stellt sich dirs nicht einmal?

Des Menschen, der die Welt durchstreift
Voll Unmut und Verdruß,
Nach Osten und nach Westen schweift,
Weil er dich lassen muß.

Mir ist es, denk ich nur an dich,
Als in den Mond zu sehn;
Ein stiller Friede kommt auf mich,
Weiß nicht, wie mir geschehn.

THE HUNTER'S SONG AT NIGHTFALL

My rifle cocked, in savage calm
I prowl the moorland here,
Your face before me everywhere,
Your vivid face, my dear.

You strolled, I'm sure, a sweeter field
In sweeter calm today.
No thought of me, or such a thought
As girls can shrug away.

No thought of one who, vexed and glum,
Has all the world to track.
The roads go east, the roads go west,
But not a road goes back.

And yet to think of you!—such peace
Around me settles soon
As if—I'm puzzled how—my gaze
Were spellbound on the moon.

AN CHARLOTTE VON STEIN

Warum gabst du uns die tiefen Blicke,
Unsre Zukunft ahnungsvoll zu schaun,
Unsrer Liebe, unserm Erdenglücke
Wähnend selig nimmer hinzutraun?
Warum gabst uns, Schicksal, die Gefühle,
Uns einander in das Herz zu sehn,
Um durch all die seltenen Gewühle
Unser wahr Verhältnis auszuspähn?

Ach, so viele tausend Menschen kennen,
Dumpf sich treibend, kaum ihr eigen Herz,
Schweben zwecklos hin und her und rennen
Hoffnungslos in unversehnem Schmerz;
Jauchzen wieder, wenn der schnellen Freuden
Unerwart'te Morgenröte tagt;
Nur uns armen Liebevollen beiden
Ist das wechselseitge Glück versagt,
Uns zu lieben, ohn uns zu verstehen,
In dem andern sehn, was er nie war,
Immer frisch auf Traumglück auszugehen
Und zu schwanken auch in Traumgefahr.

Glücklich, den ein leerer Traum beschäftigt,
Glücklich, dem die Ahndung eitel wär!
Jede Gegenwart und jeder Blick bekräftigt
Traum und Ahndung leider uns noch mehr.
Sag, was will das Schicksal uns bereiten?
Sag, wie band es uns so rein genau?
Ach, du warst in abgelebten Zeiten
Meine Schwester oder meine Frau.

TO CHARLOTTE VON STEIN

Why confer on us the piercing vision:
All tomorrow vivid in our gaze?
Not a chance to build on love's illusion?
Not a glimmer of idyllic days?
Why confer on us, O fate, the feeling
Each can plumb the other's very heart?
Always, though in storms of passion reeling,
See precisely what a course we chart?

Look at all those many thousands drudging
(Knowing even their own nature less
Than we know each other), thousands trudging,
In the dark about their own distress;
Drunk on exultation, when they're treated
Suddenly to joy's magenta dawn.
Only we unlucky lovers, cheated
Of all mutual comfort, have forgone
This: to be in love, not understanding;
This: to see the other as he's not;
Off in gaudy dreams go hand-in-handing,
In appalling dreams turn cold and hot.

Happy man, a fleeting dream engages!
Happy man, no premonitions numb!
We however—! All our looks and touches
Reaffirm our fear of days to come.
Tell me, what's our destiny preparing?
Tell me, how we're bound in such a knot?
From an old existence we are sharing?
You're the wife, the sister I forgot?

Kanntest jeden Zug in meinem Wesen,
Spähtest wie die reinste Nerve klingt,
Konntest mich mit Einem Blicke lesen,
Den so schwer ein sterblich Aug durchdringt;
Tropftest Mäßigung dem heißen Blute,
Richtetest den wilden irren Lauf,
Und in deinen Engelsarmen ruhte
Die zerstörte Brust sich wieder auf;
Hieltest zauberleicht ihn angebunden
Und vergaukeltest ihm manchen Tag.
Welche Seligkeit glich jenen Wonnestunden,
Da er dankbar dir zu Füßen lag,
Fühlt sein Herz an deinem Herzen schwellen,
Fühlte sich in deinem Auge gut,
Alle seine Sinnen sich erhellen
Und beruhigen sein brausend Blut!

Und von allem dem schwebt ein Erinnern
Nur noch um das ungewisse Herz,
Fühlt die alte Wahrheit ewig gleich im Innern,
Und der neue Zustand wird ihm Schmerz.
Und wir scheinen uns nur halb beseelet,
Dämmernd ist um uns der hellste Tag.
Glücklich, daß das Schicksal, das uns quälet
Uns doch nicht verändern mag!

Knew me then completely, every feature,
How each nerve responded and rang true;
Read me in a single glance—a nature
Others search bewildered for a clue.
To that heated blood, a cool transfusion;
To that crazy runaway, a rein;
In your clasp, what Edens of seclusion
Nursed to health that fellow, heart and brain.
Held him tightly, lightly, as enchanted;
Spirited the round of days away.
Where's a joy like this?—you'd think transplanted
At your feet the flushing lover lay;
Lay and felt his heart, against you, lighten;
Felt your eye approving: *but he's good!*
Felt his murky senses clear and brighten;
On his raging blood, a quietude.

Now, of all that was, about him hovers
Just a haze of memory, hardly there.
Still the ancient truth avails: we're lovers—
Though our new condition's a despair.
Only half a mind for earth. Around us
Twilight thickens on the brightest day.
Yet we're still in luck: the fates that hound us
Couldn't wish our love away.

DER FISCHER

Das Wasser rauscht', das Wasser schwoll,
Ein Fischer saß daran,
Sah nach dem Angel ruhevoll,
Kühl bis ans Herz hinan.
Und wie er sitzt und wie er lauscht,
Teilt sich die Flut empor;
Aus dem bewegten Wasser rauscht
Ein feuchtes Weib hervor.

Sie sang zu ihm, sie sprach zu ihm:
Was lockst du meine Brut
Mit Menschenwitz und Menschenlist
Hinauf in Todesglut?
Ach wüßtest du, wie 's Fischlein ist
So wohlig auf dem Grund,
Du stiegst herunter, wie du bist,
Und würdest erst gesund.

Labt sich die liebe Sonne nicht,
Der Mond sich nicht im Meer?
Kehrt wellenatmend ihr Gesicht
Nicht doppelt schöner her?
Lockt dich der tiefe Himmel nicht,
Das feuchtverklärte Blau?
Lockt dich dein eigen Angesicht
Nicht her in ewgen Tau?

Das Wasser rauscht', das Wasser schwoll,
Netzt' ihm den nackten Fuß;
Sein Herz wuchs ihm so sehnsuchtsvoll,
Wie bei der Liebsten Gruß.

166

THE FISHERMAN

The water washed, the water rose;
A fellow fishing sat
And watched his bobbin coolly drift.
His blood was cool as that.
A while he sits, a while he harks
—Like silk the ripples tear,
And up in swirls of foam arose
A girl with dripping hair.

She sang to him, she spoke to him:
"Cajole my minnows so
With lore of men, with lure of men,
To death's unholy glow?
If you could know my silver kin,
What cozy hours they passed,
You'd settle under, clothes and all
—A happy life at last.

"The sun, it likes to bathe and bathe;
The moon—now doesn't she?
And don't they both, to breathe the wave,
Look up more brilliantly?
You're not allured by lakes of sky,
More glorious glossy blue?
Not by your very face transformed
In this eternal dew?"

The water washed, the water rose;
It lapped his naked toe.
As longing for the one he loved
He yearned to sink below.

Sie sprach zu ihm, sie sang zu ihm;
Da wars um ihn geschehn:
Halb zog sie ihn, halb sank er hin,
Und ward nicht mehr gesehn.

She spoke to him, she sang to him;
The fellow, done for then,
Half yielded too as half she drew.
Was never seen again.

AN DEN MOND

Füllest wieder Busch und Tal
Still mit Nebelglanz,
Lösest endlich auch einmal
Meine Seele ganz;

Breitest über mein Gefild
Lindernd deinen Blick,
Wie des Freundes Auge mild
Über mein Geschick.

Jeden Nachklang fühlt mein Herz
Froh- und trüber Zeit,
Wandle zwischen Freud und Schmerz
In der Einsamkeit.

Fließe, fließe, lieber Fluß!
Nimmer werd ich froh,
So verrauschte Scherz und Kuß,
Und die Treue so.

Ich besaß es doch einmal,
Was so köstlich ist!
Daß man doch zu seiner Qual
Nimmer es vergißt!

Rausche, Fluß, das Tal entlang,
Ohne Rast und Ruh,
Rausche, flüstre meinem Sang
Melodien zu,

TO THE MOON

Flooding with a brilliant mist
Valley, bush and tree,
You release me. Oh for once
Heart and soul I'm free!

Easy on the region round
Goes your wider gaze,
Like a friend's indulgent eye
Measuring my days.

Every echo from the past,
Glum or gaudy mood,
Haunts me—weighing bliss and pain
In the solitude.

River, flow and flow away;
Pleasure's dead to me:
Gone the laughing kisses, gone
Lips and loyalty.

All in my possession once!
Such a treasure yet
Any man would pitch in pain
Rather than forget.

Water, rush along the pass,
Never lag at ease;
Rush, and rustle to my song
Changing melodies,

Wenn du in der Winternacht
Wütend überschwillst,
Oder um die Frühlingspracht
Junger Knospen quillst.

Selig, wer sich vor der Welt
Ohne Haß verschließt,
Einen Freund am Busen hält
Und mit dem genießt,

Was, von Menschen nicht gewußt
Oder nicht bedacht,
Durch das Labyrinth der Brust
Wandelt in der Nacht.

How in dark December you
Roll amok in flood;
Curling, in the gala May,
Under branch and bud.

Happy man, that rancor-free
Shows the world his door;
One companion by—and both
In a glow before

Something never guessed by men
Or rejected quite:
Which, in mazes of the breast,
Wanders in the night.

WANDRERS NACHTLIED

Über allen Gipfeln
Ist Ruh,
In allen Wipfeln
Spürest du
Kaum einen Hauch;
Die Vögelein schweigen im Walde.
Warte nur, balde
Ruhest du auch.

SONG OF THE TRAVELER AT EVENING

Over all the hills now,
Repose.
In all the trees now
Shows
Barely a breath. Birds are through
That sang in their wood to the west.
Only wait, traveler. Rest
Soon for you too.

ERLKÖNIG

Wer reitet so spät durch Nacht und Wind?
Es ist der Vater mit seinem Kind;
Er hat den Knaben wohl in dem Arm,
Er faßt ihn sicher, er hält ihn warm.

Mein Sohn, was birgst du so bang dein Gesicht?—
Siehst, Vater, du den Erlkönig nicht?
Den Erlenkönig mit Kron und Schweif?—
Mein Sohn, es ist ein Nebelstreif.—

«Du liebes Kind, komm, geh mit mir!
Gar schöne Spiele spiel ich mit dir;
Manch bunte Blumen sind an dem Strand,
Meine Mutter hat manch gülden Gewand.»

Mein Vater, mein Vater, und hörest du nicht,
Was Erlenkönig mir leise verspricht?—
Sei ruhig, bleibe ruhig, mein Kind;
In dürren Blättern säuselt der Wind.—

«Willst, feiner Knabe, du mit mir gehn?
Meine Töchter sollen dich warten schön;
Meine Töchter führen den nächtlichen Reihn,
Und wiegen und tanzen und singen dich ein.»

Mein Vater, mein Vater, und siehst du nicht dort
Erlkönigs Töchter am düstern Ort?—
Mein Sohn, mein Sohn, ich seh es genau:
Es scheinen die alten Weiden so grau.—

ERL-KING

Who spurs on the road when day is done,
Through night, through wind? A father and son.
The father's arm and his cloak enfold
The youngster, to keep him snug from cold.

"My son, why huddle and hide your eyes?"
"The King of the Darkwood, see him rise
—You don't see, father?—all sheeted, crowned?"
"Mist, my son. From the marshy ground."

Dear little fellow, come with me.
We've games to be playing, just you'll see.
I've pretty gardens along the foam,
Gold to wear in my mother's home.

"O father, father! you still can't hear
The King of the Darkwood, coaxing near?"
"Easy, my youngster. Easy there!
In twigs a-wither, a hiss of air."

Fine little fellow, off we go?
I've three tall daughters to curtsy low.
They take hands, dancing the whole night through.
They'll dance you and dandle and rock-a-by you.

"O father, father! you still can't see
His daughters there in the dark, all three?"
"Son, what I see is how they sway,
The wayside willows so old and grey."

177

«Ich liebe dich, mich reizt deine schöne Gestalt;
Und bist du nicht willig, so brauch ich Gewalt.»
Mein Vater, mein Vater, jetzt faßt er mich an!
Erlkönig hat mir ein Leids getan!—

Dem Vater grausets, er reitet geschwind,
Er hält in Armen das ächzende Kind,
Erreicht den Hof mit Mühe und Not;
In seinen Armen das Kind war tot.

I'm in love with your flesh and its human glow.
And if you're unwilling, I'll see that you go.
"O father, father! it hurts, his touch
—The King of the Darkwood!—hurts so much!"

The father shudders, the father spurs;
The boy in his arm half moans, half stirs.
Home, under stress and strain, they sped.
There in his arm the boy lay dead.

MIGNON

Kennst du das Land, wo die Zitronen blühn,
Im dunkeln Laub die Gold-Orangen glühn,
Ein sanfter Wind vom blauen Himmel weht,
Die Myrte still und hoch der Lorbeer steht,
Kennst du es wohl?
                Dahin! Dahin
Möcht ich mit dir, o mein Geliebter, ziehn.

Kennst du das Haus? Auf Säulen ruht sein Dach,
Es glänzt der Saal, es schimmert das Gemach,
Und Marmorbilder stehn und sehn mich an:
Was hat man dir, du armes Kind, getan?
Kennst du es wohl?
                Dahin! Dahin
Möcht ich mit dir, o mein Beschützer, ziehn.

Kennst du den Berg und seinen Wolkensteg?
Das Maultier sucht im Nebel seinen Weg,
In Höhlen wohnt der Drachen alte Brut,
Es stürzt der Fels und über ihn die Flut;
Kennst du ihn wohl?
                Dahin! Dahin
Geht unser Weg! o Vater, laß uns ziehn!

MIGNON

You know that land, her lemon groves in bloom?
Dark foliage of the orange, gold in gloom?
So soft a blowing air, so blue a sky
Over the myrtle hushed, the laurel high?
You know that land perhaps?
                        Oh that's the way
I'd go with you, my dearest—off today!

You know that house, how tall the pillars stand?
The halls all glossy, and the chambers grand?
The marble shapes that eye me, where I go:
"What's the world done, poor child, to hurt you so?"
You know the house perhaps?
                        Oh that's the way
I'd go with you, my guardian—off today!

You know that mountain and its cloudy track?
The drifting haze, the mule-clop echoing back?
—Old dragons and their brood in grottoes sprawl;
Each rock's a cliff; each brook, a waterfall.
You know the place perhaps?
                        Oh that's the way
Our journey goes! Good father, off today!

ANAKREONS GRAB

Wo die Rose hier blüht, wo Reben um Lorbeer sich schlingen,
    Wo das Turtelchen lockt, wo sich das Grillchen ergetzt,
Welch ein Grab ist hier, das alle Götter mit Leben
    Schön bepflanzt und geziert? Es ist Anakreons Ruh.
Frühling, Sommer und Herbst genoß der glückliche Dichter;
    Vor dem Winter hat ihn endlich der Hügel geschützt.

ANACREON'S GRAVE

Here with roses in bloom, with woodbine twining the laurel,
  Dove calling softly to dove, cricket crisp with delight—
Tell me, what grave is this, which every god of the garden
  Furbelows, lush with life? Rest for Anacreon here.
Always in luck, he loved the spring, the summer, the autumn.
  Winter he'll never know—snug in a cozier home.

DAS SONETT

Sich in erneutem Kunstgebrauch zu üben,
  Ist heilge Pflicht, die wir dir auferlegen;
  Du kannst dich auch, wie wir, bestimmt bewegen
  Nach Tritt und Schritt, wie es dir vorgeschrieben.

Denn eben die Beschränkung läßt sich lieben,
  Wenn sich die Geister gar gewaltig regen;
  Und wie sie sich denn auch gebärden mögen,
  Das Werk zuletzt ist doch vollendet blieben.

So möcht ich selbst in künstlichen Sonetten,
  In sprachgewandter Maße kühnem Stolze,
  Das Beste, was Gefühl mir gäbe, reimen;

Nur weiß ich hier mich nicht bequem zu betten,
  Ich schneide sonst so gern aus ganzem Holze,
  Und müßte nun doch auch mitunter leimen.

THE SONNET

To work away in art's traditional measure,
Renewing its vigor always—right and good!
You too can move in step, feel all the pleasure
Of dancing as ritual music says you should.

Tighten the rein—that rouses admiration
(Assuming you've racy energies to rein).
Then, when our love or hate's exasperation
Passes, the cool and perfect words remain.

I'd like, myself, to be handy with the sonnet
—Impetuous, proud, resourceful—to evoke
All of the best I throbbed to, best I knew.

Only—too snug a bunk. I'm restless on it.
Carving, I choose my one dense chunk of oak.
Sonnets I might, just maybe, patch with glue.

NATUR UND KUNST

Natur und Kunst sie scheinen sich zu fliehen,
Und haben sich, eh man es denkt, gefunden;
Der Widerwille ist auch mir verschwunden,
Und beide scheinen gleich mich anzuziehen.

Es gilt wohl nur ein redliches Bemühen!
Und wenn wir erst in abgemeßnen Stunden
Mit Geist und Fleiß uns an die Kunst gebunden,
Mag frei Natur im Herzen wieder glühen.

So ist's mit aller Bildung auch beschaffen:
Vergebens werden ungebundne Geister
Nach der Vollendung reiner Höhe streben.

Wer Großes will, muß sich zusammenraffen;
In der Beschränkung zeigt sich erst der Meister,
Und das Gesetz nur kann uns Freiheit geben.

NATURE AND ART

Genius, technique—you'd swear the pair unsuited,
Yet here they stand together, hand in hand.
Nature's in love with art. Their widely bruited
Hassle's a lie, I've come to understand.

Poet, there's one thing only works: to work.
Hours of the sweaty effort day and night
Trying it this way, that way—going berserk.
Then you can be spontaneous. You've the right.

Habits of mind we earn. To earn's laborious.
Small chance they'll make it to a difficult goal,
Those do-as-you-like "free spirits," la-dee-dee!

Nose to the grindstone first, if aims are glorious.
Mastery's much in little, tight control.
Rules! they're a springboard only, and we're *free!*

DAUER IM WECHSEL

Hielte diesen frühen Segen
Ach, nur Eine Stunde fest!
Aber vollen Blütenregen
Schüttelt schon der laue West.
Soll ich mich des Grünen freuen,
Dem ich Schatten erst verdankt?
Bald wird Sturm auch das zerstreuen,
Wenn es falb im Herbst geschwankt.

Willst du nach den Früchten greifen,
Eilig nimm dein Teil davon!
Diese fangen an zu reifen,
Und die andern keimen schon;
Gleich mit jedem Regengusse
Ändert sich dein holdes Tal,
Ach, und in demselben Flusse
Schwimmst du nicht zum zweitenmal.

Du nun selbst! Was felsenfeste
Sich vor dir hervorgetan,
Mauern siehst du, siehst Paläste
Stets mit andern Augen an.
Weggeschwunden ist die Lippe,
Die im Kusse sonst genas,
Jener Fuß, der an der Klippe
Sich mit Gemsenfreche maß,

Jene Hand, die gern und milde
Sich bewegte wohlzutun,
Das gegliederte Gebilde,
Alles ist ein andres nun.

PERMANENCE IN CHANGE

Early blossoms—could a single
Hour preserve them just as now!
But the warmer west will scatter
Petals showering from the bough.
How enjoy these leaves, that lately
I was grateful to for shade?
Soon the wind and snow are rolling
What the late Novembers fade.

Fruit—you'd reach a hand and have it?
Better have it then with speed.
These you see about to ripen,
Those already gone to seed.
Half a rainy day, and there's your
Pleasant valley not the same.
None could swim that very river
Twice, so quick the changes came.

You yourself! What all around you
Strong as stonework used to lie
—Castles, battlements—you see them
With an ever-changing eye.
Now the lips are dim and withered
Once the kisses set aglow;
Lame the leg, that on the mountain
Left the mountain goat below.

Or that hand, that knew such loving
Ways, outstretching in caress,
—Cunningly adjusted structure—
Now can function less and less.

Und was sich an jener Stelle
Nun mit deinem Namen nennt,
Kam herbei wie eine Welle,
Und so eilts zum Element.

Laß den Anfang mit dem Ende
Sich in Eins zusammenziehn!
Schneller als die Gegenstände
Selber dich vorüberfliehn.
Danke, daß die Gunst der Musen
Unvergängliches verheißt,
Den Gehalt in deinem Busen
Und die Form in deinem Geist.

All are gone; this substitution
Has your name and nothing more.
Like a wave it lifts and passes,
Back to atoms on the shore.

See in each beginning, ending,
Double aspects of the One;
Here, amid stampeding objects,
Be among the first to run,
Thankful to a muse whose favor
Grants you one unchanging thing:
What the heart can hold to ponder;
What the spirit shape to sing.

DAS TAGEBUCH

—aliam tenui, sed iam quum gaudia adirem,
Admonuit dominae deseruitque Venus.

Wir hören's oft und glauben's wohl am Ende:
Das Menschenherz sei ewig unergründlich,
Und wie man auch sich hin und wider wende,
So sei der Christe wie der Heide sündlich.
Das Beste bleibt, wir geben uns die Hände
Und nehmen's mit der Lehre nicht empfindlich;
Denn zeigt sich auch ein Dämon, uns versuchend,
So waltet was, gerettet ist die Tugend.

Von meiner Trauten lange Zeit entfernet,
Wie's öfters geht, nach irdischem Gewinne,
Und was ich auch gewonnen und gelernet,
So hatt ich doch nur immer Sie im Sinne;
Und wie zu Nacht der Himmel erst sich sternet,
Erinnrung uns umleuchtet ferner Minne:
So ward im Federzug des Tags Ereignis
Mit süßen Worten ihr ein freundlich Gleichnis.

Ich eilte nun zurück. Zerbrochen sollte
Mein Wagen mich noch eine Nacht verspäten;
Schon dacht ich mich, wie ich zu Hause rollte,
Allein da war Geduld und Werk vonnöten.
Und wie ich auch mit Schmied und Wagner tollte,
Sie hämmerten, verschmähten viel zu reden.
Ein jedes Handwerk hat nun seine Schnurren.
Was blieb mir nun? Zu weilen und zu murren.

THE DIARY

I had another girl, but as I was getting close to the blissful moment,
Venus reminded me about my true love, and went away.

Tibullus, I, 5

We've heard and heard, and finally believe:
There's no enigma like the heart of man.
The things we do! No good to twist or weave—
We're human yet, in Rome as Turkestan.
What's my advice? Forget it. Maybe heave
One sigh, and then live with it if you can.
Also, when sins come nudging with that leer,
Count on some Sturdy Virtue to appear.

Once, when I left my love and had to travel
Off on affairs a traveling man transacts,
Collecting facts and figures to unravel
(Thinking of her, *her* figure and its facts),
As always, when the night spread, thick as gravel,
Its load of stars, my mind went starry. Stacks
Of paper (balanced on my solar plexus)
Told of the day, in mostly O's and X's.

Finally I'm rolling homeward, when—you'd know it!—
Cru-ungk! and the axle goes. So one less night
Back in the bed I'm dreaming of—but stow it!
There's work now. Cross your fingers and sit tight.
Two blacksmiths come. I'm grumpy, and I show it.
Shrugging, the one spits left, the other right.
"It'll be done when done," they grunt, and batter,
Whang! at the wheel. Sparks flying. Clang and clatter.

So stand ich nun. Der Stern des nächsten Schildes
Berief mich hin, die Wohnung schien erträglich.
Ein Mädchen kam, des seltensten Gebildes,
Das Licht erleuchtend. Mir ward gleich behäglich.
Hausflur und Treppe sah ich als ein Mildes,
Die Zimmerchen erfreuten mich unsäglich.
Den sündigen Menschen der im Freien schwebet—
Die Schönheit spinnt, sie ist's die ihn umwebet.

Nun setzt ich mich zu meiner Tasch und Briefen
Und meines Tagebuchs Genauigkeiten,
Um so wie sonst, wenn alle Menschen schliefen,
Mir und der Trauten Freude zu bereiten;
Doch weiß ich nicht, die Tintenworte liefen
Nicht so wie sonst in alle Kleinigkeiten:
Das Mädchen kam, des Abendessens Bürde
Verteilte sie gewandt mit Gruß und Würde.

Sie geht und kommt; ich spreche, sie erwidert;
Mit jedem Wort erscheint sie mir geschmückter.
Und wie sie leicht mir nun das Huhn zergliedert,
Bewegend Hand und Arm, geschickt, geschickter—
Was auch das tolle Zeug in uns befiedert—
Genug ich bin verworrner, bin verrückter,
Den Stuhl umwerfend spring ich auf und fasse
Das schöne Kind; sie lispelt: «Lasse, lasse!

Die Muhme drunten lauscht, ein alter Drache,
Sie zählt bedächtig des Geschäfts Minute;
Sie denkt sich unten, was ich oben mache,
Bei jedem Zögern schwenkt sie frisch die Rute.
Doch schließe deine Türe nicht und wache,
So kommt die Mitternacht uns wohl zu Gute.»
Rasch meinem Arm entwindet sie die Glieder,
Und eilet fort und kommt nur dienend wieder;

Stuck in the sticks! With just an inn; The Star,
It says outside. Looks bearable. I'm glad
To see a girl with lantern there. So far
So good. She lifts it higher and—not bad!—
Beckons me in: nice lounge, a decent bar.
The bedroom's cozy as a travel ad.
Poor sinners! When they're wandering on the loose,
Nothing like pretty girls to jerk the noose.

I take the room, and shuffle papers out.
My diary—got to keep it up to date
The way I do just every night, about.
I like to write; my darling says I'm great.
But now, though, nothing comes. Some writer's gout?
I seem distracted, somehow. Better wait.
That girl again. She lays the table first,
Hands deft and cool. Nice manners. I'm immersed

In studying her skirt, flung out and in.
I ask. She knows the answers. That's my girl!
Can she disjoint a chicken! Flick the skin!
Those arms! And hands with fingertips in pearl!
I feel that certain stirring-up begin
And dizzy with her, crazy for—I hurl
The chair away; impulsively I twist her
Into my arms, close, closer. "Listen, mister,

Cool it," she cuddles murmuring. "My aunt,
Old hatchet face, is listening all the time.
She's down there guessing what I can or can't
Be up to every minute. Next she'll climb
Up with that cane of hers, sniff, snuffle, pant!
But look, don't lock your door. At midnight I'm
More on my own—" Untwisting (it's delicious!),
She hurries out. And hurries back with dishes.

Doch blickend auch! So daß aus jedem Blicke
Sich himmlisches Versprechen mir entfaltet.
Den stillen Seufzer drängt sie nicht zurücke,
Der ihren Busen herrlicher gestaltet.
Ich sehe, daß am Ohr, um Hals und Gnicke
Der flüchtigen Röte Liebesblüte waltet,
Und da sie nichts zu leisten weiter findet,
Geht sie und zögert, sieht sich um, verschwindet.

Der Mitternacht gehören Haus und Straßen,
Mir ist ein weites Lager aufgebreitet,
Wovon den kleinsten Teil mir anzumaßen
Die Liebe rät, die alles wohl bereitet;
Ich zaudre noch, die Kerzen auszublasen,
Nun hör ich sie, wie leise sie auch gleitet,
Mit gierigem Blick die Hochgestalt umschweif ich,
Sie senkt sich her, die Wohlgestalt ergreif ich.

Sie macht sich los: «Vergönne daß ich rede,
Damit ich dir nicht völlig fremd gehöre.
Der Schein ist wider mich, sonst war ich blöde,
Stets gegen Männer setzt ich mich zur Wehre.
Mich nennt die Stadt, mich nennt die Gegend spröde;
Nun aber weiß ich, wie das Herz sich kehre:
Du bist mein Sieger, laß dich's nicht verdrießen,
Ich sah, ich liebte, schwur dich zu genießen.

Du hast mich rein, und wenn ich's besser wüßte,
So gäb ich's dir, ich tue was ich sage.»
So schließt sie mich an ihre süßen Brüste,
Als ob ihr nur an meiner Brust behage.
Und wie ich Mund und Aug und Stirne küßte,
So war ich doch in wunderbarer Lage:
Denn der so hitzig sonst den Meister spielet,
Weicht schülerhaft zurück und abgekühlet.

Dishes—and warmer eyes. I'm in a blur.
The heavens open and the angels sing.
She sighs, and every sigh looks good on her:
It makes the heaving breast a pretty thing.
She loves me, I can tell: Such colors stir
Deeper on neck and ear—she's crimsoning!
Then sad, "Well, dinner's over, I suppose."
She goes. She doesn't want to, but she goes.

The chimes at midnight on the sleeping town!
My double bed looks wider by the minute.
"Leave half for her. That's friendlier, you clown!"
I say, and squiggle over. To begin it,
We'll leave the candles lit, I plan—when down
The hall a rustle! Slinky silk—she's in it!
My eyes devour that fully blossomed flesh.
She settles by me and our fingers mesh.

Then sweet and low: "First tell me once or twice
You love me as a person? Say you do.
As girls around here go, I'm rather nice.
Said *no* to every man, till I saw you.
Why do you think they call me 'Piece of Ice'?
Of ice, indeed! Just feel! I'm melting through.
You did it to me, darling. So be good.
And let's be lovers, do as lovers should.

"I'm starting out, remember. Make it sweet.
If I had more to give, I'd even dare."
She pressed her cooler breasts against my heat
As if she liked it and felt safer there.
Lips linger on her lips; toes reach and meet,
But—something funny happening elsewhere.
What always strutted in the leading role
Now shrank like some beginner. Bless my soul!

Ihr scheint ein süßes Wort, ein Kuß zu gnügen,
Als wär es alles was ihr Herz begehrte.
Wie keusch sie mir, mit liebevollem Fügen,
Des süßen Körpers Fülleform gewährte!
Entzückt und froh in allen ihren Zügen
Und ruhig dann, als wenn sie nichts entbehrte.
So ruht ich auch, gefällig sie beschauend,
Noch auf den Meister hoffend und vertrauend.

Doch als ich länger mein Geschick bedachte,
Von tausend Flüchen mir die Seele kochte,
Mich selbst verwünschend, grinsend mich belachte,
Nichts besser ward, wie ich auch zaudern mochte,
Da lag sie schlafend, schöner als sie wachte;
Die Lichter dämmerten mit langem Dochte.
Der Tages-Arbeit, jugendlicher Mühe
Gesellt sich gern der Schlaf und nie zu frühe.

So lag sie himmlisch an bequemer Stelle,
Als wenn das Lager ihr allein gehörte,
Und an die Wand gedrückt, gequetscht zur Hölle,
Ohnmächtig jener, dem sie nichts verwehrte.
Vom Schlangenbisse fällt zunächst der Quelle
Ein Wandrer so, den schon der Durst verzehrte.
Sie atmet lieblich holdem Traum entgegen;
Er hält den Atem, sie nicht aufzuregen.

Gefaßt bei dem, was ihm noch nie begegnet,
Spricht er zu sich: So mußt du doch erfahren,
Warum der Bräutigam sich kreuzt und segnet,
Vor Nestelknüpfen scheu sich zu bewahren.
Weit lieber da, wo's Hellebarden regnet,
Als hier im Schimpf! So war es nicht vor Jahren,
Als deine Herrin dir zum ersten Male
Vors Auge trat im prachterhellten Saale.

The girl seemed happy with a kiss, a word,
Smiling as if she couldn't ask for more.
So pure a gaze—yet every limb concurred.
So sweet a blossom, and not picked before.
Oh, but she looked ecstatic when she stirred!
And then lay back relaxing, to adore.
Me, I lay back a bit and . . . beamed away.
Nagged at my dragging actor, "Do the play!"

The more I brooded on my situation,
The more I seethed with curses, inwardly.
Laughed at myself, God knows without elation.
It got me down. And sleeping, breathing, she
Lay lovelier yet, a gilt-edged invitation.
The candles stood and burned, derisively.
Young people who work hard to earn their bread
Soon as they hit the hay are turned to lead.

She dreamed—I'd swear, an angel—flushed and snug;
Breathed easily, as if the bed were hers.
I'm scrunched up by the wall—there's *that* to hug!
Can't lift a finger. It's like what occurs
To thirsty travelers in the sands when—glug!—
There's water bubbling. But a rattler whirs!
Her lips stir softly, talking to a dream.
I hold my breath: O honeychild! And beam.

Detached—for you could call it that—I say,
Well, it's a new experience. Now you know
Why bridegrooms in a panic start to pray
They won't get spooked and see their chances go.
I'd rather be cut up in saberplay
Than in a bind like this. It wasn't so
When first I saw my real love: from the gloom
Stared at her, brilliant in the brilliant room.

Da quoll dein Herz, da quollen deine Sinnen,
So daß der ganze Mensch entzückt sich regte.
Zum raschen Tanze trugst du sie von hinnen,
Die kaum der Arm und schon der Busen hegte,
Als wolltest du dir selbst sie abgewinnen;
Vervielfacht war, was sich für sie bewegte:
Verstand und Witz und alle Lebensgeister
Und rascher als die andern jener Meister.

So immerfort wuchs Neigung und Begierde,
Brautleute wurden wir im frühen Jahre,
Sie selbst des Maien schönste Blum und Zierde;
Wie wuchs die Kraft zur Lust im jungen Paare!
Und als ich endlich sie zur Kirche führte,
Gesteh ich's nur, vor Priester und Altare,
Vor deinem Jammerkreuz, blutrünstiger Christe,
Verzeih mir's Gott, es regte sich der Iste.

Und ihr, der Brautnacht reiche Bettgehänge,
Ihr Pfühle, die ihr euch so breit erstrecktet,
Ihr Teppiche, die Lieb und Lustgedränge
Mit euren seidnen Fittichen bedecktet!
Ihr Käfigvögel, die durch Zwitscher-Sänge
Zu neuer Lust und nie zu früh erwecktet!
Ihr kanntet uns, von euerm Schutz umfriedet,
Teilnehmend sie, mich immer unermüdet.

Und wie wir oft sodann im Raub genossen
Nach Buhlenart des Ehstands heilige Rechte,
Von reifer Saat umwogt, vom Rohr umschlossen,
An manchem Unort, wo ich's mich erfrechte,
Wir waren augenblicklich, unverdrossen
Und wiederholt bedient vom braven Knechte!
Verfluchter Knecht, wie unerwecklich liegst du!
Und deinen Herrn ums schönste Glück betriegst du.

Ah, but my heart leaped then, and every sense,
My whole man's-shape a pulsing of delight.
Lord, how I swept her off in a wild dance
Light in my arms, her weight against me tight.
You'd think I fought myself for her. One glance
Would tell how I grew greater, gathered might
For her sake, mind and body, heart and soul.
That was the day my actor lived his role!

Worship and lovely lust—with both in view
I wooed her all that year, until the spring
(Violins, maestro!), when the world was new
And she outflowered, in June, the floweriest thing,
The date was set. So great our passion grew
That even in church (I blush) with heaven's King
Racked on his cross, before the priest and all,
My impudent hero made his curtain call!

And you, four-posters of the wedding night,
You pillows, that were tossed and rumpled soon,
You blankets, drawn around so our delight
Was ours alone, through morning, afternoon;
You parakeets in cages, rose and white,
Whose twitter music perked our deeper tune—
Could even you, who played your minor part,
Tell which of us was which? Or end from start?

The days of make-believe! The "Let's pretend,
Honey, we're sexy tramps!" I'd toss her there
Laughing, among the cornstalks, or we'd bend
Reeds by the river, threshing who knows where?
In public places, nearly. What a friend
My sturdy plowboy then! He wouldn't scare!
But now, with all the virgin field to reap,
Look at the lousy helper sound asleep.

Doch Meister Iste hat nun seine Grillen
Und läßt sich nicht befehlen noch verachten,
Auf einmal ist er da, und ganz im stillen
Erhebt er sich zu allen seinen Prachten;
So steht es nun dem Wandrer ganz zu Willen,
Nicht lechzend mehr am Quell zu übernachten.
Er neigt sich hin, er will die Schläferin küssen,
Allein er stockt, er fühlt sich weggerissen.

Wer hat zur Kraft ihn wieder aufgestählet,
Als jenes Bild, das ihm auf ewig teuer,
Mit dem er sich in Jugendlust vermählet?
Dort leuchtet her ein frisch erquicklich Feuer,
Und wie er erst in Ohnmacht sich gequälet,
So wird nun hier dem Starken nicht geheuer;
Er schaudert weg, vorsichtig, leise, leise
Entzieht er sich dem holden Zauberkreise,

Sitzt, schreibt: «Ich nahte mich der heimischen Pforte,
Entfernen wollten mich die letzten Stunden,
Da hab ich nun, am sonderbarsten Orte,
Mein treues Herz aufs neue dir verbunden.
Zum Schlusse findest du geheime Worte:
Die Krankheit erst bewähret den Gesunden.
Dies Büchlein soll dir manches Gute zeigen,
Das Beste nur muß ich zuletzt verschweigen.»

Da kräht der Hahn. Das Mädchen schnell entwindet
Der Decke sich und wirft sich rasch ins Mieder.
Und da sie sich so seltsam wiederfindet,
So stutzt sie, blickt und schlägt die Augen nieder;
Und da sie ihm zum letzten Mal verschwindet,
Im Auge bleiben ihm die schönen Glieder:
Das Posthorn tönt, er wirft sich in den Wagen
Und läßt getrost sich zu der Liebsten tragen.

Or was. But now he's rousing. He's the one!
You can't ignore him, and you can't command.
He's suddenly himself. And like the sun,
Is soaring full of splendor. Suave and bland.
You mean the long thirst's over with and done?
The desert traveler's at the promised land?
I lean across to kiss my sleeping girl
And—hey!—the glorious banner starts to furl!

What made him tough and proud a moment? She,
His only idol now, as long ago;
The one he took in church exultantly.
From worlds away it comes, that rosy glow.
And, as before it worried him to be
Meager, so now he's vexed at swelling so
With her afar. Soft, soft, he shrinks away
Out of that magic circle, all dismay.

That's that. I'm up and scribbling, "Close to home,
I almost thought I wouldn't make it there.
Honey, I'm yours, in Turkestan or Rome.
I'm writing you in bed, and by a bare
—Well, call it piece of luck or something, hmmm!
Impotence proved I'm superman. Now where
'S a prettier riddle? Leave it; read the rest.
Dearest, I've told you all. Except the best."

Then *cock-a-doodle-doo!* At once the girl's
Thrown off a bed sheet and thrown on a slip;
She rubs her eyes, shakes out her tousled curls,
Looks blushing at bare feet and bites her lip.
Without a word she's vanishing in swirls
Of underpretties over breast and hip.
She's dear, I murmur—rushing from above
Down to my coach. And on the road for love!

Und weil zuletzt bei jeder Dichtungsweise
Moralien uns ernstlich fördern sollen,
So will auch ich in so beliebtem Gleise
Euch gern bekennen, was die Verse wollen:
Wir stolpern wohl auf unsrer Lebensreise,
Und doch vermögen in der Welt, der tollen,
Zwei Hebel viel aufs irdische Getriebe:
Sehr viel die *Pflicht,* unendlich mehr die *Liebe!*

I'll tell you what, we writers like to bumble
Onto a moral somewhere, forehead glowing
Over a Noble Truth. Some readers grumble
Unless they feel improved. My moral's showing:
Look, it's a crazy world. We slip and stumble,
But two things, Love and Duty, keep us going.
I couldn't rightly call them hand in glove.
Duty?—who really needs it? Trust your Love.

FLIEGENTOD

(Parabolisch)

Sie saugt mit Gier verrätrisches Getränke
Unabgesetzt, vom ersten Zug verführt;
Sie fühlt sich wohl, und längst sind die Gelenke
Der zarten Beinchen schon paralysiert,
Nicht mehr gewandt, die Flügelchen zu putzen,
Nicht mehr geschickt, das Köpfchen aufzustutzen—
Das Leben so sich im Genuß verliert.
Zum Stehen kaum wird noch das Füßchen taugen;
So schlürft sie fort, und mitten unterm Saugen
Umnebelt ihr der Tod die tausend Augen.

DEATH OF A FLY

(Figurative)

He sucks with greed the treacherous attraction.
A single sip and—done for! Won't give way.
Never was half so happy—all the action
Gone from his limbs, long paralyzed. They'd play
Brisk on the little wing—no more though, never.
Won't slick the little head, so pert and clever.
Life, in his fit of pleasure, slips away.
The tiny feet, enfeeble-ing, go slack;
Toppled, he sucks the more, goes blacker black,
Death in his thousand eyes like cataract.

GEFUNDEN

Ich ging im Walde
So für mich hin,
Und nichts zu suchen,
Das war mein Sinn.

Im Schatten sah ich
Ein Blümchen stehn,
Wie Sterne leuchtend,
Wie Äuglein schön.

Ich wollt es brechen,
Da sagt' es fein:
Soll ich zum Welken
Gebrochen sein?

Ich grubs mit allen
Den Würzlein aus,
Zum Garten trug ichs
Am hübschen Haus.

Und pflanzt es wieder
Am stillen Ort;
Nun zweigt es immer
Und blüht so fort.

FOUND

Off in the forest,
Any old way;
Nothing in mind but
Mosey and stray—

Saw there a blossom
Hid amid plants,
Lovely as starlight,
Bright as a glance.

Reckoned to pick it;
Heard a small cry:
"I'm to be broken
Only to die?"

Stooping I dug it
Rootlets and all—
I've a fine cottage,
Fine garden-wall;

Planted it back there,
Half in the sun.
Look at her prosper
—Blossomy one!

SELIGE SEHNSUCHT

Sagt es niemand, nur den Weisen,
Weil die Menge gleich verhöhnet,
Das Lebendge will ich preisen
Das nach Flammentod sich sehnet.

In der Liebesnächte Kühlung,
Die dich zeugte, wo du zeugtest,
Überfällt dich fremde Fühlung
Wenn die stille Kerze leuchtet.

Nicht mehr bleibest du umfangen
In der Finsternis Beschattung,
Und dich reißet neu Verlangen
Auf zu höherer Begattung.

Keine Ferne macht dich schwierig,
Kommst geflogen und gebannt,
Und zuletzt, des Lichts begierig,
Bist du Schmetterling verbrannt.

Und so lang du das nicht hast,
Dieses: Stirb und werde!
Bist du nur ein trüber Gast
Auf der dunklen Erde.

ECSTATIC LONGING

Not a word, or to the knowing
Only (most would jeer with *Liar!*):
How I'd praise a life that's glowing
With the passion: die in fire.

When the love-nights settle, chilling
You they sowed, and you the sower,
All at once the strangest feeling,
And the candle low and lower.

Out of time, and no returning
To this night of smothered covers:
Earth, to your intenser yearning,
Too confined a groove for lovers.

Far in space and borne above it,
Flying with a blind desire
For the holocaust you covet:
Moth in ecstasy afire!

Till you grapple this to heart:
Death's a further birth!
You're a drifter, pale, apart,
On the murky earth.

TRILOGIE DER LEIDENSCHAFT

AN WERTHER

Noch einmal wagst du, vielbeweinter Schatten,
Hervor dich an das Tageslicht,
Begegnest mir auf neu beblümten Matten,
Und meinen Anblick scheust du nicht.
Es ist, als ob du lebtest in der Frühe,
Wo uns der Tau auf Einem Feld erquickt
Und nach des Tages unwillkommner Mühe
Der Scheidesonne letzter Strahl entzückt;
Zum Bleiben ich, zum Scheiden du erkoren,
Gingst du voran—und hast nicht viel verloren.

Des Menschen Leben scheint ein herrlich Los:
Der Tag wie lieblich, so die Nacht wie groß!
Und wir, gepflanzt in Paradieses Wonne,
Genießen kaum der hocherlauchten Sonne,
Da kämpft sogleich verworrene Bestrebung
Bald mit uns selbst und bald mit der Umgebung;
Keins wird vom andern wünschenswert ergänzt,
Von außen düsterts, wenn es innen glänzt,
Ein glänzend Äußres deckt ein trüber Blick,
Da steht es nah—und man verkennt das Glück.

Nun glauben wirs zu kennen! Mit Gewalt
Ergreift uns Liebreiz weiblicher Gestalt:
Der Jüngling, froh wie in der Kindheit Flor,
Im Frühling tritt als Frühling selbst hervor,
Entzückt, erstaunt, wer dies ihm angetan?
Er schaut umher, die Welt gehört ihm an.

TRILOGY OF PASSION

TO WERTHER

So once again, poor much-lamented shadow,
You venture in the light of day?
And here, in blossoms of the fresher meadow,
Confront me and not turn away?
Alive as in the early dawn, when tender
Chill of a misty field bestirred the two,
When both were dazzled by the west in splendor
After the drudging summer days were through.
My doom: endure. And yours: depart forlorn.
Is early death, we wonder, much to mourn?

In theory how magnificent, man's fate!
The day agreeable, the night so great.
Yet we, in such a paradise begun,
Enjoy but briefly the amazing sun,
And then the battle's on: vague causes found
To struggle with ourself, the world around.
Neither completes the other as it should:
The skies are gloomy when our humor's good;
The vista glitters and we're glum enough.
Joy near at hand, but we—at blindman's buff.

At times we think it ours: some darling girl!
Borne on a fragrant whirlwind, off we whirl.
The young man, breezy as in boyhood's prime,
Like spring itself goes strutting in springtime.
Astounded, charmed, "Who's doing this, all for me?"
Claims like a cocky heir the land and sea.

Ins Weite zieht ihn unbefangne Hast,
Nichts engt ihn ein, nicht Mauer, nicht Palast;
Wie Vögelschar an Wäldergipfeln streift,
So schwebt auch er, der um die Liebste schweift,
Er sucht vom Äther, den er gern verläßt,
Den treuen Blick, und dieser hält ihn fest.

Doch erst zu früh und dann zu spät gewarnt,
Fühlt er den Flug gehemmt, fühlt sich umgarnt.
Das Wiedersehn ist froh, das Scheiden schwer,
Das Wieder-Wiedersehn beglückt noch mehr,
Und Jahre sind im Augenblick ersetzt;
Doch tückisch harrt das Lebewohl zuletzt.

Du lächelst, Freund, gefühlvoll, wie sich ziemt:
Ein gräßlich Scheiden machte dich berühmt;
Wir feierten dein kläglich Mißgeschick,
Du ließest uns zu Wohl und Weh zurück.
Dann zog uns wieder ungewisse Bahn
Der Leidenschaften labyrinthisch an;
Und wir, verschlungen wiederholter Not,
Dem Scheiden endlich—Scheiden ist der Tod!
Wie klingt es rührend, wenn der Dichter singt,
Den Tod zu meiden, den das Scheiden bringt!
Verstrickt in solche Qualen, halbverschuldet,
Geb ihm ein Gott zu sagen, was er duldet.

ELEGIE

Und wenn der Mensch in seiner Qual verstummt,
Gab mir ein Gott zu sagen, was ich leide.

Was soll ich nun vom Wiedersehen hoffen,
Von dieses Tages noch geschloßner Blüte?

Goes footloose anywhere, without a thought;
No wall, no palace holds him, even if caught.
As swallows skim the treetops in a blur,
He hovers round, in rings, that certain her.
Scans, from the height he means to leave at last,
Earth for an answering gaze, that holds him fast.

First warned too soon, and then too late, he'll swear
His feet are bound, traps planted everywhere.
Sweet meetings are a joy, departure's pain.
Meeting again—what hopes we entertain!
Moments with her make good the years away.
Yet there's a treacherous parting, come the day.

You smile, my friend, eyes welling. Still the same!
Yours, what a ghastly avenue to fame.
We dressed in mourning when your luck ran out
And you deserted, leaving ours in doubt.
For us, the road resuming God knows where,
Through labyrinths of passion, heavy air,
Still drew us on, bone-tired, with desperate breath
Up to a final parting. Parting's death!
True: it's affecting when the poet sings
To wish away the death that parting brings.
Some god—though man's half guilty, hurt past cure—
Grant him a tongue to murmur: I endure.

ELEGY

Though most men suffer dumbly, yet a god
Gave me a tongue to utter all my pain.

What's to be hoped from seeing her again?
Hoped from the still-shut blossoms of today?

215

Das Paradies, die Hölle steht dir offen;
Wie wankelsinnig regt sichs im Gemüte!—
Kein Zweifeln mehr! Sie tritt ans Himmelstor,
Zu ihren Armen hebt sie dich empor.

So warst du denn im Paradies empfangen,
Als wärst du wert des ewig schönen Lebens;
Dir blieb kein Wunsch, kein Hoffen, kein Verlangen,
Hier war das Ziel des innigsten Bestrebens,
Und in dem Anschaun dieses einzig Schönen
Versiegte gleich der Quell sehnsüchtiger Tränen.

Wie regte nicht der Tag die raschen Flügel,
Schien die Minuten vor sich her zu treiben!
Der Abendkuß, ein treu verbindlich Siegel:
So wird es auch der nächsten Sonne bleiben.
Die Stunden glichen sich in zartem Wandern
Wie Schwestern zwar, doch keine ganz den andern.

Der Kuß, der letzte, grausam süß, zerschneidend
Ein herrliches Geflecht verschlungner Minnen.
Nun eilt, nun stockt der Fuß, die Schwelle meidend,
Als trieb' ein Cherub flammend ihn von hinnen;
Das Auge starrt auf düstrem Pfad verdrossen,
Es blickt zurück, die Pforte steht verschlossen.

Und nun verschlossen in sich selbst, als hätte
Dies Herz sich nie geöffnet, selige Stunden
Mit jedem Stern des Himmels um die Wette
An ihrer Seite leuchtend nicht empfunden;
Und Mißmut, Reue, Vorwurf, Sorgenschwere
Belastens nun in schwüler Atmosphäre.

Ist denn die Welt nicht übrig? Felsenwände,
Sind sie nicht mehr gekrönt von heiligen Schatten?
Die Ernte, reift sie nicht? Ein grün Gelände,

Which opens, heaven or hell, around me? When
I guess, my thoughts go wandering every way.
But steady—there! She's there, at heaven's door;
Her arms enfold and raise me, as before.

So then the heavens are open, take me in
As if deserving life forever blest.
No wish, no longing, and no might-have-been
Stinted: the very goal of all my quest.
Eyes dwell delighted on that loveliest thing,
Their tears subsiding at the passionate spring.

Didn't the day go by on flashing feathers!
Didn't it send the minutes skimming there!
Our sign, the kiss at evening—and what weathers
It promised: fair tonight, tomorrow fair.
Hours were like sisters, lingering as they passed,
Each face alike, each different from the last.

Our final kiss, so shuddering sweet, it tore
The sheerest of all fiber, heart's desire.
My foot, abrupt or dragging, dodged her door
As if an angel waved that sword of fire.
Eyes frozen on the dusky ruts go glum.
Turn, and her door's a darkness, shut and dumb.

My soul's a darkness, shut and dumb—as though
This heart had never opened, never found
Hours of delight beside her, such a glow
As all the stars of heaven let dance around.
Now gloom, remorse, self-mockery—clouds of care
Clutch at it, sluggish, in the sluggish air.

What of the world—it's done for? Cliffs of granite
Crowned shadowy with the sacred grove—they're vapor?
No harvest-moon? Green delta country (can it?)

Zieht sichs nicht hin am Fluß durch Busch und Matten?
Und wölbt sich nicht das überweltlich Große,
Gestaltenreiche, bald Gestaltenlose?

Wie leicht und zierlich, klar und zart gewoben
Schwebt, seraphgleich, aus ernster Wolken Chor,
Als glich' es ihr, am blauen Äther droben
Ein schlank Gebild aus lichtem Duft empor!
So sahst du sie in frohem Tanze walten,
Die lieblichste der lieblichsten Gestalten.

Doch nur Momente darfst dich unterwinden,
Ein Luftgebild statt ihrer festzuhalten;
Ins Herz zurück! dort wirst dus besser finden,
Dort regt sie sich in wechselnden Gestalten:
Zu Vielen bildet Eine sich hinüber,
So tausendfach, und immer, immer lieber.

Wie zum Empfang sie an den Pforten weilte
Und mich von dannauf stufenweis beglückte,
Selbst nach dem letzten Kuß mich noch ereilte,
Den letztesten mir auf die Lippen drückte:
So klar beweglich bleibt das Bild der Lieben
Mit Flammenschrift ins treue Herz geschrieben.

Ins Herz, das fest, wie zinnenhohe Mauer,
Sich ihr bewahrt und sie in sich bewahret,
Für sie sich freut an seiner eignen Dauer,
Nur weiß von sich, wenn sie sich offenbaret,
Sich freier fühlt in so geliebten Schranken
Und nur noch schlägt, für alles ihr zu danken.

War Fähigkeit zu lieben, war Bedürfen
Von Gegenliebe weggelöscht, verschwunden,
Ist Hoffnungslust zu freudigen Entwürfen,

Turn with its trees to ash, like burning paper?
That grandeur curved above us—all undone?—
Now with its thousand clouds, and now with none.

A form there!—rare and airy, silken, bright,
Floats forth, among the clouds in grave ballet,
An angel in blue noon, or—? No, a white
Slim body—hers!—inclining far away.
You saw her lean so at the gala ball;
Among the loveliest, lovelier far than all.

A ruse for moments only. Don't suppose
The empty air a match for her embraces.
Back to your heart of hearts, that better knows
Her and the changing miracle her face is.
In every guise she's greater. Like a flame,
Forever varying and the very same.

Once by the gate she waited; in she brought me;
Onward from joy to keener joy we passed.
The last last kiss—but how she ran and caught me,
Pressed to my mouth an even laster last.
Still that indelible image of desire
Burns on my heart in script of living fire—

My heart (its battlement a height securing
Her for itself alone, itself for her)
Only for her is happy in enduring;
Knows it has life by stirring if she stir.
Confined in love, is free and on its own;
Praising, with each pulsation, her alone,

Because: when dead to love, and hardly caring
Whether another's love could sink or save it
—She came. And my old verve in dreaming, daring,

219

Entschlüssen, rascher Tat sogleich gefunden!
Wenn Liebe je den Liebenden begeistet,
Ward es an mir aufs lieblichste geleistet;

Und zwar durch sie!—Wie lag ein innres Bangen
Auf Geist und Körper, unwillkommner Schwere:
Von Schauerbildern rings der Blick umfangen
Im wüsten Raum beklommner Herzensleere;
Nun dämmert Hoffnung von bekannter Schwelle,
Sie selbst erscheint in milder Sonnenhelle.

Dem Frieden Gottes, welcher euch hienieden
Mehr als Vernunft beseliget—wir lesens—
Vergleich ich wohl der Liebe heitern Frieden
In Gegenwart des allgeliebten Wesens;
Da ruht das Herz, und nichts vermag zu stören
Den tiefsten Sinn, den Sinn: ihr zu gehören.

In unsers Busens Reine wogt ein Streben,
Sich einem Höhern, Reinern, Unbekannten
Aus Dankbarkeit freiwillig hinzugeben,
Enträtselnd sich den ewig Ungenannten;
Wir heißens: fromm sein!—Solcher seligen Höhe
Fühl ich mich teilhaft, wenn ich vor ihr stehe.

Vor ihrem Blick, wie vor der Sonne Walten,
Vor ihrem Atem, wie vor Frühlingslüften,
Zerschmilzt, so längst sich eisig starr gehalten,
Der Selbstsinn tief in winterlichen Grüften;
Kein Eigennutz, kein Eigenwille dauert,
Vor ihrem Kommen sind sie weggeschauert.

Es ist, als wenn sie sagte: «Stund um Stunde
Wird uns das Leben freundlich dargeboten.
Das Gestrige ließ uns geringe Kunde,

Resolving, up-and-doing—this she gave it.
If ever love restored a human soul,
It took my shrunken self and made it whole.

And all through her! In mind and body's gloom
I mooned lugubrious, lurching and agrope.
Look where I would, saw shuddering visions loom
Over the heart's eroded acres. Hope
—Suddenly, out of hopelessness—was there:
A girl with the light of morning on her hair.

To God's own peace, the peace that here below
Passeth all understanding (so the preacher)
I'm minded to compare that heady glow
Of fervor, being near a certain creature.
The heart's at ease; not one distraction blurs
That deepest sense, the sense of *wholly hers*.

In the pure ocean of the soul, a comber
Flings itself, out of thankfulness, self-giving,
Toward something Purer, Higher—Grand Misnomer
However named—to approach the ever-living.
We call it, *being reverent*. And its flight
Sweeps me, when I'm beside her, height to height.

Before her gaze, like sun where winter lingers,
Before her breathing, like the stir of May,
Self-love, that steely ice that digs its fingers
Deep in our rigid psyche, melts away.
No self-concern, no self-importance where
She sets a foot. They squirm away, that pair.

As if I heard her, urgent: "Hour by hour
Life gives itself, exuberant, unbidden.
Yesterday's meaning is a withered flower;

221

Das Morgende—zu wissen ists verboten;
Und wenn ich je mich vor dem Abend scheute,
Die Sonne sank und sah noch, was mich freute.

Drum tu wie ich und schaue, froh verständig,
Dem Augenblick ins Auge! Kein Verschieben!
Begegn ihm schnell, wohlwollend wie lebendig,
Im Handeln seis, zur Freude seis dem Lieben.
Nur wo du bist, sei alles, immer kindlich,
So bist du alles, bist unüberwindlich.»

Du hast gut reden, dacht ich: zum Geleite
Gab dir ein Gott die Gunst des Augenblickes,
Und jeder fühlt an deiner holden Seite
Sich augenblicks den Günstling des Geschickes;
Mich schreckt der Wink, von dir mich zu entfernen—
Was hilft es mir, so hohe Weisheit lernen!

Nun bin ich fern! Der jetzigen Minute,
Was ziemt denn der? Ich wüßt es nicht zu sagen;
Sie bietet mir zum Schönen manches Gute,
Das lastet nur, ich muß mich ihm entschlagen.
Mich treibt umher ein unbezwinglich Sehnen,
Da bleibt kein Rat als grenzenlose Tränen.

So quellt denn fort! und fließet unaufhaltsam;
Doch nie gelängs, die innre Glut zu dämpfen!
Schon rasts und reißt in meiner Brust gewaltsam,
Wo Tod und Leben grausend sich bekämpfen.
Wohl Kräuter gäbs, des Körpers Qual zu stillen;
Allein dem Geist fehlts am Entschluß und Willen,

Fehlts am Begriff: wie sollt er sie vermissen?
Er wiederholt ihr Bild zu tausendmalen.
Das zaudert bald, bald wird es weggerissen,

Tomorrow!—who can live there? Where's it hidden?
Today though—if I quailed with sunset near
Never a sun but showed me something dear.

"Then do as I do: Look with knowing pride
Each moment in the face. But no evasion!
Keep every nerve a-tingle! Open-eyed
Rush to it all: day's effort, love's elation.
But where you are, be wholly. Be a child.
You're *all* then. Undefeatable," she smiled.

Easy, I thought, for you to say! Some grace
Shows you forever as the moment's friend.
Anyone near you for a moment's space
Is fortune's favorite—till the moment end.
As end it does! In panic I depart:
You and your pretty wisdom break the heart!

Now miles and miles between us. If I could,
How should I live this minute? Who's to say?
It offers much desirable and good
—All like a shabby pack to shrug away.
Invincible longing dogs me as I go.
Tears are the one philosophy I know.

So let them have their way now, unrepressed.
No chance they'll damp the furnaces within.
Embattled there, all's berserk in my breast
With life and death locked grisly. Which to win?
Herbs dull our suffering when the body's ill,
But if the soul lack nerve, lack even will—?

Or worse, lack understanding? Years without her!
Whose image haunts me in a thousand ways.
Sun on her hair, the falling dusk about her—

Undeutlich jetzt und jetzt im reinsten Strahlen;
Wie könnte dies geringstem Troste frommen,
Die Ebb und Flut, das Gehen wie das Kommen?

♦   ♦

Verlaßt mich hier, getreue Weggenossen!
Laßt mich allein am Fels, in Moor und Moos;
Nur immer zu! euch ist die Welt erschlossen,
Die Erde weit, der Himmel hehr und groß;
Betrachtet, forscht, die Einzelnheiten sammelt,
Naturgeheimnis werde nachgestammelt.

Mir ist das All, ich bin mir selbst verloren,
Der ich noch erst den Göttern Liebling war;
Sie prüften mich, verliehen mir Pandoren,
So reich an Gütern, reicher an Gefahr;
Sie drängten mich zum gabeseligen Munde,
Sie trennen mich, und richten mich zugrunde.

AUSSÖHNUNG

Die Leidenschaft bringt Leiden!—Wer beschwichtigt,
Beklommnes Herz, dich, das zu viel verloren?
Wo sind die Stunden, überschnell verflüchtigt?
Vergebens war das Schönste dir erkoren!
Trüb ist der Geist, verworren das Beginnen;
Die hehre Welt, wie schwindet sie den Sinnen!

Da schwebt hervor Musik mit Engelsschwingen,
Verflicht zu Millionen Tön um Töne,
Des Menschen Wesen durch und durch zu dringen,
Zu überfüllen ihn mit ewger Schöne:
Das Auge netzt sich, fühlt im höhern Sehnen
Den Götter-Wert der Töne wie der Tränen.

The memories lag, or dwindle off in haze.
What good's all this? What comfort? shaken so
By all this coming, going, ebb and flow?

♦   ♦

Well, leave me, good companions, to endure it
Here on the moor alone, with rocks and moss.
But you, the world's before you. On! Explore it,
The whole wide earth, the heaven so broad across!
Make your investigations, scour and scout.
Nature has clues to shuffle and sort out.

I've lost it all, earth, heaven, self. Ignore a
Man the gods coddled with a "lucky star"!
They put me to the proof with that Pandora
So rich in gifts, in havoc richer far.
They pressed me to sweet lips that gave and gave;
Then crushed and flung me headlong. Toward the grave.

RECONCILIATION

Passion, and then the anguish. And with whom
To soothe you, heavy heart that lost so much?
Love's hour escaped, unstoppered like perfume?
The loveliest—all for nothing—within touch?
Cloudy the mind; mere muddle all it tries.
And the great world adrift before the eyes.

Then music to the fore like angels swarming,
A million tones in galaxy. We surrender
All of our inner fort to forces storming
—Irresistibly overrun with splendor.
The eye goes damp: in longings past tomorrow
We guess at the infinite worth of song and sorrow.

Und so das Herz erleichtert merkt behende,
Daß es noch lebt und schlägt und möchte schlagen,
Zum reinsten Dank der überreichen Spende
Sich selbst erwidernd willig darzutragen.
Da fühlte sich—o daß es ewig bliebe!
Das Doppel-Glück der Töne wie der Liebe.

And so the heart, disburdened, in a flash
Knows: I endure, and beat, and pound with pleasure!
Gives itself over utterly, in rash
Thanks for the windfall, life. No common treasure.
Then came—could it only last!—that feeling of
Double delight from music and from love.

IX

Rosalía de Castro

(1837–1885)

Rosalía de Castro is the third poet represented here who suffers from linguistic underprivilege. Although she wrote poetry in Spanish, her best work was in her native Galician, which is not unlike medieval Portuguese. Had it been in Spanish, Gerald Brenan is convinced, she would long since have been recognized as "the greatest woman poet of modern times." Nor is her eminence only among women: Salvador de Madariaga thinks her poetry "the best written in Spain in the nineteenth century."

Galicia, the green rainy northwestern corner of Spain, is more like Ireland than like austere Castile; Galicians, typically and racially, are more Celtic than Spanish—melancholy, intuitive, rather given to superstition. Expressed long before in medieval poetry, the Galician mood of *morriña*—the passionate dark longing for something loved and absent—found its most eloquent voice in Rosalía de Castro.

Her life was a sorrowful one. Troubles began with her birth in Compostela: her mother, whose name she had, was of good family; her father was unknown. After the youthful years she remembers so often, years of fiestas and outings and romances on her strange haunted seacoast, there was little but suffering for Rosalía. In Castile, which she found unsympathetic, she made a troubled marriage, had six children, knew years of domestic grief, and was consumed with longing for her homeland.

Her poetry might remind us of Sappho's. Her language too was "the most simple and natural imaginable; her diction almost that used every day," says V. García Martí, her editor and biographer, "the language of a sensitive child."

It is rich in echoes of folk song and folk sayings; rich in allusions to the scenery and folkways of her region. Sound—the translator's despair—is used musically and suggestively; one feels that for some combination of reasons it is *right* for what is said: these are the words to remember forever for some simple detail—how fine and gentle the rain, for example, that falls around Laiño and Lestrobe:

Cómo chove mihudiño,
cómo mihudiño chove ...
pó-la banda de Laiño,
pó-la banda de Lestrobe ...

And one remembers the moody internal *m*'s (which can be sounded with lips closed) and the clinging repetitions of "Cando penso ..."

In her honesty too she is like Sappho: the combination of romance and grating realism that runs through "Nasín cand' as prantas nasen ..." is unusual in poetry.

The Galician text is from Rosalía de Castro, *Obras completas*. Edited by V. García Martí. Aguilar, Madrid. 1958.

I was born
at birth of
blossoms

NASÍN CAND' AS PRANTAS NASEN

Nasín cand' as prantas nasen,
no mes das froles nasín,
nunh' alborada mainiña,
nunh' alborada d' abril.
Por eso me chaman Rosa,
mais á dó triste sorrir,
con espiñas para todos,
sin ningunha para ti.
Dés que te quixen, ingrato,
tod' acabou para min,
qu' eras ti para min todo,
miña groria e meu vivir.
¿De qué, pois, te queixas, Mauro?
¿De qué, pois, te queixas, di,
cando sabes que morrera
por te contemplar felís?
Duro crabo me encrabaches
con ese teu maldesir,
con ese teu pedir tolo
que non sei qué quer de min,
pois dinche canto dar puden
avariciosa de ti.

O meu corasón che mando
c' unha chave par' ó abrir;
nin eu teño máis que darche,
nin ti máis que me pedir.

I WAS BORN AT BIRTH OF BLOSSOMS

I was born at birth of blossoms,
born when all the gardens grew,
on so very soft a morning,
on a morning April-blue.
So I'm Rosa—that's the reason—
of the lonely smile, it's true.
I'm a thorny rose for others;
never had a thorn for you.
When I fell in love—and little
thanks I had of it—I threw
all my life away, believing
you my earth and heaven too.
Why then this complaining, Mauro?
Why are loving looks so few?
If my dying made you happy,
dying's what I'd learn to do.
All these bitter words about me,
bitter, barbed! I never knew
what it was you really wanted.
Lunacies you've put me through!
All I had I gave you. Couldn't
dull my hungering for you.

Even now, my heart I'm sending,
with the one key fits it true.
Nothing left to give you, nothing;
nothing you could ask me to.

AQUEL ROMOR DE CÁNTIGAS E RISAS

Aquel romor de cántigas e risas,
ir, vir, algarear;
aquel falar de cousas que pasaron
y outras que pasarán;
aquela, en fin, vitalidade inquieta
xuvenil, tanto mal
me fixo, que lles dixen:
"Ivos e non volvás."

Un a un desfilaron silenciosos
por aquí, por alá,
tal como cando as contas d'un rosario
s' espallan pol-o chán:
y ò romor d' os seus pasos, mentres s' iñan,
de tal modo hastra min veu resoar,
que non máis tristemente
resoará quisáis
n' ò fondo d' os sepulcros
ò último adiós qu' un vivo ôs mortos dá.

Y ô fin soya quedéi, pero tan soya,
qu' oyo d' a mosca ò inquieto revoar,
d' o ratiño ò roer terco e constante,
e d' o lume ò "chis chas,"
cando d' a verde pónla
o fresco zugo devorando vai,
parece que me falan, qu' os entendo,
que compaña me fan;

NOW ALL THAT SOUND OF LAUGHTER, SOUND OF SINGING

Now all that sound of laughter, sound of singing,
going, coming, happy stir!
that talk of *Know what happened? What's about to?*
the breathless *Have you heard?*
all of that bright vitality, so restless,
of boys and girls
—too much to bear. I begged
"Please leave me. Don't return."

So one by one they left me, left in silence
this way or that. Alone.
Beads of a broken rosary rolled and scattered
across the floor.
And as they left, the brush of footsteps moving
away, went softly eddying round me, so
softly who'd ever heard
such lonely tones?
No, not the last farewell
the living give their hollow dead below.

And finally left alone here, so alone
I heard the restless fly buzz to and fro,
heard the rat gnaw, his purpose one thing only,
heard the thin sticks aglow
hiss on the hearth, the fire protest, consuming
raw logs of greener oak.
I dream they're talking to me, dream I listen,
know I've no other folk,

y este meu coraçón lles di tembrando:
"¡Por Dios,… non vos vayáis!"

¡Qué doçe, mais que triste,
tamén é a soedad!

and so I urge them one and all, heart skipping,
"Don't you leave. Don't you go."

All's well with me. No grieving.
This solitude's my home.

CANDO PENSO QUE TE FUCHES

Cando penso que te fuches,
negra sombra que m' asombras,
ô pe d' os meus cabezales
tornas facéndome mofa.

Cando maxino qu' és ida
n' ò mesmo sol te m' amostras,
y eres á estrela que brila,
y eres ò vento que zoa.

Si cantan, ês ti que cantas;
si choran, ês ti que choras,
y ês o marmurio d' o rio
y ês á noite y és á aurora.

En todo estás e ti ès todo,
pra min y en min mesma moras,
nin m' abandonarás nunca,
sombra que sempre m' asombras.

BLACK MOOD

When I think you're somewhere yonder,
dark penumbra, so benumbing
—back again! and by my bedside
hunched to mock with: "Trouble coming!"

Half imagining you vanish
—in the sun, that shadow massing!
You're a glumness in the starlight,
glumness where the winds are passing.

When there's singing, you're the singer;
when there's sorrowing, the sorrow.
You're the brooks that murmur darkly:
gloom this evening, gloom tomorrow.

You're in all. Are all. Marooning
me in me myself. Moroser
moods that never long unloosen—
dark penumbra close and closer.

X

Two Twentieth-Century Spanish Poets

Antonio Machado (1875–1939)
Federico García Lorca (1898–1936)

If one had to select, from the dazzling poetic spectrum of twentieth-century Spain, two of the most brilliant poets, one could probably not do better than to take Antonio Machado and Federico García Lorca. Both belonged to famous "generations": Machado, like Unamuno, to that of '98, whose shock and sense of disillusion at the suddenly revealed weakness of their country led to a tough-minded soul-searching that found its hope partly in the spirit symbolized by the stern Castilian landscape; García Lorca, like Gerardo Diego, Alberti, Guillén, Salinas, and Dámaso Alonso, belonged to the generation of the mid-twenties—of '27, as most would call it—whose spectacular achievement was in many ways the result of the effort and aspiration of the earlier generation. Both poets were victims of the civil war. García Lorca, no political activist although against repression and for the people, was shot in Granada under circumstances that may never be entirely clear; Machado died of exposure and neglect soon after the painful retreat from Catalonia into France with the forces and sympathizers of the Republic.

If García Lorca is the better known outside of Spain, it may be in part because his vivid imagery (though not his incantation) survives translation better than the racy rhythms and idiom of the older poet—whose best work has been compared to that of the late Yeats. It may also be because a publicity-conscious age like our own judges poetry partly in terms of the figure the poet cuts—and who would think that the work of a seedy old philosopher-teacher rather behind the times could be as good as that of a brilliant young man murdered mysteriously in a tragic war? And yet Machado's poems may prove fully as tough and enduring.

The Spanish texts are from Antonio Machado, *Poesías completas.* Espasa-Calpe, Madrid. 1955; and from Federico García Lorca, *Obras completas.* Volume IV, *Romancero Gitano,* etc. Losada, Buenos Aires. 1938.

Portrait

Antonio Machado

RETRATO

Mi infancia son recuerdos de un patio de Sevilla,
y un huerto claro donde madura el limonero;
mi juventud, veinte años en tierra de Castilla;
mi historia, algunos casos que recordar no quiero.

Ni un seductor Mañara, ni un Bradomín he sido
—ya conocéis mi torpe aliño indumentario—,
mas recibí la flecha que me asignó Cupido,
y amé cuanto ellas pueden tener de hospitalario.

Hay en mis venas gotas de sangre jacobina,
pero mi verso brota de manantial sereno;
y, más que un hombre al uso que sabe su doctrina,
soy, en el buen sentido de la palabra, bueno.

Adoro la hermosura, y en la moderna estética
corté las viejas rosas del huerto de Ronsard;
mas no amo los afeites de la actual cosmética,
ni soy un ave de esas del nuevo gay-trinar.

Desdeño las romanzas de los tenores huecos
y el coro de los grillos que cantan a la luna.
A distinguir me paro las voces de los ecos,
y escucho solamente, entre las voces, una.

¿Soy clásico o romántico? No sé. Dejar quisiera
mi verso, como deja el capitán su espada:
famosa por la mano viril que la blandiera,
no por el docto oficio del forjador preciada.

Antonio Machado

PORTRAIT

My childhood is all memories of a patio in Sevilla,
A garden where the summer sun meant lemons in the fall.
My youth: some twenty years or so in regions of Castilla.
My history: a turn or two I've no wish to recall.

I'm no seducer, never been Don Juan or Casanova
—Dull of dress and dull of mien, I little fit the part—
Yet Cupid had a shaft for me, shot, and I endured it.
But took no more than they could give that had a friendly heart.

Although my veins have blood enough ripe for revolution,
My poetry comes flowing from some untroubled well.
I'm not the chap we see around can chant the catechism,
Yet dare say I'm as good of heart, if "good" be taken well.

Beauty—there's the saint I serve. To click of modern scissors
I cut the ancient roses in gardens of Ronsard,
No lover of the current muse who prinks amid beauticians;
I'm not a swan of *those* swans who warble avant-garde.

But devil take the tremolo of certain whiskey tenors,
The choir of all those katydids who twitter at the moon.
I pause apart, to ascertain true voices from the echoes,
And—out of all the voices there—care for only one.

Am I romantic, classical? I shrug. But know I'd leave it,
My poetry, in much the way a captain leaves his sword:
Famous for the manly hand that made the good air whistle,
And not the scientific fist that buffed it at the forge.

Converso con el hombre que siempre va conmigo
—quien habla solo espera hablar a Dios un día—;
mi soliloquio es plática con este buen amigo
que me enseñó el secreto de la filantropía.

Y al cabo, nada os debo; debéisme cuanto he escrito.
A mi trabajo acudo, con mi dinero pago
el traje que me cubre y la mansión que habito,
el pan que me alimenta y el lecho en donde yago.

Y cuando llegue el día del último viaje,
y esté al partir la nave que nunca ha de tornar,
me encontraréis a bordo ligero de equipaje,
casi desnudo, como los hijos de la mar.

My conversation's leveled at a fellow always with me
—Who holds a parley with his soul may talk with God some day—
And what appears soliloquy is chat with this companion
Who taught me how to love the race, and taught the only way.

I owe you nothing, after all. You owe me for my volumes.
I go about my work with care, with my resources buy
The suit of clothes that covers me, the roof that I live under,
The bread that keeps my flesh alive, the pillow where I lie.

And when the sailing day arrives, the day of the last voyage,
The ship that never comes again will cast the anchor free—
You'll find me waiting safe aboard, and find I travel lightly,
With scarce a rag upon my back, like children of the sea.

A ORILLAS DEL DUERO

Mediaba el mes de julio. Era un hermoso día.
Yo, solo, por las quiebras del pedregal subía,
buscando los recodos de sombra, lentamente.
A trechos me paraba para enjugar mi frente
y dar algún respiro al pecho jadeante;
o bien, ahincando el paso, el cuerpo hacia adelante
y hacia la mano diestra vencido y apoyado
en un bastón, a guisa de pastoril cayado,
trepaba por los cerros que habitan las rapaces
aves de altura, hollando las hierbas montaraces
de fuerte olor —romero, tomillo, salvia, espliego—.
Sobre los agrios campos caía un sol de fuego.

Un buitre de anchas alas con majestuoso vuelo
cruzaba solitario el puro azul del cielo.
Yo divisaba, lejos, un monte alto y agudo,
y una redonda loma cual recamado escudo,
y cárdenos alcores sobre la parda tierra
—harapos esparcidos de un viejo arnés de guerra—,
las serrezuelas calvas por donde tuerce el Duero
para formar la corva ballesta de un arquero
en torno a Soria. —Soria es una barbacana,
hacia Aragón, que tiene la torre castellana—.
Veía el horizonte cerrado por colinas
obscuras, coronadas de robles y de encinas;
desnudos peñascales, algún humilde prado
donde el merino pace y el toro, arrodillado
sobre la hierba, rumia; las márgenes del río
lucir sus verdes álamos al claro sol de estío,
y, silenciosamente, lejanos pasajeros,

ON THE BANKS OF THE DUERO

We were halfway through July. Handsome afternoon!
All alone I rambled up hills of broken stone.
Favoring the nooks of shade, lingering as I would.
Stood a while to mop my brow, maybe a while stood
Breathing deep and breathing deep in my laboring lungs.
Maybe, hurrying my pace, body forward flung
Panting hard and pressing hard on a thorny stick
In my right hand for support—like a shepherd's crook—
I went climbing for the heights, haunt of snatching birds
Native to the keener air—scuffing mountain herbs,
Sage and lavender and thyme, odors brash and sweet.
Over all the angry land fires of heaven beat.

A vulture on enormous wing at a lordly height
Sailed across the utter blue in its lonely flight.
In the distance one great peak blazing high and keen
And one low and rolling knoll, shield of damascene.
Many a lilac rise above leopard-colored ground,
Scraps of an old suit of mail thrown haphazard down.
Bare sierras far and wide. Duero, twisting river,
Draws a mighty crossbow back, to the full, forever
Rounding Soria: Soria, barbican to seal
In despite of Aragon the fortress of Castile.
Saw the far horizons were locked in mountain ranges
Crowned with oak—the evergreen or the oak that changes.
Naked areas of shale, scanty grass in these
Feeding the merino sheep; the black bull on his knees
In the verdure, ruminant; where the waters run
The brilliance of green poplars shone, in the summer sun.
Saw, without a breath of sound, travelers far away

¡tan diminutos! —carros, jinetes y arrieros—
cruzar el largo puente, y bajo las arcadas
de piedra ensombrecerse las aguas plateadas
del Duero.

        El Duero cruza el corazón de roble
de Iberia y de Castilla.
             ¡Oh, tierra triste y noble,
la de los altos llanos y yermos y roquedas,
de campos sin arados, regatos ni arboledas;
decrépitas ciudades, caminos sin mesones,
y atónitos palurdos sin danzas ni canciones
que aun van, abandonando el mortecino hogar,
como tus largos ríos, Castilla, hacia la mar!

    Castilla miserable, ayer dominadora,
envuelta en sus andrajos desprecia cuanto ignora.
¿Espera, duerme o sueña? ¿La sangre derramada
recuerda, cuando tuvo la fiebre de la espada?
Todo se mueve, fluye, discurre, corre o gira;
cambian la mar y el monte y el ojo que los mira.

    ¿Pasó? Sobre sus campos aun el fantasma yerra
de un pueblo que ponía a Dios sobre la guerra.

    La madre en otro tiempo fecunda en capitanes
madrastra es hoy apenas de humildes ganapanes.
Castilla no es aquella tan generosa un día,
cuando Myo Cid Rodrigo el de Vivar volvía,
ufano de su nueva fortuna y su opulencia,
a regalar a Alfonso los huertos de Valencia;
o que, tras la aventura que acreditó sus bríos,
pedía la conquista de los inmensos ríos
indianos a la corte, la madre de soldados,

—Shrunk to almost nothing, those!—horseman, driver, dray
Trail across the span of bridge; by its vaulted floor
Saw the waters turn to black that ran bright before.
Duero waters!

    Heart of oak where the Duero ran,
Old Iberia, Castile!
     Great and sorry land!
Land of the high wailing plain, waste of crag and crater;
Fields without a single plow, tree, or spurt of water;
Cities peeling tumbledown, roads without a tavern;
Yokels without song or dance, at a loss and sullen,
Who flee their homes as one might flee dying things—who flee
Even as Spanish rivers go pouring to the sea.

Castile so miserable now, and before so grand,
Wrapped in its rags and scorning all it scorns to understand.
Lagging, dozing, dreaming now? All that blood you poured
Forgot, when mightily you raged with fever of the sword?
All's turnabout: all flees and flows and runs in raveling eddies—
Sea and mountain not the same, nor the eye that held them steady.

Vanished? And across the land a phantom moves, no more—
The ghost of folk who set God's flag victorious over war.

Mother who another time sent captains north and south
Is a poor mother now to grubs living hand to mouth.
Castile is not that noble land of centuries before,
When Myo Cid Rodrigo once, returning to Vivar,
In glory of new fortune and exuberant conquering
Gave all Valencia's fertile earth as keepsake to the king.
Not the Castile—when many a risk had proved its fervor true—
Could yearn to follow to the source the worldwide rivers, sue
For Indian kingdoms to the court, that mother of steel men,

guerreros y adalides que han de tornar, cargados
de plata y oro, a España, en regios galeones,
para la presa cuervos, para la lid leones.
Filósofos nutridos de sopa de convento
contemplan impasibles el amplio firmamento;
y si les llega en sueños, como un rumor distante,
clamor de mercaderes de muelles de Levante,
no acudirán siquiera a preguntar ¿qué pasa?
Y ya la guerra ha abierto las puertas de su casa.

Castilla miserable, ayer dominadora,
envuelta en sus harapos desprecia cuanto ignora.

El sol va declinando. De la ciudad lejana
me llega un armonioso tañido de campana
—ya irán a su rosario las enlutadas viejas—.
De entre las peñas salen dos lindas comadrejas;
me miran y se alejan, huyendo, y aparecen
de nuevo ¡tan curiosas!... Los campos se obscurecen.
Hacia el camino blanco está el mesón abierto
al campo ensombrecido y al pedregal desierto.

Of warriors and commanders come laden back to Spain
Bringing in galleons of the king their gold and silver freight:
No hawk was keener for the kill, no lion for the fight.
Now syllogizing men, grown fat lapping pap of abbeys,
Scan the enormous firmament, eyelids hanging flabby,
And if they catch, as in a dream, certain distant whispers
Of uproar on the eastern quay, where furious seamen cluster,
Rarely care to shift a ham or yawn out, "What's the matter?"
Again the portals of the war go wide with iron clatter!

Castile so miserable now, and before so grand,
Wrapped in its scraps and scorning all it scorns to understand.

Low and lower now, the sun. From villages afar
A trill of bells is spilling soft chorals in my ear
—Now gather for their rosary-beads the grannies all in black—.
Suddenly two lissom mink glitter from the rock,
Look at me with jewel eyes, flash away, and come
Back at once—so interested! Darkening fields are dumb.
The tavern door is open now to where the road lies white:
Many a mile of lonely stone; overpowering night.

PARÁBOLAS, I

Era un niño que soñaba
un caballo de cartón.
Abrió los ojos el niño
y el caballito no vió.
Con un caballito blanco
el niño volvió a soñar;
y por la crin lo cogía...
¡Ahora no te escaparás!
Apenas lo hubo cogido,
el niño se despertó.
Tenía el puño cerrado.
¡El caballito voló!
Quedóse el niño muy serio
pensando que no es verdad
un caballito soñado.
Y ya no volvió a soñar.
Pero el niño se hizo mozo
y el mozo tuvo un amor,
y a su amada le decía:
¿Tú eres de verdad o no?
Cuando el mozo se hizo viejo
pensaba: todo es soñar,
el caballito soñado
y el caballo de verdad.
Y cuando vino la muerte,
el viejo a su corazón
preguntaba: ¿Tú eres sueño?
¡Quién sabe si despertó!

PARABLES, I

Once a little boy was dreaming
of a hobby horse—you know?
Popped his sleepy eyelids open;
couldn't see the pony though.
Back to sleep again, and dreamed a
finer bronco, white as snow.
By the very mane he caught it—
Now I'll never let you go!
Hardly had he time to catch it,
when, excited, he awoke;
fist in fist was doubled, clutching,
but the snowy creature—flown!
So he thought and thought about it
gravely: *They're not really so,*
pretty horses one can dream of.
No more use in dreaming, no.
Well, the lad became a lover
later on, as youngsters do,
and he whispered to his darling,
Darling, are you really you?
Years go by, and he's a grandpa;
All's a dream—he brooded so—
both the little horse I dreamed of,
and the horse the meadows show.
Then when finally death took him,
to his heart he murmured low:
You a dream like all the others?
And awakened? Who's to know?

From *PROVERBIOS Y CANTARES*

XV

Cantad conmigo en coro: Saber, nada sabemos,
de arcano mar vinimos, a ignota mar iremos...
Y entre los dos misterios está el enigma grave;
tres arcas cierra una desconocida llave.
La luz nada ilumina y el sabio nada enseña.
¿Qué dice la palabra? ¿Qué el agua de la peña?

XXI

Ayer soñé que veía
a Dios y que a Dios hablaba;
y soñé que Dios me oía...
Después soñé que soñaba.

L

—Nuestro español bosteza.
¿Es hambre? ¿Sueno? ¿Hastío?
Doctor, ¿tendrá el estómago vacío?
—El vacío es más bien en la cabeza.

From PROVERBS AND SONGS

XV

Come sing with me in chorus: it's nothing, all we know;
we come from a mysterious sea, to unknown oceans go . . .
Mystery first and mystery last—mystery in between;
closets locked, all three of them. Not a key been seen.
The light enlightens nothing; the knowing, all they've known
is nothing. What do words say? Or water from a stone?

XXI

Yesterday, dreamed He was near me;
spoke to Him clearly, it seemed.
Moreover, dreamed He could hear me . . .
thereupon dreamed that I dreamed.

L

Look, our Spaniard's yawning.
Hunger? Boredom? Bed?
Empty stomach, doctor?
No sir: empty head.

LIV

Ya hay un español que quiere
vivir y a vivir empieza,
entre una España que muere
y otra España que bosteza.

Españolito que vienes
al mundo, te guarde Dios.
Una de las dos Españas
ha de helarte el corazón.

LIV

Here's another Spaniard! Welcome!
as your day of living dawns,
in between a Spain expiring
and a Spain that yawns and yawns.

Little Spaniard, new on earth now,
God be with you from the start.
Till the one Spain or the other
turn to ice your very heart.

Federico García Lorca

PRECIOSA Y EL AIRE

Su luna de pergamino
Preciosa tocando viene
por un anfibio sendero
de cristales y laureles.
El silencio sin estrellas,
huyendo del sonsonete,
cae donde el mar bate y canta
su noche llena de peces.
En los picos de la sierra
los carabineros duermen
guardando las blancas torres
donde viven los ingleses.
Y los gitanos del agua
levantan por distraerse
glorietas de caracolas
y ramas de pino verde.

◆　　◆

Su luna de pergamino
Preciosa tocando viene.
Al verla se ha levantado
el viento que nunca duerme.
San Cristobalón desnudo,
lleno de lenguas celestes,
mira a la niña tocando
una dulce gaita ausente.

—Niña, deja que levante
tu vestido para verte.
Abre en mis dedos antiguos
la rosa azul de tu vientre.

Federico García Lorca

PRECIOSA AND THE WIND

Jingling her moon of parchment,
along comes Preciosa,
through the laurel leaves, through crystal,
a land-and-water road.
The hush of the starless dark
that shrank from her *ching-chang,* chose
to flee where the sea beats, crooning
its fish-thick night below.
Above, in the high sierras,
the revenue men are dozing,
their carbines guarding the towered white
houses the English own.
And gypsy forms in the water
make, for amusement only,
many a green pavilion,
their pine-and-seashell homes.

◆　　◆

Jingling her moon of parchment,
along comes Preciosa.
The wind, at sight of her, stiffens;
he's never napping, no.
Big St. Christopher, naked,
his tongues all heavenly, coaxing
with faraway bagpipe music,
eyes on the girl alone.

"Let me whisk, little girl, your skirt up,
the better to see you. Open
once for my ancient fingers
your lap and its cool-blue rose."

Preciosa tira el pandero
y corre sin detenerse.
El viento-hombrón la persigue
con una espada caliente.

Frunce su rumor el mar.
Los olivos palidecen.
Cantan las flautas de umbría
y el liso gong de la nieve.

¡Preciosa, corre, Preciosa,
que te coge el viento verde!
¡Preciosa, corre, Preciosa!
¡Míralo por dónde viene!
Sátiro de estrellas bajas
con sus lenguas relucientes.

♦   ♦

Preciosa, llena de miedo,
entra en la casa que tiene,
más arriba de los pinos,
el cónsul de los ingleses.

Asustados por los gritos
tres carabineros vienen,
sus negras capas ceñidas
y los gorros en las sienes.

El inglés da a la gitana
un vaso de tibia leche,
y una copa de ginebra
que Preciosa no se bebe.

Y mientras cuenta, llorando,
su aventura a aquella gente,
en las tejas de pizarra
el viento, furioso, muerde.

Her tambourine a-tumble,
she's off and away, Preciosa.
That buck of a wind pants after,
his sword a live-red coal.

The sea makes a frown of its rumble;
olives go pale in their grove.
Flutes in the shadows chatter
to the tool-smooth gong of the snow.

Preciosa, run, Preciosa,
he'll get you, the wind, old goat!
Preciosa, run, Preciosa!
Over there now, look at him lope!
A satyr of low-hung planets,
his glittering tongues aglow.

◆   ◆

Preciosa, half in a panic,
ducks in a doorway close,
over the dark pine forest
—the English consul's home.

Up in alarm at her screams, three
men of the special patrol
come with their black capes muffled,
caps to their ears pulled low.

The Englishman offers the gypsy
lukewarm milk in a bowl;
offers her gin if she'd rather.
She isn't drinking it, though,

and while she bewails her adventure,
all sobs, to the foreign folk,
the wind's at the roof, in fury,
teeth in its slate and oak.

ROMANCE SONÁMBULO

Verde que te quiero verde.
Verde viento. Verdes ramas.
El barco sobre la mar
y el caballo en la montaña.
Con la sombra en la cintura
ella sueña en su baranda,
verde carne, pelo verde,
con ojos de fría plata.
Verde que te quiero verde.
Bajo la luna gitana,
las cosas la están mirando
y ella no puede mirarlas.

♦   ♦

Verde que te quiero verde.
Grandes estrellas de escarcha
vienen con el pez de sombra
que abre el camino del alba.
La higuera frota su viento
con la lija de sus ramas,
y el monte, gato garduño,
eriza sus pitas agrias.
Pero ¿quién vendrá? ¿Y por dónde?...
Ella sigue en su baranda,
verde carne, pelo verde,
soñando en la mar amarga.

♦   ♦

—Compadre, quiero cambiar
mi caballo por su casa,

SLEEPWALKERS' BALLAD

Green it's your green I love.
Green of the wind. Green branches.
The ship far out at sea.
The horse above on the mountain.
Shadows dark at her waist,
she's dreaming there on her terrace,
green of her cheek, green hair,
with eyes like chilly silver.
Green it's your green I love.
Under that moon of the gypsies
things are looking at her
but she can't return their glances.

◆ ◆

Green it's your green I love.
The stars are frost, enormous;
a tuna cloud floats over
nosing off to the dawn.
The fig tree catches a wind
to grate in its emery branches;
the mountain's a wildcat, sly,
bristling its acrid cactus.
But—who's on the road? Which way?
She's dreaming there on her terrace,
green of her cheek, green hair,
she dreams of the bitter sea.

◆ ◆

"Friend, what I want's to trade
this horse of mine for your house here,

mi montura por su espejo,
mi cuchillo por su manta.
Compadre, vengo sangrando,
desde los puertos de Cabra.
—Si yo pudiera, mocito,
este trato se cerraba.
Pero yo ya no soy yo,
ni mi casa es ya mi casa.
—Compadre, quiero morir
decentemente en mi cama.
De acero, si puede ser,
con las sábanas de holanda.
¿No ves la herida que tengo
desde el pecho a la garganta?
—Trescientas rosas morenas
lleva tu pechera blanca.
Tu sangre rezuma y huele
alrededor de tu faja.
Pero yo ya no soy yo,
ni mi casa es ya mi casa.
—Dejadme subir al menos
hasta las altas barandas;
¡dejadme subir!, dejadme
hasta las verdes barandas.
Barandales de la luna
por donde retumba el agua.

◆　　◆

Ya suben los dos compadres
hacia las altas barandas.
Dejando un rastro de sangre.
Dejando un rastro de lágrimas.
Temblaban en los tejados
farolillos de hojalata.
Mil panderos de cristal
herían la madrugada.

this saddle of mine for your mirror,
this knife of mine for your blanket.
Friend, I come bleeding, see,
from the mountain pass of Cabra."
"I would if I could, young man;
I'd have taken you up already.
But I'm not myself any longer,
nor my house my home any more."
"Friend, what I want's to die
in a bed of my own—die nicely.
An iron bed, if there is one,
between good linen sheets.
I'm wounded, throat and breast,
from here to here—you see it?"
"You've a white shirt on; three hundred
roses across—dark roses.
There's a smell of blood about you;
your sash, all round you, soaked.
But I'm not myself any longer,
nor my house my home any more."
"Then let me go up, though; let me!
at least to the terrace yonder.
Let me go up then, let me!
up to the high green roof.
Terrace-rails of the moonlight,
splash of the lapping tank."

◆   ◆

So they go up, companions,
up to the high roof-terrace;
a straggle of blood behind them,
behind, a straggle of tears.
Over the roofs, a shimmer
like little tin lamps, and glassy
tambourines by the thousand
slitting the glitter of dawn.

♦　♦

Verde que te quiero verde,
verde viento, verdes ramas.
Los dos compadres subieron.
El largo viento dejaba
en la boca un raro gusto
de hiel, de menta y de albahaca
¡Compadre! ¿Dónde está, díme,
dónde está tu niña amarga?
¡Cuántas veces te esperó!
¡Cuántas veces te esperara,
cara fresca, negro pelo,
en esta verde baranda!

♦　♦

Sobre el rostro del aljibe
se mecía la gitana.
Verde carne, pelo verde,
con ojos de fría plata.
Un carámbano de luna
la sostiene sobre el agua.
La noche se puso íntima
como una pequeña plaza.
Guardias civiles borrachos
en la puerta golpeaban.
Verde que te quiero verde.
Verde viento. Verdes ramas.
El barco sobre la mar.
Y el caballo en la montaña.

◆   ◆

Green it's your green I love,
green of the wind, green branches.
They're up there, two companions.
A wind from the distance leaving
its tang on the tongue, strange flavors
of bile, of basil and mint.
"Where is she, friend—that girl
with the bitter heart, your daughter?"
"How often she'd wait and wait,
how often she'd be here waiting,
fresh of face, hair black,
here in green of the terrace."

◆   ◆

There in her terrace pool
was the gypsy girl, in ripples.
Green of her cheek, green hair,
with eyes of chilly silver.
Icicles from the moon
held her afloat on the water.
Night became intimate then—
enclosed, like a little plaza.
Drunken, the Civil Guard
had been banging the door below them.
Green it's your green I love.
Green of the wind. Green branches.
The ship far out at sea.
The horse above on the mountain.

LA CASADA INFIEL

Y que yo me la llevé al río
creyendo que era mozuela,
pero tenía marido.
Fué la noche de Santiago
y casi por compromiso.
Se apagaron los faroles
y se encendieron los grillos.
En las últimas esquinas
toqué sus pechos dormidos,
y se me abrieron de pronto
como ramos de jacintos.
El almidón de su enagua
me sonaba en el oído
como una pieza de seda
rasgada por diez cuchillos.
Sin luz de plata en sus copas
los árboles han crecido,
y un horizonte de perros
ladra muy lejos del río.

Pasadas las zarzamoras,
los juncos y los espinos,
bajo su mata de pelo
hice un hoyo sobre el limo.
Yo me quité la corbata.
Ella se quitó el vestido.
Yo, el cinturón con revólver.
Ella, sus cuatro corpiños.
Ni nardos ni caracolas
tienen el cutis tan fino,

THE UNFAITHFUL WIFE

. . . so I walked her down to the river.
I was really the first, she said
—forgetting the fact of a husband.
On the night of the patron of Spain—
I was merely trying to oblige.
As the streetlamps all went black and
crickets came afire.
When we reached the end of the sidewalk
I touched her breasts: sleeping.
They blossomed for me promptly,
no hyacinth so sweet.
The slip she wore, starched cotton,
hissed in my ear excitement.
As a piece of silk would, ripped to
ribbons by ten knives.
No silver catching the branches,
the trees loomed enormous.
And a skyline of hounds yowling
very far from the shore.

Passing the blackberry bushes,
passing the reeds and the bracken,
under her cover of hair I
scooped a hole in the clay.
I unfastened my necktie.
She unfastened her skirt.
I, my belt and revolver.
She, her petticoats—four.
Neither camellia, seashell
such delight to the finger.

ni los cristales con luna
relumbran con ese brillo.
Sus muslos se me escapaban
como peces sorprendidos,
la mitad llenos de lumbre,
la mitad llenos de frío.
Aquella noche corrí
el mejor de los caminos,
montado en potra de nácar
sin bridas y sin estribos.
No quiero decir, por hombre,
las cosas que ella me dijo.
La luz del entendimiento
me hace ser muy comedido.
Sucia de besos y arena,
yo me la llevé del río.
Con el aire se batían
las espadas de los lirios.

Me porté como quien soy.
Como un gitano legítimo.
La regalé un costurero
grande, de raso pajizo,
y no quise enamorarme
porque teniendo marido
me dijo que era mozuela
cuando la llevaba al río.

Never a moon on water
shone as she did then.
Her thighs in my clutch, elusive
as bass you catch bare-handed.
Half, they were fire and splendor;
chilly as winter, half.
That night I went riding
the finest of all our journeys,
fast on a filly of pearl, that
never knew stirrup or curb!
I'm man enough not to be breathing
certain words she uttered.
I'm a clean straight-thinking fellow
with a decent tongue in love.
She was slubbered with kisses and sand
when I took her home from the river.
The air was a melee of sabers:
lilies raged at the wind.

I behaved like the man I am:
hundred-percent gypsy.
And presented her with a saffron
satiny case, de luxe.
But for falling in love?—not me!
She with a husband, yet
to say I was really the first
as I walked her down to the river!

ROMANCE DE LA PENA NEGRA

Las piquetas de los gallos
cavan buscando la aurora,
cuando por el monte oscuro
baja Soledad Montoya.
Cobre amarillo, su carne
huele a caballo y a sombra.
Yunques ahumados sus pechos,
gimen canciones redondas.
—Soledad, ¿por quién preguntas
sin compaña y a estas horas?
—Pregunte por quien pregunte,
díme: ¿a ti qué se te importa?
Vengo a buscar lo que busco,
mi alegría y mi persona.
—Soledad de mis pesares,
caballo que se desboca
al fin encuentra la mar
y se lo tragan las olas.
—No me recuerdes el mar
que la pena negra brota
en las tierras de aceituna
bajo el rumor de las hojas.
—¡Soledad, qué pena tienes!
¡Qué pena tan lastimosa!
Lloras zumo de limón
agrio de espera y de boca.
—¡Qué pena tan grande! Corro
mi casa como una loca,
mis dos trenzas por el suelo,
de la cocina a la alcoba.

BALLAD OF BLACK GRIEF

The little picks of the roosters
are chipping holes for the dawn.
Down the dark of the mountain
comes Soledad Montoya.
Saffron copper her flesh
with a smell of the woods and horses.
Anvil and smoke, her breasts,
heaving their rounded songs.
"Soledad, you're looking for what
at a time like this, alone here?"
"Looking for never you mind!
What's it to *you,* my business?
I'm looking for just one thing:
to find myself. To be happy."
"Soledad my exasperation!
a horse that seizes the bit will
come at last to the seashore,
founder out in the surf."
"Never you mind about seashore!
Bitter grief comes welling,
back in lands of the olive,
under a whisper of leaves."
"Soledad, what grief you're suffering!
grief that I feel for, deeply.
Bitter as lemon, your tears,
bitter as waiting lips."
"Awful to bear! I run
through my house like a thing possessed,
tresses trailing the floor,
kitchen to bedroom and back.

¡Qué pena! Me estoy poniendo
de azabache carne y ropa.
Ay, ¡mis camisas de hilo!
Ay, ¡mis muslos de amapola!
—Soledad, lava tu cuerpo
con agua de las alondras,
y deja tu corazón
en paz, Soledad Montoya.

◆   ◆

Por abajo canta el río:
volante de cielo y hojas.
Con flores de calabaza
la nueva luz se corona.
¡Oh pena de los gitanos!
Pena limpia y siempre sola.
¡Oh pena de cauce oculto
y madrugada remota!

Awful. I'm turning fast
—skirt, flesh—to a thing of jet.
Too bad for my pretty slips!
Too bad for my thighs' silk poppy!"
"Soledad, go bathe your limbs
in pools of dew with the skylark.
Leave it in peace, your heart,
in peace, Soledad Montoya!"

◆　　◆

Below there's a river singing
in eddies of heaven and leaves.
A new day dawns to be crowned with
blossoms of pumpkin and squash.
O grief of the gypsy heart!
grief pure and forever lonely.
Grief from a source unknown, its
hour of dawn remote.

XI

Four Twentieth-Century Italian Poets

Saba, Campana, Ungaretti, Montale

Umberto Saba (1883–1957) felt himself, as a native of Trieste, out of the mainstream of contemporary Italian letters. If not revolutionary, he is staunchly independent and individual; his *Canzoniere* is a record of his life and feelings over fifty years.

Dino Campana (1885–1932), inspired and erratic, worked at many jobs in Europe and Argentina. A compulsive wanderer, he was driven, he said, by a "mania di vagabondaggio." The last years of his life were spent in a psychiatric hospital near Florence.

Giuseppe Ungaretti was born in Egypt in 1888, educated chiefly in the Paris of Gide and Valéry. He became interested in poetry while a soldier during the first World War. For some years he was professor of Italian Literature in Brazil (the setting of "Tu ti spezzasti," which is about the death of his son there); and later at the University of Rome. Ungaretti has done a good deal of translating from the poetry of Shakespeare, Góngora, Racine, Mallarmé, and others. He died in 1970.

Eugenio Montale was born in 1896 at Genova; the Ligurian coast, not unlike that of Valéry's Sète, has provided the imagery for some of his poems. When opposition to the party in power lost him his directorship of a library, he turned to journalism, particularly for Milan's *Corriere della Sera,* and to translation. Montale has translated, he says, "un po' di tutto," including Marlowe, Shakespeare, Thomas Hardy, Emily Dickinson, Hopkins, and T. S. Eliot. In 1975 he received the Nobel Prize for literature; he died in 1981.

The Italian texts are from Umberto Saba, *Il canzoniere.* Giulio Einaudi,

Rome. Fourth Edition, 1958; Dino Campana, *Canti orfici*. Vallecchi, Florence. Fourth Edition, 1952; Giuseppe Ungaretti, *Il dolore*. Arnoldo Mondadori, Rome. 1947; Eugenio Montale, *La bufera e altro*. Arnoldo Mondadori, Rome. 1957.

Winter Noon

Umberto Saba

MEZZOGIORNO D'INVERNO

In quel momento ch'ero già felice
(Dio mi perdoni la parola grande
e tremenda) chi quasi al pianto spinse
mia breve gioia? Voi direte: "Certa
bella creatura che di là passava,
e ti sorrise." Un palloncino invece,
un turchino vagante palloncino
nell'azzurro dell'aria, ed il nativo
cielo non mai come nel chiaro e freddo
mezzogiorno d'inverno risplendente.
Cielo con qualche nuvoletta bianca,
e i vetri delle case al sol fiammanti,
e il fumo tenue d'uno due camini,
e su tutte le cose, le divine
cose, quel globo dalla mano incauta
d'un fanciullo sfuggito (egli piangeva
certo in mezzo alla folla il suo dolore,
il suo grande dolore) tra il Palazzo
della Borsa e il Caffè dove seduto
oltre i vetri ammiravo io con lucenti
occhi or salire or scendere il suo bene.

Umberto Saba

WINTER NOON

That wink of time when I was happy still
(happy!—may God forgive the grand rash word)
what was it dashed to the very brink of tears
my momentary joy? You'll say, "Oh some
pretty young thing just happened to be passing
with a bright smile for you." No, a toy balloon
rather, a turquoise wandering balloon
up high in the azure air, and the skies of home
never so wholly brilliant as that day—
very cold they were, very clear, that winter noon.
A heaven with just a trace of fine white cloud,
and the city windows bright as fire in the sun,
and a wisp of smoke from a chimney or maybe two—
and up there high over all those things—divine
things!—that globe that had slipped from the heedless hand
of a little boy (he was all in tears, I'm sure,
in the thick of the crowd somewhere, for his grief, his grief,
for his mighty grief)—slipped into the sky between
the Commercial Bank and the Coffee House I sat in,
staring there, lost in reverie, through the pane,
eyes bright, as it dipped and soared away—his treasure.

Dino Campana

L'INVETRIATA

La sera fumosa d'estate
Dall'alta invetriata mesce chiarori nell'ombra
E mi lascia nel cuore un suggello ardente.
Ma chi ha (sul terrazzo sul fiume si accende una lampada) chi ha
A la Madonnina del Ponte chi è chi è che ha acceso la lampada?—c'è
Nella stanza un odor di putredine: c'è
Nella stanza una piaga rossa languente.
Le stelle sono bottoni di madreperla e la sera si veste di velluto:
E tremola la sera fatua: è fatua la sera e tremola ma c'è
Nel cuore della sera c'è,
Sempre una piaga rossa languente.

Dino Campana

THE WINDOW

The smoky summer evening
Riddles the gloom with a dazzle of glass from the window above,
Sears a token of fire in my heart.
But who has (on the terrace on the river there's lamplight) who has
To the Little Madonna of the Bridge who is it who is it who's lighted the
    lamp?—there's
An odor of rot in the room: there's
A lagging red wound in the room.
The stars are mother-of-pearl and the evening is dressing in velvet:
And it shimmers, an evening all folly and will-o'-the-wisp: it shimmers,
    but there's
In the heart of the evening there's
Forever a lagging red wound.

GIARDINO AUTUNNALE

(Firenze)

Al giardino spettrale al lauro muto
De le verdi ghirlande
A la terra autunnale
Un ultimo saluto!
A l'aride pendici
Aspre arrossate nell'estremo sole
Confusa di rumori
Rauchi grida la lontana vita:
Grida al morente sole
Che insanguina le aiole.
S'intende una fanfara
Che straziante sale: il fiume spare
Ne le arene dorate: nel silenzio
Stanno le bianche statue a capo i ponti
Volte: e le cose già non sono più.
E dal fondo silenzio come un coro
Tenero e grandioso
Sorge ed anela in alto al mio balcone:
E in aroma d'alloro,
In aroma d'alloro acre languente,
Tra le statue immortali nel tramonto
Ella m'appar, presente.

AUTUMN GARDEN

(Florence)

To the ghostly garden to the laurel mute
Green garlands shorn
To the autumnal country
Now a last salute!
Up the parched falling lawns
Harsh scarlet in the sun's last rays
Struggles a torn
Deep-throated roar—life crying far away:
It cries to the dying sun that sheds
Dark blood on the flower-beds.
A brass band saws
The air: the river's gone
Between its golden sands: in a great calm
The dazzling statues that the bridgehead bore
Are turned away: there's nothing any more.
Out of profound silence, something like
A chorus soft and grand,
Longing, soars to the terrace where I stand:
And in redolence of laurel,
Of laurel languorous, laurel piercing, where
Those statues in the sunset loom immortal,
She appears, present there.

Giuseppe Ungaretti

TU TI SPEZZASTI

I

I molti, immani, sparsi, grigi sassi
Frementi ancora alle segrete fionde
Di originarie fiamme soffocate
Od ai terrori di fiumane vergini
Ruinanti in implacabili carezze,
—Sopra l'abbaglio della sabbia rigidi
In un vuoto orizzonte, non rammenti?

E la recline, che s'apriva all'unico
Raccogliersi dell'ombra nella valle,
Araucaria, anelando ingigantita,
Volta nell'ardua selce d'erme fibre
Piú delle altre dannate refrattaria,
Fresca la bocca di farfalle e d'erbe
Dove dalle radici si tagliava,
—Non la rammenti delirante muta
Sopra tre palmi d'un rotondo ciottolo
In un perfetto bilico
Magicamente apparsa?

Di ramo in ramo fiorrancino lieve,
Ebbri di meraviglia gli avidi occhi
Ne conquistavi la screziata cima,
Temerario, musico bimbo,
Solo per rivedere all'imo lucido
D'un fondo e quieto baratro di mare
Favolose testuggini
Ridestarsi fra le alghe.

Giuseppe Ungaretti

YOU WERE BROKEN

I

The many, monstrous, tumbled, dun-gray boulders
Stunned even yet from the catapults that flung them
From the ancient fires of earth, long dungeoned, or
From terror of raw cataracts, virgin surge
Hauling off all in the hug that nothing softens:
—Over the dazzle of sand, on a blind horizon
Looming stiff in their trance—you don't remember them?

And that jutting hunchback, swollen over the only
Clotting of gloom in the hollow, the araucaria
—Wild pine—racked by its anguish to great size,
But, tougher than other victims of that inferno,
Its exiled fibers turning to fierce flint;
The dark maw, rotted out where the roots were wounded
Now all a freshness of butterflies and grasses:
—Its silent contortion of madness, not remember?
Perched on a ball of a boulder three palms wide
Balanced uncannily,
Trick of a witch?

Gay little light little bird, from branch to branch,
With eyes that were giddy with wonder, never weary,
You mounted in triumph to its tettered top,
Rash little song-loving boy,
Only to see again in the glossy gulf
Of a sunk and silent crater in the ocean,
The fabulous murk of turtles
Stirring to life in the seaweed.

Della natura estrema la tensione
E le subacquee pompe,
Funebri moniti.

2

Alzavi le braccia come ali
E ridavi nascita al vento
Correndo nel peso dell'aria immota.

Nessuno mai vide posare
Il tuo lieve piede di danza.

3

Grazia felice,
Non avresti potuto non spezzarti
In una cecità tanto indurita
Tu semplice soffio e cristallo,

Troppo umano lampo per l'empio
Selvoso, accanito, ronzante
Ruggito d'un sole ignudo.

Tension of nature wrought to extremes
And that solemn ado in the deep,
Funereal premonitions.

2

You lifted your arms like wings
And called every breeze into being
As you sprinted in lulls of the air.

Nobody ever saw lagging
Your light little foot in its dance.

3

Happy grace,
No way but for you to be broken
In a blindness denser than stone,
You, simple breath, and a crystal,

Too human a glow for the rancorous,
Shaggy, berserk, and reverberant
Roar of the stark-naked sun.

Eugenio Montale

L'ANGUILLA

L'anguilla, la sirena
dei mari freddi che lascia il Baltico
per giungere ai nostri mari,
ai nostri estuarî, ai fiumi
che risale in profondo, sotto la piena avversa,
di ramo in ramo e poi
di capello in capello, assottigliati,
sempre piú addentro, sempre piú nel cuore
del macigno, filtrando
tra gorielli di melma finché un giorno
una luce scoccata dai castagni
ne accende il guizzo in pozze d'acquamorta,
nei fossi che declinano
dai balzi d'Appennino alla Romagna;
l'anguilla, torcia, frusta,
freccia d'Amore in terra
che solo i nostri botri o i disseccati
ruscelli pirenaici riconducono
a paradisi di fecundazione;
l'anima verde che cerca
vita là dove solo
morde l'arsura e la desolazione,
la scintilla che dice
tutto comincia quando tutto pare
incarbonirsi, bronco seppellito;
l'iride breve, gemella
di quella che incastonano i tuoi cigli
e fai brillare intatta in mezzo ai figli
dell'uomo, immersi nel tuo fango, puoi tu
non crederla sorella?

Eugenio Montale

THE EEL

The eel, the
siren of sleety seas, abandoning
the Baltic for our waters,
our estuaries, our
freshets, to lash upcurrent under the brunt
of the flood, sunk deep, from brook to brook and then
trickle to trickle dwindling,
more inner always, always more in the heart
of the rock, thrusting
through ruts of the mud, until, one day,
explosion of splendor from the chestnut groves
kindles a flicker in deadwater sumps,
in ditches pitched
from ramparts of the Apennine to Romagna;
eel: torch and whip,
arrow of love on earth,
which nothing but our gorges or bone-dry
gutters of the Pyrenees ushers back
to edens of fertility;
green soul that probes
for life where only
fevering heat or devastation preys,
spark that says
the whole commences when the whole would seem
charred black, an old stick buried;
brief rainbow, twin
to that within your lashes' dazzle, to that
you keep alive, inviolate, among
the sons of men, steeped in your mire—in this
not recognize a sister?

XII

Five Contemporary Mexican Poets

Paz, Bonifaz Nuño, Castellanos, Pacheco, Aridjis

In an article on Mexican poetry in a "Mexico Today" supplement which *The Atlantic* published in March 1964 (an issue for which the following translations were made), Ramón Xirau declared that Octavio Paz "has achieved one of the highest peaks of lyric poetry written in Spanish in the twentieth century." Paz, born in 1914, spent many years in the diplomatic service. Among the contributors to his anthology *Poesía en movimiento* (*Mexico 1915–1966*) are the other four poets translated here. Rubén Bonifaz Nuño, born in 1923, is a professor of Latin; a poet in his own right, he has also translated Catullus, Horace, and Virgil. Rosario Castellanos was born in 1925; she is a well-known novelist and poet. Among the works of José Emilio Pacheco is a recent translation of Samuel Beckett's *Comment c'est*. Pacheco, born in 1939, and Homero Aridjis, a year younger, are both regarded as outstanding among the newer poets; they have been especially active as journalists and editors.

Octavio Paz

AQUÍ

Mis pasos en esta calle
Resuenan
      en otra calle
donde
    oigo mis pasos
pasar en esta calle
donde

Sólo es real la niebla

Octavio Paz

HERE

My footsteps in this street
Re-echo
      in another street
where
      I hear my footsteps
passing in this street
where

Nothing is real but the fog

PAUSA

A la memoria de Pierre Reverdy

Llegan
unos cuantos pájaros
y una idea negra.

Rumor de árboles,
rumor de trenes y motores,
¿va o viene este instante?

El silencio del sol
traspasa risas y gemidos,
hunde su pica
hasta el grito de piedra de las piedras.

Sol-corazón, piedra que late,
piedra de sangre que se vuelve fruto:
las heridas se abren y no duelen,
mi vida fluye parecida a la vida.

PAUSE

In memory of Pierre Reverdy

There come to me
certain birds
and a black idea.

Murmur of trees,
murmur of trains and motors,
this moment, is it arriving? leaving?

The silence of the sun
penetrates laughter and sighs,
sinks its goad
deep as the stony cry of the stones.

Sun-heart, stone that pulses,
stone of blood that matures in fruit:
the wounds open and do not hurt,
my life, very much like life, is flowing on.

NIÑA

Entre la tarde que se obstina
y la noche que se acumula
hay la mirada de una niña.

Deja el cuaderno y la escritura,
todo su ser dos ojos fijos.
En la pared la luz se anula.

¿Mira su fin o su principio?
Ella dirá que no ve nada.
Es transparente el infinito.

Nunca sabrá lo que miraba.

GIRL

The afternoon, its lazy ways,
and night, the shadows that amass.
Between the two, a girl. Her gaze.

Forgets her essay, work for class,
soul in that staring reverie.
Light on the wall goes black at last.

On dawn of life, on dark to be
poring? "Oh nowhere"—vaguely, though.
Transparent, that infinity.

Was gazing where she'll never know.

SOLO A DOS VOCES

En ninguna otra lengua occidental son tantas
las palabras fantasmas...

J. Corominas, Diccionario Crítico-
Etimológico de la Lengua Castellana

Si decir No
al mundo al presente
hoy (solsticio de invierno)
no es decir
      Sí
decir es solsticio de invierno
hoy en el mundo
          no
es decir
     Sí
decir mundo presente
no es decir
     ¿qué es
Mundo Solsticio Invierno?
¿Qué es decir?

     Desde hace horas
oigo caer, en el patio negro,
una gota de agua.
Ella cae y yo escribo.

Solsticio de invierno:
sol parado,
     mundo errante.
Sol desterrado,
     fijeza al rojo blanco.
La tierra blanca negra,
dormida,
sobre sí misma echada,
es una piedra caída.

SOLO FOR TWO VOICES

*In no other occidental language are there so
many ghost words . . .*

> J. Corominas, Diccionario Crítico-
> Etimológico de la Lengua Castellana

If saying No
to the world to the present
this day (the winter solstice)
is not saying
            Yes if
saying is the winter solstice
today in the world
                        it is not
saying
            Yes if
saying the world the present
is not saying
            what is
Winter Solstice World?
What is saying?

*For hours now
I've heard falling, in the black patio,
a drop of water.
It falls and I write.*

Winter solstice:
sun stopped,
            world wandering.
Sun in exile,
            fixity at white heat.
The black white earth,
asleep,
flung on itself,
is a fallen stone.

Ánima en pena
        el mundo,
peña de pena
        el alma,
pena entrañas de piedra.

Cae la gota invisible
sobre el cemento húmedo.
Cae también en mi cuarto.
A la mitad del pensamiento
me quedo, como el sol,
parado
en la mitad de mí,
separado.

        Mundo mondo,
sonaja de semillas semánticas:
vírgenes móndigas
                (múndicas,
las que llevan el *mundum*
el día de la procesión),
muchachas cereales
ofrendan a Ceres panes y ceras;
muchachas trigueñas,
entre el pecho y los ojos
alzan la monda,
Pascua de Resurrección:
Señora del Prado,
                sobre tu cabeza,
como una corona cándida,
la canasta del pan.
Incandescencias del candeal,
muchachas, cestas de panes,
pan de centeno y pan de cebada,
pan de abejas, pan de flor,
altar vivo los pechos,

Soul in purgatory
                    the world,
purgatorial stone
                    the soul,
stone with stony heart.

The drop falls unseen
on the wet cement.
It falls too in my room.
Midway in thought
I stay, like the sun,
stopped
midway in myself,
separated.

            Mundo mondo, clean world,
rattle of semantic seeds:
virgin *móndigas*
                    (*mundicas,*
those that carry the *mundum*
the day the procession is held),
girls of the grain
offer to Ceres loaves and beeswax;
girls like tawny wheat,
between their breasts and their eyes
lift the offering,
at Eastertide:
Our Lady of the Meadow,
                            on your head,
as if crowned with candor,
the basket of bread.
Incandescences of white bread,
girls, baskets of loaves,
rye bread and barley bread,
bread with a bee design, the fine white bread,
the breasts a living altar,

sobre mesa de tierra vasos de sol:
como y bebo, hombre soy.

Sonaja de simientes, poema:
enterrar la palabra,
el grano de fuego,
en el cuerpo de Ceres
tres veces arado;
enterrarla en el patio,
horadar el cemento
con la gota tenaz,
con la gota de tinta.
Para la diosa negra,
piedra dormida en la nieve,
dibujar un caballo de agua,
dibujar en la página
un caballo de yerba.

Hoy es solsticio de invierno:
canta el gallo,
                 el sol despierta.
Voces y risas, baile y panderos,
sobre el suelo entumido
rumor de faldas de muchachas
como el viento corriendo entre espadañas,
como el agua que brota de la peña.
Muchachas,
            cántaros penantes,
el agua se derrama,
el vino se derrama,
el fuego se derrama,
penetra las entrañas,
la piedra se despierta:
lleva un sol en el vientre.
Como el pan en el horno,

goblets of sun on the table of earth:
I eat and I drink, am a man.

Rattle of seeds, poem:
to bury the word in earth,
the kernel of fire,
in the body of Ceres
three times plowed;
to bury it in the patio,
drill through the cement
with the persistent drop,
with the drop of ink.
For the dark goddess,
stone asleep in the snow,
to sketch a horse of water,
to scrawl on the page
a horse of grass.

Today is the winter solstice:
the rooster crows
                    the sun awakens.
Voices and laughter, dancing and tambourines.
Over the numb earth
rustle of skirts of girls
like the wind as it runs through the rushes,
like the water that bursts from the rock.
Girls,
        jars, slender-throated,
the water runs over,
the wine runs over,
the fire runs over,
goes deep into the body,
the stone awakens:
bears a sun in its womb.
Like a loaf in the oven,

el hijo de la piedra incandescente
es el hijo de nadie.

A solas con el diccionario
agito el ramo seco,
palabras, muchachas, semillas,
sonido de guijarros
sobre la tierra negra y blanca,
inanimada.
En el aire frío del patio
se dispersan las vírgenes.
Humedad y cemento.

El mundo
no es tortas y pan pintado.
El diccionario
es un mundo no dicho:
de solsticio de invierno
a pascua de resurrección,
en dirección inversa
a las agujas del cuadrante,
hay: "sofisma, símil, selacio, salmo,
rupestre, rosca, ripio, réprobo,
rana, Quito, quejido,
pulque, ponzoña, picotín, peluca . . ."
Desandar el camino,
volver a la primera letra
en dirección inversa
al sol,
         hacia la piedra:
simiente,
                gota de energía,
joya verde
entre los pechos negros de la diosa.

the child of the white-hot stone,
is the child of no one.

Alone with the dictionary
I shake the dry branch,
words, girls, seeds,
the rattle of pebbles
on the earth black and white,
without life.
In the cold air of the patio
the virgins scatter.
Wetness and cement.

The world
is not all cakes and fancy bread.
The dictionary
is a world not spoken:
From the winter solstice
to the resurrection of Easter,
in a direction contrary
to that of the sundial-marker,
occur: "spiral, sophism, similar, selachian,
rocky, reprobate, refuse, Quito,
querulous, quartern, pulque, psalm,
pollywog, poison, periwig . . ."
Retracing the road,
going back to the first letter
in a direction contrary
to that of the sun,
                    toward the stone:
seed,
        drop of energy,
green jewel
between the dark breasts of the goddess.

Escribo contra la corriente,
contra la aguja hipnotizada
y los sofismas del cuadrante:
como la sombra, la aguja
sigue al sol,
             un sol sin cuerpo,
sombra de sol,
                  siempre futuro;
como un perro, la aguja
tras los pasos del sol,
                  sol ido,
desvanecido, sol de sombra.

No el movimiento del círculo,
maestro de espejismos:
                      la quietud
en el centro del movimiento.
No predecir: decir.
Mundo suspendido en la sombra,
mundo mondo, pulido como hueso,
decir es mondadura,
poda del árbol de los muertos.
Decir es penitencia de palabras,
la zona negra y blanca,
el húmedo cemento, el patio,
el no saber qué digo
entre la ausencia y la presencia
de este mundo, echado
sobre su propio abandono,
caído como gota de tinta.

La letra no reposa en la página:
memoria la levanta,
monumento de viento.
¿Y quién recuerda a la memoria,

I write against the current,
against the mesmerized marker
and the plausible lies of the sundial:
like the shadow, the marker
follows the sun,
                    a sun without body,
shade of a sun,
                    forever future;
like a dog, the marker
hard on the heels of the sun,
                              a sun gone,
vanished, sun of shade.

Not the movement of the circle,
master of mirages:
                    the quietude
at the center of the movement.
Not to foretell: to tell.
World suspended in the shadow,
clean world, clean as bone,
saying is a paring away,
a pruning of the tree of the dead.
Saying is a penance of words,
the black-and-white zone,
the wet cement, the patio,
the not knowing what I say
between the absence and the presence
of this world, flung
on its own abandonment,
fallen like a drop of ink.

The letter does not lie still on the page:
memory arouses it,
monument of wind.
And who is the reminder of memory,

quién la levanta, dónde se implanta?
Frente de claridad, alumbramiento,
la memoria es raíz en la tiniebla.

Come tiniebla,
>   come olvido:
no lo que dices, lo que olvidas,
es lo que dices:
>   hoy es solsticio de invierno
en el mundo
>   hoy estás separado
en el mundo
>   hoy es el mundo
ánima en pena en el mundo.

who raises it, where is it planted?
Brow of brightness, the lightening womb,
memory is a root in the dark.

Feed on the dark,
          feed on forgetfulness:
not what you say, what you forget,
is what you say:
          today is the winter solstice
in the world
          today you are separated
in the world
          today is the world
purgatorial soul in the world.

Rubén Bonifaz Nuño

HUMO

Humo la estrella, escoba
de humo sólo, su lumbre; de agua oscura
su nube de serpiente, su sonaja.

Y alguien tirita de sentirse a medias
borracho, a medias solo, amado a medias,
y siendo yo, completamente a medias.

Pues cuando de mi mano doy la vuelta
por la esquina que quiero, y cuando llueve
y espero alguna cosa, algún milagro
en ruedas grises, a destiempo, y miro,
hallo mi espejo, rostro a rostro
desmantelado, abriéndose de risa.

Y así se llama, así se nombra mía
mi casa, mi alimento, mi brasero:
cara de humo, cueva de humo, tigre
de humo reluciente, tigre joya,
joya de humo resonante, escudo.

Tal vez si comprendieras, si supieras,
tal vez, hacia qué rumbo, vencedora
de la serpiente la paloma
del espírito fuera, y la purísima
concepción del guerrero coronado
de sangre hasta el sabor de la garganta.

Y un sol en cruz para salvarme,
y un collar degollado y una sarta

Rubén Bonifaz Nuño

SMOKE

It's smoke, the star, a broom
of nothing but smoke, its light; of dusky water
its serpent cloud, its jingle bell.

And someone shudders to feel himself
half drunk, half by himself, half loved,
and if I'm the one, at halves completely.

For when with a gesture of my hand I turn
the corner I had in mind, and when it's raining
and there's something I'm waiting for, some miracle
in the gray streets, at the wrong time, and I'm staring,
I find my mirror, face to ravaged face,
and each goes wide with laughter.

And thus they call it, refer to it as *mine*
my house, my food, my little stove:
a face of smoke, a den of smoke, a tiger
of glittering smoke, jewel tiger,
jewel of sonorous smoke, a coat of arms.

Perhaps if you understood, if you knew
perhaps, in what direction—then the dove
of the spirit would rise triumphant
over the serpent, and the most immaculate
conception of the warrior crowned
with blood to the taste of his throat.

And a sun hung crosswise there for my salvation,
and a necklace guillotined and a string

de calaveras, y tendría
la mazorca de dientes amarillos
y las hambrientas órbitas.

Tú fuiste lo que somos; antes
que bebiera mi sangre en tu cuchara,
tú fuiste, ya, la sed que multiplica
por cero el canto de la dicha
y salve el cetro de la cólera.

Yo, qué diré; qué mando yo, qué entrego,
qué abandono, si el hambre fué la herencia;
y el hambre de mi hermano, el hambre a medias
de mis abuelos chicos, de mis nietos.

Junto a la guerra se asentó mi casa;
arde el escudo ronco entre la lluvia.
Todo es tierra florida bajo el humo,
todo es maizal de llamas.

Y es la batalla. Nadie en adelante
comprenderá, tal vez, que tenga fuerzas
mi corazón para voltear; que envíe
su plumaje de fuego, su árbol rojo,
su tren de escamas póstumas brillando.

of skulls, and I'd have
the ear of corn with its yellow teeth
and the hungry orbits.

The thing we are, you were; before
I sipped my blood from your tablespoon,
you were, already, the thirst that multiplies
by exactly zero the chant of happiness
and rescues the choleric scepter.

I—what's to say; or what orders give, what charges,
what should I leave, with hunger for all my inheritance;
and the hunger of my brother, the half hunger
of my father's poor little parents, of my grandsons.

Next to the war my house was situated;
its coat of arms burns hoarsely in the rain.
All is a land in blossom under the smoke,
all is a cornfield of fire.

Is the battle too. Not a man to come
will understand, perhaps, that my heart has strength
to turn back round; is sending forth
its plumage all of flame, its scarlet tree,
its train with the posthumous scales a-glitter.

Rosario Castellanos

TESTAMENTO DE HECUBA

A Ofelia Guilmain, homenaje.

Torre, no hiedra, fuí. El viento nada pudo
rondando en torno mío con sus cuernos de toro:
alzaba polvaredas desde el norte y el sur
y aún desde otros puntos que olvidé o que ignoraba.
Pero yo resistía, profunda de cimientos,
ancha de muros, sólida
y caliente de entrañas, defendiendo a los míos.

El dolor era un deudo más de aquella familia.
No el predilecto ni el mayor. Un deudo
comedido en la faena, humilde comensal,
oscuro relator de cuentos junto al fuego.
Cazaba, en ocasiones, lejos, y por servir
su instinto de varón
que tiene el pulso firme y los ojos certeros.
Volvía con la presa y la entregaba al hábil
destazador y al diestro
afán de las mujeres.

Al recogerme yo decía: qué hermosa
labor están tejiendo con las horas mis manos.
Desde la juventud tuve frente a mis ojos
un hermoso dechado
y no ambicioné más que copiar su figura.

En su día fuí casta
y después fiel al único, al esposo.
Nunca la aurora me encontró dormida
ni me alcanzó la noche

318

Rosario Castellanos

HECUBA'S TESTAMENT

For Ofelia Guilmain

A tower, no ivy, I. The wind was powerless,
horns lunging round and round me like a bull's.
It stirred up clouds of dust to north and south
and in quarters I've forgotten or never knew.
But I endured, foundations deep in earth,
walls broad, heart strong
and warm within, defending my own brood.

Sorrow was closer kin than any of those.
Not the favorite; not the eldest. But a kinsman
agreeable in the chores, humble at table,
a shadowy teller of tales beside the fire.
There were times he went off hunting far away
at the masculine call
of his steady pulse, his eye sharp on the target.
He returned with game, consigned it
to a helper shrewd with the knife
and the zealous care of women.

On retiring I'd say: What a fine
piece of work my hands are weaving out of the hours.
From girlhood on I kept before my eyes
a handsome sampler;
was ambitious to copy its figure; wished no more.

Unmarried, I lived chaste while that was right;
later was loyal to one, to my own husband.
Never a dawn that found me still asleep,
never a night that overtook me till

antes que se apagara mi rumor de colmena.
La casa de mi dueño se llenó de mis obras
y su campo llegó hasta el horizonte.

Y para que su nombre no acabara
al acabar su cuerpo,
tuvo hijos en mí, valientes, laboriosos,
tuvo hijas de virtud,
desposadas con yernos aceptables
(excepto una, virgen, que se guardó a sí misma
tal vez como la ofrenda para un dios).

Los que me conocieron me llamaron dichosa
y no me contenté con recibir
la feliz alabanza de mis iguales
sino que me incliné hasta los pequeños
para sembrar en ellos gratitud.

Cuando vino el relámpago buscando
aquel árbol de las conversaciones
clamó por la injusticia el fulminado.

Yo no dije palabras, porque es condición mía
no entender otra cosa sino el deber y he sido
obediente al desastre:
viuda irreprensible, reina que pasó a esclava
sin que su dignidad de reina padeciere
y madre, ay, y madre
huérfana de su prole.

Arrastré la vejez como una túnica
demasiado pesada.
Quedé ciega de años y de llanto
y en mi ceguera ví
la visión que sostuvo en su lugar mi ánimo.

the beehive hum of my home had sunk to rest.
The house of my lord was rich with works of my hand;
his lands stretched out to horizons.

And so that his name would not die
when his body died,
he had sons of me; they were valiant sons; had stamina.
Of me he had virtuous girls
that all made a suitable match
(except for one, a virgin, that held aloof,
as offering, it well may be, to a god himself).

Those who knew me called me fortunate.
Not satisfied with receiving
the happy praise of my equals,
I leaned to the little ones,
to sow in these a harvest of gratitude.

When the lightning bolt came probing
that tree of the conversations,
he who was struck by it raged about injustice.

I said not a word, for my way is
to listen to one thing only: bounden duty.
Disaster spoke; I obeyed:
a widow without reproach, a queen made slave
without loss to her queenly pride,
and mother, ah, and mother
orphaned of all her brood.

I dragged along old age like a tunic
too heavy to wear.
I was blind with years and weeping
and in my blindness saw
the vision that sustained my soul at its post.

Vino la invalidez, el frío, el frío
y tuve que entregarme a la piedad
de los que viven. Antes
me entregué así al amor, al infortunio.

Alguien asiste mi agonía. Me hace
beber a sorbos una docilidad difícil
y yo voy aceptando
que se cumplan en mí los últimos misterios.

Helplessness came, the cold, the cold,
and I had to surrender myself to the charity
of those alive. As before I had
surrendered myself to love, and to misfortune.

Someone cares for me in my final sufferings. Makes me
drink down a harsh docility,
which I more and more learn to accept
so that all be fulfilled in me: those ultimate mysteries.

José Emilio Pacheco

CANCIÓN PARA ESCRIBIRSE EN UNA OLA

I

Ante la soledad
se extienden días quemados,
luces de carnaval que los recuerdos cubren
con huellas de ceniza;
pez abierto
por cuya hueca sombra el mar navega
en sus horas de espuma y torbellinos.
Agua marcada por un buque aciago
y en su sentina, ratas, criaturas de lo antiguo
como remotos juegos de una mujer ahogada
en la mano sin líneas de un hosco dios marino
que proyecta sus horas de salitre y hastío
en el óxido muerto, en la piedra anegada
con cabellos de algas y peces vegetales,
disueltos en la arena de una playa dormida
en boca de la tarde,
del momento más hondo
en que forma el cangrejo
húmedas galerías que las olas destruyen.

II

El mar tiene palabras que se mezclan y estallan
cuando la tierra escucha
su canción repetida
en piedra, ola tras hora.

José Emilio Pacheco

SONG TO BE WRITTEN ON A WAVE

I

Confronting the solitude
the burnt out days extend,
carnival lights that recollections cover
with cindery prints;
a fish split wide
through whose hollow gloom the great sea cruises yet
in its hours of foam and whirlwinds.
Water scored by an ill-fated ketch
and rats in its bilge, creatures of long ago
like the faraway games of a woman drowned
in the unlined palm of a somber marine deity
who projects his hours of boredom and saltpeter
in the lifeless oxide, in the stone engulfed
with its seaweed hair and vegetable fishes,
dissolved in the sand of a sleeping beach
in the very mouth of the afternoon,
that deepest moment
when the crab is at work
on his dripping tunnels the combers wreck.

II

The sea has words that fuse and explode
when earth attends
to her song twice-told
in stone, wave after hour.

El viento vibra, inflama la piel de los océanos
que persiguen su oleaje, su huraño ser rugoso.
La curva singladura del aire se repite,
un caracol eterno son el mar y su nombre
y sobre él las palabras se mecen siempre iguales.
El viento las deshace, las incluye en la noche;
iniciales gastadas de un lejano retorno,
cementerio de voces que trabajan su muerte.
desde el centro responden sus péndulos de espuma,
—plurales descendencias que en el tiempo se agitan.
En su cuerpo varado encalla toda noche:
el mar es roto espejo de la luna desierta.

The wind is vibrant, inflames the skin of the seas
that go on with their surging, their diffident wrinkled ways.
The curving runs of the air are made over and over,
sea and its name are an everlasting snail,
and above it the same words undulate, ever the same.
Wind blows them apart, enfolds them in the night;
the worn initials of a far return,
a cemetery of voices drudging at death.
Its pendulums of foam reply from the center
—manifold genealogies ruffled by time.
On its body driven aground, all nights are stranded;
the sea is a shattered glass of the lone moon.

DEL FRÁGIL LABERINTO

Como la lluvia tercamente se detiene en el río
—minuciosa, veloz, hecha de mil pronombres—
los mundos atraviesan la sorpresiva fecha,
y dejan como estela, como ruinosa huella,
los instintos del polvo.

En la serena fuga de la tarde
miro alzarse las horas como llamas o mástiles;
el sol como un gran toro luminoso y desértico
al que el viento circunda,
leve materia de alas que en su vuelo se apaga.

Así, los vastos, frágiles, laberintos del aire
dulcemente se inundan del ruido y el amor,
de un eco que propaga sus cautivos silencios.
Es el cercado reino que instauró los secretos
de su nombre y su dádiva.

En la ribera de mirarla, digo:
sobre dormidas hojas y entre escollos floridos
ven a la dócil costa donde el mar va naciendo,
al cantil de la brisa, a este jardín de arena,
al desierto marino
donde la ola termina su condición de oveja
y el alba se corona
con los blandos rumores de la luz y la espuma.

Lento, el mar pastorea
el litoral, las islas.
Mientras el día se incendia

ON THE FRAGILE LABYRINTH

As the rain is lagging, wayward, in the river
—meticulous, swift, made up of a thousand pronouns—
the worlds cross the astonishing dateline,
and leave as a wake, as ruinous traces,
the instincts of the dust.

In the quiet flight of the evening
I see the hours arise like flames or mastheads:
the sun like a great bull of desert brilliance
that the wind edges round,
light stuff of wings that in its flight dissolves.

So the fragile vast labyrinths of the air
are softly flooded with noise and love,
with an echo that propagates the dungeoned lulls.
Here's the kingdom under siege that restored the secrets
of its name and of its gift.

Here on the sands of scrutiny, I say:
over sleeping leaves and between the reefs in blossom
come to the docile coast where the sea is born forever,
to the shelf of the breeze, to this garden of sand,
to the desert along the surf
where the wave gives over its sheeplike ways
and the dawn is crowned
with the intonations of light and foam—more suave.

Slowly, the ocean is shepherding
island and shore.
Meanwhile the day takes fire

va creando su linaje —emblemas, luces, rostros
profanación de espejos.

Su resplandor mitiga esta hora que se inmensa,
este rito de instantes que en su oquedad se pierden,
tal humo que deshace su momentánea hiedra.

and continues creating its lineage: emblems, faces,
lights, profanation of mirrors.

Its radiance softens this hour which spreads immense,
this ritual of instants lost in their own vacuity,
such smoke as unravels its momentaneous ivy.

LÍMITES

Todo lo que has perdido, me dijeron, es tuyo.
Y ninguna memoria recordaba que es cierto.
Estuve vivo, amé, dije palabras
que las horas borraron.
Sentí una honda piedad
por los años que faltan.

Todo lo que destruyes, me dijeron, te hiere.
Traza una cicatriz que no lava el olvido;
renace cada día dentro de ti,
desborda
esos muros de sal que no pueden cubrirte.

Todo lo que has amado, me dijeron, ha muerto.
Y no sé definirlo,
pero hay algo en el tiempo
que zarpó para siempre.
Hay rostros que ya nunca
volveré a recordar;
y hay acaso un espejo, una calle, un verano
que ya ha cubierto el eco de otra sombra baldía.

Todo lo que creíste, repitieron, es falso.
Ningún dios te protege,
sólo te ampara el viento.
Y el viento es, ya lo sabes,
una oquedad sin límite,
el ruido que hace el mundo
cuando muere un instante.

BOUNDARIES

All that you have lost, they told me, is yours.
And no memory remembered that, yes, it's true.
I was alive, I loved, I uttered words
the hours erased,
I felt a profound pity
for the years to come.

All you destroy, they told me, injures you.
Traces a scar forgetfulness won't cleanse;
is born again each day within you,
spreads beyond
those salty walls unable to contain you.

All you have loved, they told me, is now dead.
And I can't describe it quite,
but there's something in time
that has sailed away forever.
There are faces now I'll never
see in my mind again;
and perhaps there's a mirror, a summer, a street
that already go under the echo of one more futile shade.

All you created, they kept repeating, is false.
No god protects you,
only the wind is your shelter.
And the wind, as well you know,
is a boundless vacancy,
the sound the world makes
when a moment dies.

Todo lo que has perdido, concluyeron, es tuyo.
Es tu sola heredad, tu recuerdo, tu nombre.
Ya no tendrás el día
que rechazaste.
El tiempo
te ha dejado en la orilla
de esta noche
y acaso
una luz fugitiva
anegará el silencio.

All you have lost, they concluded, is your own.
Your sole estate, your memory, your name.
You won't have, now, the day
you once refused.
Time
has left you on the shore
of this night
and perhaps
a fleeting light
will drown the silence.

Homero Aridjis

EPITAFIO PARA UN POETA

Antes de que las nieblas descendieran a tu cuerpo
mucho antes del grumo de vacilación en los ojos de tu máscara
antes de la muerte de tus hijos primeros y de los bajos fondos
antes de haber equivocado la tristeza y la penuria
y el grito salvaje en el candor de un hombre
antes de haber murmurado la desolación sobre los puentes
y lo espurio de la cópula tras la ventana sin vidrios

casi cuando tus lagos eran soles
y los niños eran palabras en el aire
y los días eran la sombra de lo fácil

cuando la eternidad no era la muerte exacta que buscábamos
ni el polvo era más verosímil que el recuerdo
ni el dolor era nuestra crueldad de ser divinos

entonces cuando se pudo haber dicho todo impunemente
y la risa como una flor de pétalos cayendo

entonces cuando no debías más que la muerte de un poema
eras tuyo y no mío y no te había perdido

Homero Aridjis

EPITAPH FOR A POET

Before the mists descended on your body
long before hesitations clotted in the eyes of your mask
before the death of your first sons and the lower depths
before a confusion of sadness and destitution
and the savage cry in the frankness of a man
before having murmured of desolation on the bridges
and the falsity of a cupola through the window that had no glass

almost when your lakes were suns
and the children were words in the air
and the days were the shadow of what was easy

when eternity was not the exact death we were looking for
nor the dust more likely than memory
nor sorrow our cruelty for being divine

then when all could have been said with impunity
and laughter like a flower of petals falling

then when you owed nothing but the death of a poem
you were your own and not mine and I had not lost you

CAE LA LLUVIA SOBRE JUNIO

Cae la lluvia sobre junio
y los signos se contienen
en toda puerta que se colabora

Al fondo de ti ríen las doncellas

El espíritu de la mujer que ama
corre en tu cuerpo   se desnuda en las calles

No hay desengaño en este día
sólo una luz   fuego secreto
y un grito que se exorcisa adentro

En todo está el hombre
y el espíritu de la mujer que ama

La vida en los rincones
sostiene el equilibrio del mundo
con un algo de Dios que asciende de las ruinas

Los hijos del hombre hacen su universo
sobre un barco de papel que se destroza
pero la alegría no está precisamente ahí
sino en la proyección de otro universo

Nada debe detenerse
volverá septiembre y después abril
y los amigos que no acudieron esta primavera
estarán con nosotros en un invierno previsible

THE RAIN IS FALLING

Over the month of June the rain is falling
tokens posted
on every door that has a hand in the matter

Deep in your heart the young girls laugh

The spirit of woman in love
runs in your flesh—takes off its clothes in the streets

No disenchantment in this day
only a brightness—secret fire
and within you a cry as of spirits laid to rest

In everything man
and the spirit of woman in love

Life in the corners
sustains the world's equilibrium
with a something of God that rises out of the ruins

The sons of man make their universe
on a paper boat that founders
yet happiness is not precisely there
but in the projection of another universe

Nothing should postpone its going
September will return and April later
and the friends that were not at our side this spring
these will be with us in a foreseeable winter

339

Así he reencontrado imágenes perdidas
hogueras muertas de otras intemperies
y lutos tardíos por bienamados yertos

Amo este tiempo
donde los perros son sagrados
y los insectos titubean en los vidrios

Te amo a ti por efímera   por susceptible al frío

La ciudad se ilumina para nuevas proezas

Thus I have come again on the lost images
dead bonfires from other seasons of bad weather
and mourning long delayed for the stiffened limbs we cherished

I love this time
when dogs are holy
and insects hesitate at the pane

I love you—you as ephemeral—as suffering the cold

The lights of the city come on for further exploits

XIII

A Miscellany

Plato (c. 429–347 B.C.)

GREEK ANTHOLOGY, V,78

Τὴν ψυχήν, Ἀγάθωνα φιλῶν, ἐπὶ χείλεσιν ἔσχον·
ἦλθε γὰρ ἡ τλήμων ὡς διαβησομένη.

Plato

THE KISS

That was my very soul that stole to the lips in our kissing.
Thinking to pass—poor thing!—over from me into you.

Rufinus (2d century A.D.?)

GREEK ANTHOLOGY, V,14

Εὐρώπης τὸ φίλημα, καὶ ἢν ἄχρι χείλεος ἔλθῃ,
ἡδύ γε, κἂν ψαύσῃ μοῦνον ἄκρου στόματος·
ψαύει δ᾽ οὐκ ἄκροις τοῖς χείλεσιν, ἀλλ᾽ ἐρίσασα
τὸ στόμα τὴν ψυχὴν ἐξ ὀνύχων ἀνάγει.

Rufinus

A KISS FROM HER

A kiss from her! Her mouth, coming even close to your own, how
  Sweet! How sweet if it brush ever so lightly the lip.
But that's not her kind of kiss. No: drawing your mouth close, closer,
  She drinks of your soul; it flows—currents from finger and toe.

Anonymous

LA LAVANDERA

Yo me levantara, madre,—mañanica de Sant Juan:
vide estar una doncella—ribericas de la mar:
sola lava y sola tuerce,—sola tiende en un rosal:
mientras los paños se enjugan,—dice la niña un cantar:
"¿Dó los mis amores, dó los?—¿dó los andaré a buscar?"
Mar abajo, mar arriba,—diciendo iba el cantar,
peine de oro en las sus manos—por sus cabellos peinar.
"Dígasme tú, el marinero,—sí, Dios te guarde de mal,
si los viste, mis amores,—si los viste allá pasar."

Anonymous

LASS A-LAUNDERING

Rose and went a-roving, mother,
On the morning of St. John.
Rose and saw a lass a-laundering
On the ocean sands alone.
Lone she wrings and lone she rinses,
Lone extends them on a thorn;
All the while the clothes are sunning,
Sings a solitary song:

"Where's my darling, where, I wonder?
How to wander where he's gone?"

Up the ocean, down the ocean,
Still the girl goes singing on.
With a gold comb in her fingers
For her tresses ocean-blown.
"You, you sailor, tell me truly,
True as heaven steer you home,
Have you seen him pass, my darling,
Seen him faring on the foam?"

Pierre de Ronsard (1524–1585)

LES AMOURS DE MARIE, XIX

Marie, levez-vous, ma jeune paresseuse!
Jà la gaie alouette au ciel a fredonné,
Et jà le rossignol doucement jargonné,
Dessus l'épine assis, sa complainte amoureuse.
Sus, debout! allons voir l'herbelette perleuse,
Et votre beau rosier de boutons couronné
Et vos œillets mignons auxquels aviez donné
Hier au soir de l'eau d'une main si soigneuse.
Harsoir en vous couchant vous jurâtes vos yeux
D'être plus tôt que moi ce matin éveillée;
Mais le dormir de l'aube aux filles gracieux
Vous tient d'un doux sommeil encor les yeux sillée.
Çà, çà! que je les baise et votre beau tétin
Cent fois, pour vous apprendre à vous lever matin.

Pierre de Ronsard

TIME TO BE UP, MARIE, YOUNG SLEEPYHEAD

Time to be up, Marie, young sleepyhead!
The meadowlark's already in the sky;
The nightingale that keeps her thorny bed
Already's sung and hushed the lovelorn cry.
Let's revel now in grassiness and dew
And hail your rosebush with its corals crowned;
Your clove pinks too—I watched, last evening, you
Water with loving hand the garden 'round.
Last night, on going to bed, Lord! Lord! you swore
That you'd be up and doing, the first to rise.
Yet slumber on at dawn? Sink more and more
In morning-sleep girls love? A kiss for eyes;
For breasts, here, there a kiss. Some hundred strewing,
I'll teach you, dreamer, to be up and doing.

Lope de Vega (1562–1635)

SONETO DE REPENTE

Un soneto me manda hacer Violante,
que en mi vida me he visto en tal aprieto;
catorce versos dicen que es soneto;
burla burlando van los tres delante.

Yo pensé que no hallara consonante,
y estoy a la mitad de otro cuarteto;
mas si me veo en el primer terceto,
no hay cosa en los cuartetos que me espante.

Por el primer terceto voy entrando,
y aun parece que entré con pie derecho,
pues fin con este verso le voy dando.

Ya estoy en el segundo, y aun sospecho
que estoy los trece versos acabando;
contad si son catorce, y está hecho.

Lope de Vega

SONNET RIGHT OFF THE BAT

"Write me a sonnet. On the spot," said she.
Now there's a bind I wasn't in before.
A sonnet's fourteen lines, I hear—no more
No less. But look, just jabbering I did three.
You'd think the rhymes would have me up a tree,
But here I'm halfway through the second four.
So, if I up by two my present score
The octave's a dead duck. No stopping me!

Well look at Lope entering line nine!
I must have knocked it off in nothing flat
And breezed half through the sestet. Doing fine
Nearing the finish. As to where I'm at,
I rather think it's—hmmm—the thirteenth line.
Here's fourteen. Care to count them? And that's that.

Paul Valéry (1871–1945)

LA DISTRAITE

Daigne, Laure, au retour de la saison des pluies,
Présence parfumée, épaule qui t'appuies
Sur ma tendresse lente attentive à tes pas,
Laure, très beau regard qui ne regarde pas,
Daigne, tête aux grands yeux qui dans les cieux t'égares,
Tandis qu'à pas rêveurs, tes pieds voués aux mares
Trempent aux clairs miroirs dans la boue arrondis,
Daigne, chère, écouter les choses que tu dis…

Paul Valéry

GIRL WITH MIND WANDERING

Deign, Laura—now again the rainy season's here—
Beside me all perfume, your shoulder leaning, dear,
On my indulgent love attentive as you go,
Laura, all soulful look that looks at nothing though,
Deign, brow and the wide eyes so lost in heaven's own blue,
Even while your dreaming feet, as fated to, splash through
Pools mirrored lush in mud you wade and set a-spraying,
Deign, dear, to listen once to what your lips are saying . . .

Hugo Von Hofmannsthal (1874–1929)

DIE BEIDEN

Sie trug den Becher in der Hand
—Ihr Kinn und Mund glich seinem Rand—
So leicht und sicher war ihr Gang,
Kein Tropfen aus dem Becher sprang.

So leicht und fest war seine Hand:
Er ritt auf einem jungen Pferde,
Und mit nachlässiger Gebärde
Erzwang er, daß es zitternd stand.

Jedoch, wenn er aus ihrer Hand
Den leichten Becher nehmen sollte,
So war es beiden allzu schwer:
Denn beide bebten sie so sehr,
Daß keine Hand die andre fand
Und dunkler Wein am Boden rollte.

Hugo Von Hofmannsthal

THE TWO OF THEM

Her fingers bore the winecup in,
Rim shapely as her lip, her chin.
So easy and assured her air
That not a drop fell anywhere.

So easy and so firm his hand
—He rode a stallion, fiery, young,
And nonchalant, wrist flickering, swung
Its crupper, quivering, to a stand.

But when he leaned to take the cup
Her fingers held so lightly up,
They found it such a burden there
With both atremble so, that pair,
That neither hand the other found;
Dark wine rolled spattering the ground.

Jacques Prévert (1900–1977)

JE SUIS COMME JE SUIS

Je suis comme je suis
Je suis faite comme ça
Quand j'ai envie de rire
Oui je ris aux éclats
J'aime celui qui m'aime
Est-ce ma faute à moi
Si ce n'est pas le même
Que j'aime chaque fois
Je suis comme je suis
Je suis faite comme ça
Que voulez-vous de plus
Que voulez-vous de moi

Je suis faite pour plaire
Et n'y puis rien changer
Mes talons sont trop hauts
Ma taille trop cambrée
Mes seins beaucoup trop durs
Et mes yeux trop cernés
Et puis après
Qu'est-ce que ça peut vous faire
Je suis comme je suis
Je plais à qui je plais

Qu'est-ce que ça peut vous faire
Ce qui m'est arrivé
Oui j'ai aimé quelqu'un
Oui quelqu'un m'a aimée
Comme les enfants qui s'aiment
Simplement savent aimer

Jacques Prévert

I'M THE WAY I AM

I'm the way I am
Way I'm made and so
When I want to laugh
Man do I let go
I'm a girl that loves
Someone who loves me
My fault if at times
He's a different he
I'm the way I am
Way I'm made and so
You expected more
What, I'd like to know

Made for giving joy
Not that I could choose
Me with nifty hips
Me in ritzy shoes
Breasts quite tough enough
Eyelids ringed with blue
After all
What's it then to you
I'm the way I am
Pleasing where I please

What's it then to you
If I've memories
Sure I loved a man
Sure a man loved me
The way kids in love
Irregardlessly

Aimer aimer . . .
Pourquoi me questionner
Je suis là pour vous plaire
Et n'y puis rien changer.

Love love love . . .
Keep your "Why don't you . . ." s
I'm for giving joy
Not that I could choose

INVENTAIRE

Une pierre
deux maisons
trois ruines
quatre fossoyeurs
un jardin
des fleurs

un raton laveur

une douzaine d'huîtres un citron un pain
un rayon de soleil
une lame de fond
six musiciens
une porte avec son paillasson
un monsieur décoré de la légion d'honneur

un autre raton laveur

un sculpteur qui sculpte des Napoléon
la fleur qu'on appelle souci
deux amoureux sur un grand lit
un receveur des contributions une chaise trois dindons
un ecclésiastique un furoncle
une guêpe
un rein flottant
une écurie de courses
un fils indigne deux frères dominicains trois sauterelles un strapontin
deux filles de joie un oncle Cyprien
une Mater dolorosa trois papas gâteau deux chèvres de Monsieur Seguin

INVENTORY

One stone
two houses
three ruins
four gravediggers
a garden
some flowers

one raccoon

a dozen oysters a lemon a loaf of bread
a ray of sunshine
a groundswell
six musicians
a door complete with doormat
a gentleman wearing the ribbon of the legion of honor

another raccoon

a sculptor who sculpts napoleons
the flower they call Mary Gold
two lovers on a king-size bed
a tax collector a chair three turkey-gobblers
a member of the clergy a boil
a wasp
a floating kidney
a racing stable
one unworthy son two dominican friars three grasshoppers a jump-seat
two women of pleasure an Uncle Cyprian type
a Sorrowful Mother three doting daddies two goats from a story-book

un talon Louis XV
un fauteuil Louis XVI
un buffet Henri II deux buffets Henri III trois buffets Henri IV
un tiroir dépareillé
une pelote de ficelle deux épingles de sûreté un monsieur âgé
une Victoire de Samothrace un comptable deux aides-comptables un
    homme du monde deux chirurgiens trois végétariens
un cannibale
une expédition coloniale un cheval entier une demi-pinte de bon sang une
    mouche tsé-tsé
un homard à l'américaine un jardin à la française
deux pommes à l'anglaise
un face-à-main un valet de pied un orphelin un poumon d'acier
un jour de gloire
une semaine de bonté
un mois de Marie
une année terrible
une minute de silence
une seconde d'inattention
et…

cinq ou six ratons laveurs

un petit garçon qui entre à l'école en pleurant
un petit garçon qui sort de l'école en riant
une fourmi
deux pierres à briquet
dix-sept éléphants un juge d'instruction en vacances assis sur un pliant
un paysage avec beaucoup d'herbe verte dedans
une vache
un taureau
deux belles amours trois grandes orgues un veau marengo
un soleil d'Austerlitz
un siphon d'eau de Seltz
un vin blanc citron

a Louis XV heel
a Louis XVI armchair
one Henry II buffet two Henry III buffets three Henry IV buffets
a drawer that doesn't match
a ball of string two safety-pins a gentleman on in years
a Victory of Samothrace an accountant two assistant accountants
a man of the world two surgeons three vegetarians
a cannibal
a colonial expedition one whole horse one half horse-laugh
   a tsetse fly
a lobster à l'américaine a garden à la française
two potatoes à l'anglaise
a lorgnette for the hand a footman on foot an orphan an iron lung
a day of glory
a week of Sundays
a Month of our Mother
a terrible year
a moment of silence
a second of inattention
and . . .

five or six raccoons

a little boy who goes into the school crying
a little boy who comes out of the school laughing
one ant
two flints
seventeen elephants a vacationing legal expert on a campstool
a landscape with lots of green grass in it
a cow
a bull
two grand passions three grand pianos one veal marengo
an Austerlitz sun
a bottle of soda water
a lemon-yellow white wine

un Petit Poucet un grand pardon un calvaire de pierre une échelle de corde
deux sœurs latines trois dimensions douze apôtres mille et une nuits trente-
deux positions six parties du monde cinq points cardinaux dix ans de
bons et loyaux services sept péchés capitaux deux doigts de la main dix
gouttes avant chaque repas trente jours de prison dont quinze de cellule
cinq minutes d'entr'acte

et...

plusieurs ratons laveurs.

a little Thumb (Tom) a big Kippur (Yom) a stone calvary a rope ladder
two Roman sisters three dimensions twelve apostles a thousand and one
nights thirty-two positions six continents five points of the compass ten
years of good and faithful service seven deadly sins two fingers of the
hand ten drops before each meal thirty days in jail fifteen of them in
solitary five-minute intermission

and . . .

raccoons, quite a few of them.

Sandro Penna (1906–1976)

DONNA IN TRAM

Vuoi baciare il tuo bimbo che non vuole:
ama guardare la vita, di fuori.
Tu sei delusa allora, ma sorridi:
non è l'angoscia della gelosia
anche se già somiglia egli all'altr'uomo
che per "guardare la vita, di fuori"
ti ha lasciata così ...

Sandro Penna

LADY ON STREETCAR

You'd like to kiss your little boy but he doesn't want to:
he likes to look at life, outside there.
You are disappointed then, but you smile:
it doesn't hurt the way jealousy does
even though he already looks like the other man
who "to look at life, outside there"
left you in just this way . . .

Sappho: the papyrus text of Fragment 16 ("Some prefer a glory of horsemen . . .").
Oxyrhynchus Papyri, 1231, Fr. 1, col. 1. British Museum.

XIV

Sappho, Catullus, Horace

About the lives of Sappho and Catullus, probably the greatest lyric poets of antiquity, we know very little beyond what their own poems tell us. Sappho was born in the seventh century B.C. on the island of Lesbos, just off the coast of Asia Minor, and there she spent most of her life.

I explain in the essay on translation why I think that Greek and Latin poetry presents special problems for the translator, chiefly for metrical reasons.

The first five poems of Sappho here are translated in the metrical swing of her own "Sapphic" stanzas: in lines of eleven and five syllables, in which my pattern of stressed and unstressed syllables corresponds to her own pattern of long and short ones. The metric line of Number 55 could be described as a series of three choriambic feet ($-\cup\cup-$) preceded and followed by two freer syllables. Number 94 (in which the first line, and much more, is missing) is made up of three-line stanzas, their first two lines each consisting of two syllables (either long or short) followed by an Aeolic glyconic unit ($-\cup\cup-\cup-$). The longer third line inserts a dactyl before the glyconic. These rhythmical systems are clearly more complicated than anything we are used to in English.

With Sappho, another problem arises. The translator either has to be something of a paleographer of ancient Greek or has to know what paleographers he can count on; otherwise he may find that he is not translating Sappho at all, but merely some nineteenth-century clergyman whose hobby was "restoring" fragmentary texts. Only one of Sappho's poems (Number 1, here) has survived intact, or nearly so, because an ancient rhetorician quoted it in his textbook. Another is almost complete, though we are not sure of the ending. Number 16 exists only in a papyrus of the second century A.D.; that is, of some seven or

371

eight hundred years after her death. It is obvious from the reproduction of this text (shown on page 362) that some lines are incomplete. They can be filled in only by guesswork. Suppose a single surviving copy of a poem by Robert Frost, a copy as tattered as the Sappho is, were found about the year 4570, and suppose a foreign scholar, who had shown no particular talent as poet, and of course had never heard anything like twentieth-century English, tried to fill in the gaps—! Besides these three poems, we have only about two hundred complete lines—pieces of over fifty poems, and a grab-bag of shreds and patches on pieces of papyrus and broken pottery: single words that some lexicographer quoted as an example of something, phrases used to illustrate a meter, or even mere tatters in which not one word is complete. Over these fragments there has been a great deal of ecstasizing: one of our most famous critics lets himself say that Sappho's voice "has so articulate an identity that we recognize it in the least fragment." Nonsense: there are fragments by the hundred that Sappho herself could not recognize as her own, let alone detect the articulate identity in. Here is a snippet of an English poem, about the size and shape of one of the Sappho fragments, and by no means the least of them:

If-impose
    king
that in fai
  stars th
    serv

Can anyone say he feels in this the articulate identity of Shakespeare? Could he even tell Shakespeare's voice from Edgar Guest's?—whose "Just Folks," as a matter of fact, does yield the above fragment.

Some translators treat the scraps as if they were little haiku-like poems on their own. But Sappho did not write haiku; she did not write imagistic mini-poems like those of H.D. Her work was formally structured, tightly organized, shaped by physical rhythms of some intricacy, though she seems to handle them with ease. It is wrong to make her seem wispy, wrong to make poems out of a series of half lines—as if our imaginary translator of the future, with only a torn piece of the sixth stanza of "Ode to a Nightingale," would have Keats write:

Many a time,
    Easeful death!
Musèd rhyme,
    Quiet breath!
Rich to die
    With no pain!
Soul abroad,
    Ears in vain.

Pick up some translations of Sappho, and you find yourself as far from her manner as the above jingle is from that of Keats.

Sappho was universally admired, almost idolized, in antiquity, and by connoisseurs too independent and hardheaded to jump on bandwagons. What kind of poetry does come through the few intact stanzas and the many fragments? A poetry preeminently "simple, sensuous, and passionate," as Milton thought poetry, in comparison with rhetoric, ought to be. Her simplicity comes through in the word order, which is that of common sense (of impassioned common sense). Her poems are almost without literary artifice; it has been pointed out that she did not even need understatement, recently so much in vogue. Her vocabulary was simple, colloquial—she was perhaps the only Greek poet to use the very words she heard around her. One of her greatest modern editors, Edgar Lobel, says it is hard to resist the impression that her language was "nonliterary, and represents, as nearly as the nature of the case admits, the contemporary speech of her country and class." The first obligation of a translator, then, would seem to be to use words *we* really use in emotional situations. Sappho should be in colloquial—but not hey like slangy—English.

Sappho's poetry is also rich, but not lush, with sense detail, with the things of this world and the response of our senses to them. Her description of a pleasant garden, with its musical brook-water, incense, apple-branches, roses, sunlight in foliage, drowsiness, involves every one of the senses. She describes the effect of an uncomfortable love in terms of its physical symptoms: a pounding heart, chills and fever, a lump in the throat, weak knees, profuse sweat, ringing ears, blurred vision, a pallor like that of grass—the greenish pallor of Mediterranean complexions. When she says Aphrodite is ποικιλόθρον', she does not mean any vague effulgence like "on a many-splendored throne"—she refers to actual furniture, with its wood inlaid with ivory or mother-of-pearl, or gaudily painted, as early Greek artifacts indeed were, or perhaps upholstered or pillowed with fancy needlepoint. But an actual throne; she was not a poet to use expressions like "many-splendored." There is a slight dig in the word too: ποικίλος meant not only *many-colored* or *intricately made* but also suggested *cunning, contrived,* or *tricky,* as Aphrodite herself was.

Sappho is sensuous too in the music of her lines, so much praised in antiquity; in the skill with which appropriate sounds are set together so that they seem inevitable, without any little log-jams of consonants unless these are functional, as in the consonant-dense line about Aphrodite's sparrows with their densely beating wings.

Her poetry is passionate, almost exclusively about her loves and hates. Even when carried away by emotion, however, she is coolly objective about herself; sees herself as she is, with something like rueful amusement. This is the tone of her one complete poem, the hymn to Aphrodite (Number I). Sometimes mistranslated as a rather stiffly liturgical poem full of the pathos of love-longing, this is in part a poem of self-mockery. Here I am, laments Sappho, again in love, again in agony: I've been through all this before, more than once; I know I'll get over it this time too, but meanwhile it's almost more than I can bear. Even Aphrodite is mournfully amused, or rather is remembered as having been mournfully amused on other occasions: Who is it *this* time? She tries to console Sappho by pointing out how changeable lovers are, and how different it will all be tomorrow, when Sappho may not even want the love she wants now.

Reasonable guesses for the birth- and death-dates of Catullus would be 84 B.C. and 55 B.C. His poem V is translated here in eleven-syllable lines like those used for Sappho. Number VIII is done in lines of five iambic feet for his six, without the final reversed or "limping" foot. Catullus too, except in his learned poems, is a colloquial poet; it is of curious interest that he uses a word for kiss (*basium*) not known to have been used before in writing: it became the common word for kiss in most of the European languages. His tone, his colloquial but I think not slangy simplicity, makes him difficult to translate. Ezra Pound said "I have failed forty times myself" in efforts to translate Catullus; he adds that "even Landor turned back from an attempt." The failure I am most conscious of is a failure to find an equivalent for the melancholy long, long *oo* that results from the elision of the *a* of *perpetua* in "Nox est perpetu' una dormienda." And perhaps not enough is done with the burlesque bookkeeping of V with which Catullus teases his elders. The trouble here is that one can easily overdo and vulgarize: "Pay to Bearer One Hundred Thousand Kisses"—that sort of thing.

The "strangest of all Catullus's poems," as Gilbert Highet has called Number 63, is the poet's version of the story of Attis, the Phrygian fertility figure that corresponds to the Syrian Adonis. In a fit of religious mania, Attis castrates himself for Cybele. As Frazer says in *The Golden Bough:* "When the tumult of emotion had subsided, and the man had come to himself again, the irrevocable sacrifice must often have been followed by passionate sorrow and lifelong regret . . . powerfully depicted by Catullus in a celebrated poem." The galliambic rhythm, which Highet finds "fantastically difficult," is based on this metrical scheme:

$$\cup\cup-\cup\,|\,-\cup-\breve{\cup}\,\|\,\cup\cup-\cup\cup\,|\,\cup\cup\breve{\cup}$$

L. P. Wilkinson (*Golden Latin Artistry*) says it "was invented to express . . . the orgiastic dance to Cybele—the essentials beneath the variations are the anapaestic tread of the wild dance and the short rattling syllables of the tambourine or castanets at the end." These runs of short syllables sometimes led Catullus to make use of, or make up, words not found elsewhere in Latin poetry: *hederigerae, properipedem, nemoriuagus,* etc. I thought I detected a touch of irony in the way Catullus handled his subject; this suspicion of mine may show, here and there, in the diction of the translation.

Horace was born in 65 B.C.; he died in 8 B.C. He has probably been more preyed on by translators than any other Latin poet, although his extreme terseness and the interlocking effects of Latin word order offer peculiar difficulties, probably less evident in the last two poems here translated than in more famous ones. These two, both written in Sappho's stanza form, are translated in a metrically freer manner than her own are, with an attempt to give something like the swing of the rhythm, but without any exact syllabic correspondence. The first two of the four poems keep to his metrical patterns (Alcaic in the first, Fifth or Greater Asclepiadean in the second), with English stress substituting for Latin length.

The Greek text is based on *Poetarum Lesbiorum Fragmenta,* edited by E. Lobel and Denys Page (Oxford, 1955), as printed, with simpler paleographic indications and some emendations, in *Lyrica Graeca Selecta,* by D. L. Page (Oxford, 1968). Passages where the text is corrupt are obelized. I have left ἐθέλοισα in line 24 of Number 1, but have translated it as if it had the final *nu* of the accusative, which some have suggested gives us a better reading.

The Latin texts are from *Q. Valerii Catulli Carmina,* edited by R. A. B. Mynors, Oxford, 1958; and *Q. Horati Flacci Opera,* edited by E. C. Wickham and H. W. Garrod, Oxford, 1901.

375

Sappho

I

ποικιλόθρον᾽ ἀθανάτ᾽ Ἀφρόδιτα,
παῖ Δίος δολόπλοκε, λίσσομαί σε·
μή μ᾽ ἄσαισι μηδ᾽ ὀνίαισι δάμνα,
πότνια, θῦμον,

ἀλλὰ τυίδ᾽ ἔλθ᾽, αἴ ποτα κἀτέρωτα
τὰς ἔμας αὔδας ἀίοισα πήλοι
ἔκλυες, πάτρος δὲ δόμον λίποισα
χρύσιον ἦλθες

ἄρμ᾽ ὑπασδεύξαισα· κάλοι δέ σ᾽ ἆγον
ὤκεες στροῦθοι περὶ γᾶς μελαίνας
πύκνα δίννεντες πτέρ᾽ ἀπ᾽ ὠράνωἴθε-
ρος διὰ μέσσω·

αἶψα δ᾽ ἐξίκοντο, σὺ δ᾽ ὦ μάκαιρα
μειδιαίσαισ᾽ ἀθανάτωι προσώπωι
ἤρε᾽ ὄττι δηὖτε πέπονθα κὤττι
δηὖτε κάλημμι

κὤττι μοι μάλιστα θέλω γένεσθαι
μαινόλαι θύμωι· τίνα δηὖτε πείθω
†.. σαγην† ἐς σὰν φιλότατα; τίς σ᾽ ὦ
Ψάπφ᾽ ἀδικήει;

καὶ γὰρ αἰ φεύγει, ταχέως διώξει,
αἰ δὲ δῶρα μὴ δέκετ᾽, ἀλλὰ δώσει,
αἰ δὲ μὴ φίλει, ταχέως φιλήσει
κοὐκ ἐθέλοισα.

ἔλθε μοι καὶ νῦν, χαλέπαν δὲ λῦσον
ἐκ μερίμναν, ὄσσα δέ μοι τέλεσσαι
θῦμος ἰμέρρει, τέλεσον, σὺ δ᾽ αὖτα
σύμμαχος ἔσσο.

376

Sappho

I

On your throne, a marvel of art, immortal
Aphrodite, daughter of Zeus, amused to
lead us on through folly and pain—you'd doom me
    body and soul now?
Come with help, if ever in days gone-by you
heard me praying desperately in the distance—
heard and hurried, leaving your father's home to
    harness your golden
car up. Had it yoked in a moment. Gamy
sparrows flew you quick as a wink around the
dusky earth, their wings in a blur, and sky-high
    diving through cover
spiraled down here. You (your immortal features
hid a half smile stirring the dimple) asked me:
"What's it now, love? Trouble again? And this time
    why the commotion?
What's your wild heart heaving to have, I wonder,
this time? Only tell me her name, the one you'd
have me wheedle round to your love. She's being
    cruel to you, Sappho?
Running off now? Soon she'll be running after.
Won't take gifts? Tomorrow she will—and give them.
Just can't love? Tomorrow she'll love—but you'll see—
    like it or not, dear."
Even so, though! Now's when I need you. End this
tossing, turning! All that I'm mad to have, you
know so well! Then work for it, standing with me
    shoulder to shoulder.

2

δεῦρύ μ' ἐκ Κρήτας ἐπ[ὶ τόνδ]ε ναῦον
ἄγνον, ὄππ[αι τοι] χάριεν μὲν ἄλσος
μαλί[αν], βῶμοι δὲ τεθυμιάμε-
νοι [λι]βανώτωι,

ἐν δ' ὔδωρ ψῦχρον κελάδει δι' ὔσδων
μαλίνων, βρόδοισι δὲ παῖς ὁ χῶρος
ἐσκίαστ', αἰθυσσομένων δὲ φύλλων
κῶμα κατέρρει,

ἐν δὲ λείμων ἰππόβοτος τέθαλεν
ἠρίνοισιν ἄνθεσιν, αἰ δ' ἄηται
μέλλιχα πνέοισιν [   ]
[   ]

ἔνθα δὴ σὺ στέμ⟨ματ'⟩ ἔλοισα Κύπρι
χρυσίαισιν ἐν κυλίκεσσιν ἄβρως
ὀμ⟨με⟩μείχμενον θαλίαισι νέκταρ
οἰνοχόαισον

378

2

Leaving Crete, come visit again our temple,
please, for me. So holy a place, a pleasant
stand of apple trees, and the altar wreathed in
   cedary incense.
Once within, you've water that chuckles cool through
mazy apple paths, with a dusk of roses
overgrown. There's sleep in the air: the wind and
   leaves are like magic.
Once within, you've pasture for horses grazing;
Maytime flowers are rich in the grass, the friendly
heavens breathe . . . . . .
     .   .   . . .
Once within, O .   .   . adored in Cyprus,
poise and pour, by turns, in that pretty way that
you know well—rejoicing our golden cups—your
   headiest nectar .   .   .

ο]ἰ μὲν ἰππήων στρότον, οἰ δὲ πέσδων,
οἰ δὲ νάων φαῖσ᾿ ἐπ[ὶ] γᾶν μέλαι[ν]αν
ἔ]μμεναι κάλλιστον, ἔγω δὲ κῆν᾿ ὄτ-
τω τις ἔραται·

πά]γχυ δ᾿ εὔμαρες σύνετον πόησαι
π]άντι τ[ο]ῦτ᾿, ἀ γὰρ πόλυ περσκέθοισα
κάλλος [ἀνθ]ρώπων Ἐλένα [τὸ]ν ἄνδρα
τὸν [πανάρ]ιστον

καλλ[ίποι]σ᾿ ἔβα ᾿ς Τροΐαν πλέοι[σα
κωὐδ[ὲ πα]ῖδος οὐδὲ φίλων το[κ]ήων
πά[μπαν] ἐμνάσθη, ἀλλὰ παράγαγ᾿ αὔταν
[   ]σαν

[   ]αμπτον γὰρ [
[   ]... κούφως τ[   ]οη.[.]ν
..]με νῦν Ἀνακτορί[ας ὀ]νέμναι-
σ᾿ οὐ] παρεοίσας,

τᾶ]ς κε βολλοίμαν ἔρατόν τε βᾶμα
κἀμάρυχμα λάμπρον ἴδην προσώπω
ἢ τὰ Λύδων ἄρματα καὶ πανόπλοις
πεσδομ]άχεντας.

Some prefer a glory of horsemen; warships,
some; a phalanx, some—as the dark horizon's
finest sight. No—listen to me!—the best is
  what you're in love with.
Easy truth to prove to you one and all. Just
think of this: how Helen, the most delightful
girl of girls and queen to a hero, chose to
  break with that husband,
sailing off for Troy on the salty water.
Mother, father, daughter a darling—these she
stood to lose, but—irresistible impulse

     . . . . . .
  . . . . lightly . . . . .
  . . . . that's why
Anaktoria mostly I remember
  —she's gone away now.
Seeing her! her walk and the glow it gave, her
breathing cheek, alive in its light—I'd sooner
far see these than chariots of the king, than
  armor in mêlée.

φαίνεταί μοι κῆνος ἴσος θέοισιν
ἔμμεν᾽ ὤνηρ, ὄττις ἐνάντιός τοι
ἰσδάνει καὶ πλάσιον ἆδυ φωνεί-
σας ὐπακούει

καὶ γελαίσας ἰμέροεν, τό μ᾽ ἦ μὰν
καρδίαν ἐν στήθεσιν ἐπτόαισεν·
ὡς γὰρ ἔς σ᾽ ἴδω βρόχε᾽, ὤς με φώναι-
σ᾽ οὐδ᾽ ἒν ἔτ᾽ εἴκει,

ἀλλ᾽ ἄκαν μὲν γλῶσσα †ἔαγε†, λέπτον
δ᾽ αὔτικα χρῶι πῦρ ὐπαδεδρόμηκεν,
ὀππάτεσσι δ᾽ οὐδ᾽ ἒν ὄρημμ᾽, ἐπιρρόμ-
βεισι δ᾽ ἄκουαι,

†έκαδε μ᾽ ἴδρως ψῦχρος κακχέεται†, τρόμος δὲ
παῖσαν ἄγρει, χλωροτέρα δὲ ποίας
ἔμμι, τεθνάκην δ᾽ ὀλίγω ᾽πιδεύης
φαίνομ᾽ ἔμ᾽ αὔται·

ἀλλὰ πὰν τόλματον ἐπεὶ †καὶ πένητα†

There's a man, I really believe, compares with
any god in heaven above! To sit there
knee to knee so close to you, hear your voice, your
    cozy low laughter,
close to *you*—enough in the very thought to
put my heart at once in a palpitation.
I, come face to face with you even briefly,
    stand in a stupor:
tongue a lump, unable to lift; elusive
little flames play over the skin and smolder
under. Eyes go blind in a flash; and ears hear
    only their own din.
Head to toe I'm cold with a sudden moisture;
knees are faint; my cheeks, in an instant, drain to
green as grass. I think to myself, the end? I'm
    really going under?
Well, endure is all I can do, reduced to . . .

34

ἄστερες μὲν ἀμφὶ κάλαν σελάνναν
ἂψ ἀπυκρύπτοισι φάεννον εἶδος
ὅπποτα πλήθοισα μάλιστα λάμπηι
γᾶν [   ]

34

Stars around the luminous moon—how soon they
hide away their glitter of diamond light, when
she floats over, and at the full, refulgent,
   glamors the landscape . . .

55

κατθάνοισα δὲ κείσηι οὐδέ ποτα μναμοσύνα σέθεν
ἔσσετ' οὐδέ †ποκ'† ὔστερον· οὐ γὰρ πεδέχηις βρόδων
τὼν ἐκ Πιερίας· ἀλλ' ἀφάνης κἀν Ἀίδα δόμωι
φοιτάσηις πεδ' ἀμαύρων νεκύων ἐκπεποταμένα.

55 (ON A LADY INDIFFERENT TO POETRY)

You though! Die and you'll lie dumb in the dirt; nobody care, and none
Miss you ever again, knowing there's no rapture can stir your soul;
You've no love for the Muse, none for her flowers. Even in hell you'll be
Not worth anyone's glance, lost in the vague colorless drifting dead.

94

• • •

τεθνάκην δ' ἀδόλως θέλω·
ἄ με ψισδομένα κατελίμπανεν

πόλλα καὶ τόδ' ἔειπ .[
ὤιμ' ὡς δεῖνα πεπ[όνθ]αμεν·
Ψάπφ', ἦ μάν σ' ἀέκοισ' ἀπυλιμπάνω.

τὰν δ' ἔγω τάδ' ἀμειβόμαν·
χαίροισ' ἔρχεο κἄμεθεν
μέμναισ'· οἶσθα γὰρ ὥς σε πεδήπομεν.

αἰ δὲ μή, ἀλλά σ' ἔγω θέλω
ὄμναισαι[...(.)] [..(.)]..αι
..[   ] καὶ κάλ' ἐπάσχομεν·

πό[λλοις γὰρ στεφάν]οις ἴων
καὶ βρ[όδων   ]κίων τ' ὔμοι
κα..[   ] πὰρ ἔμοι περεθήκαο,

καὶ πόλλαις ὑπαθύμιδας
πλέκταις ἀμφ' ἀπάλαι δέραι
ἀνθέων .[   ] πεποημμέναις,

καὶ π.....[   ]. μύρωι
βρενθείωι .[   ]ρυ[..]ν
ἐξαλείψαο καὶ βασιληίωι,

καὶ στρώμν[αν ἐ]πὶ μολθάκαν
ἀπάλαν πα.[   ]...ων
ἐξίης πόθο[ν   ].νιδων,

κωὔτε τις [   ]..τι
ἶρον οὐδυ[   ]
ἔπλετ' ὄππ[οθεν ἄμ]μες ἀπέσκομεν,

οὐκ ἄλσος .[   ].ρος
                    ]ψοφος
                    ]...οιδιαι

94

. . . . .
Honestly I'd as soon be dead!
She's gone, tears in her eyes as they lingered last
on me, and she said . . .
"Sappho, this is our darkest day!
Heaven knows it's no wish of mine to be
leaving you!" and I answered her,
"Fare well, fare very well, and still
think of me, for you know you were cherished here.
Don't remember? Well, if you don't
I'd remind you of . . .
 . . . and how it was lovely then.
Wreathes of flowers! and the way we wove
violets . . roses
 . . . . you'd loop them round,
chains and leis of them, full festoons
draped in fragrance about your smooth
throat and shoulder. . .
and . . . . with perfume
culled from blossoms . . laid lavish on,
auras even a queen would have gloried in;
then soft beds that were spread, on those
 . . . tenderest touch . .
 . . . . you, whatever you wanted, had.
And no . . . . at all
no holy . . . . .
 . . . no occasion, with us away,
no grove . . . .
 . . . "

Catullus

V

Vivamus, mea Lesbia, atque amemus,
rumoresque senum seueriorum
omnes unius aestimemus assis!
soles occidere et redire possunt:
nobis cum semel occidit breuis lux,
nox est perpetua una dormienda.
da mi basia mille, deinde centum,
dein mille altera, dein secunda centum,
deinde usque altera mille, deinde centum.
dein, cum milia multa fecerimus,
conturbabimus illa, ne sciamus,
aut ne quis malus inuidere possit,
cum tantum sciat esse basiorum.

Catullus

V

So let's live—really live!—for love and loving,
honey! Guff of the grumpy old *harrumph!*-ers
—what's it worth? Is it even worth a penny?
Suns go under and bubble bright as ever
up but—smothered, our little light, the night's one
sudden plunge—and oblivion forever.
Kiss me! kiss me a thousand times! A hundred!
Now a thousand again! Another hundred!
Don't stop yet. Add a thousand. And a hundred.
So. Then post, sitting pretty on our millions,
sums that none—we the least—make head or tail of.
Don't let's know, even us. Or evil eyes might
glitter green, over such a spell of kisses.

VIII

Miser Catulle, desinas ineptire,
et quod vides perisse perditum ducas.
fulsere quondam candidi tibi soles,
cum uentitabas quo puella ducebat
amata nobis quantum amabitur nulla.
ibi illa multa cum iocosa fiebant,
quae tu uolebas nec puella nolebat,
fulsere uere candidi tibi soles.
nunc iam illa non uolt: tu quoque inpote[ns noli],
nec quae fugit sectare, nec miser uiue,
sed obstinata mente perfer, obdura.
uale, puella. iam Catullus obdurat,
nec te requiret nec rogabit inuitam.
at tu dolebis, cum rogaberis nulla.
scelesta, uae te, quae tibi manet uita?
quis nunc te adibit? cui uideberis bella?
quem nunc amabis? cuius esse diceris?
quem basiabis? cui labella mordebis?
at tu, Catulle, destinatus obdura.

VIII

O poor Catullus, stupid long enough!
See what's before your face now: gone is gone.
Once how the sunlight sparkled, gorgeous weather
When you went strolling out with her, a girl
Loved as no other ever was or will be.
Fun enough then, the things we did together,
Some that I thought of first; she nodded, laughing.
Then how the sunlight sparkled—gorgeous weather.
Now she'll have none of it. Be tough yourself;
Don't tag as she goes gadding; don't sit moping.
Learn to stand staunch, learn courage to endure.
Tell her: Good-bye, girl. Show her what you're made of.
Tell her right out: Don't need you; won't come begging.
Then you'll be sorry, never hearing from me,
Wondering—damned, abandoned—what's to live for.
Who'll hover round you? Coo about your beauty?
Who's he, the new man? Who'll your name be linked with?
Your lips on—whose? teeth, teasing tongue—O stop it,
Stupid Catullus! Stubborn soul, endure.

Paene insularum, Sirmio, insularumque
ocelle, quascumque in liquentibus stagnis
marique uasto fert uterque Neptunus,
quam te libenter quamque laetus inuiso,
uix mi ipse credens Thuniam atque Bithunos
liquisse campos et uidere te in tuto.
o quid solutis est beatius curis,
cum mens onus reponit, ac peregrino
labore fessi uenimus larem ad nostrum,
desideratoque acquiescimus lecto?
hoc est quod unum est pro laboribus tantis.
salue, o uenusta Sirmio, atque ero gaude
gaudete, uosque, o Lydiae lacus undae,
ridete quidquid est domi cachinnorum.

XXXI

Jewel of the almost islands and the isles,
Whichever, Sirmio, by sweetwater lakes
Or the wide ocean versatile Neptune holds,
Oh but I'm glad to see you once again!
Hardly believing, even myself, I'm back
Now safe and sound from remote plains of Asia.
What greater joy on earth than, duties done,
All pressure off a mind still overtired
With gadding aggravations, to come home
And, on the bed long dreamed of, sink to rest?
Just that, just that alone, is compensation.
Greetings, enchanted spot; be glad I'm back.
Chuckle with joy; cavort, Etruscan waters;
If the old home can laugh, let's hear it now.

LXIII

Super alta uectus Attis celeri rate maria
Phrygium ut nemus citato cupide pede tetigit
Adiitque opaca siluis redimita loca deae,
Stimulatus ibi furenti rabie, uagus animis
Deuoluit ili acuto sibi pondera silice.
Itaque ut relicta sensit sibi membra sine uiro,
Etiam recente terrae sola sanguine maculans
Niueis citata cepit manibus leue typanum,
Typanum, tubam Cybelles, tua, mater, initia,
Quatiensque terga tauri teneris caua digitis
Canere haec suis adorta est tremebunda comitibus.

'Agite ite ad alta, Gallae, Cybeles nemora simul,
Simul ite, Dindymenae dominae uaga pecora,
Aliena quae petentes uelut exsules loca
Sectam meam exsecutae duce me mihi comites
Rapidum salum tulistis truculentaque pelagi
Et corpus euirastis Veneris nimio odio,
Hilarate erae citatis erroribus animum.
Mora tarda mente cedat; simul ite, sequimini
Phrygiam ad domum Cybelles, Phrygia ad nemora deae,
Vbi cymbalum sonat uox, ubi tympana reboant,
Tibicen ubi canit Phryx curuo graue calamo,
Vbi capita maenades ui iaciunt hederigerae,
Vbi sacra sancta acutis ululatibus agitant,
Vbi sueuit illa diuae uolitare uaga cohors,
Quo nos decet citatis celerare tripudiis.'

Simul haec comitibus Attis cecinit notha mulier,
Thiasus repente linguis trepidantibus ululat,

ATTIS

Over oceans sped he, Attis, in the speediest of the ships,
Till ashore by Phrygian forests, feet impetuous with desire,
He drew near the gloomy purlieus of the goddess within the wood,
There, his mind at sixes, sevens, he, hysterical in his zeal,
With a flintstone cropped his pendules, the appurtenance of his groin,
Whereupon he, sensing there where once luxuriance was, a lack,
And the earth around him spangled with a bounteousness of blood,
He—a she now—lily fingers on the shivery tambourine,
Tambourine, your music, Cybele, in the mysteries of your cult,
Diddled with it, delicate touches on the leatheriness of bulls,
And began to sway and singsong, in a rapture amid the troop:

"On your feet now! Scurry, she-priests, off to Cybele on the heights,
All together, gadding cattle of the Lady of Dindymon,
Herds that sought a foreign haven, like all wanderers of the earth,
You, companions of The Way here, you, stampeding about my heels,
Who endured the foaming ocean and the truculence of the tide,
Lost your lappets, loathing Venus, all that languoring in morass,
Come, delight the Lady's spirit by our snake-dance into the woods,
Not a thought to spare for dawdling, all together and after me
To her Phrygian home, the Lady's, Phrygian woodlands of the Queen,
Where the brassy cymbal shivers, where there's jangle of tambourines,
Where the Phrygian flutist hoohoos through the flues of the embouchure,
Where the Maenads shake wild tresses and the ivy on their batons,
Where they celebrate the mysteries, ululating with hoots of glee,
Shadowy figures flitting, fading, all the revelry of the Queen,
There it leads, our tarantella, in an ecstasy all the way."

She no sooner sang so, Attis, only by legerdemain a she,
Than her cronies yowled and yodeled, riffing tremolos off the tongue,

Leue tympanum remugit, caua cymbala recrepant,
Viridem citus adit Idam properante pede chorus.
Furibunda simul anhelans uaga uadit animam agens
Comitata tympano Attis per opaca nemora dux,
Veluti iuuenca uitans onus indomita iugi:
Rapidae ducem secuntur Gallae properipedem.
Itaque, ut domum Cybelles tetigere lassulae,
Nimio e labore somnum capiunt sine Cerere.
Piger his labante langore oculos sopor operit:
Abit in quiete molli rabidus furor animi.

Sed ubi oris aurei Sol radiantibus oculis
Lustrauit aethera album, sola dura, mare ferum,
Pepulitque noctis umbras uegetis sonipedibus,
Ibi Somnus excitam Attin fugiens citus abiit:
Trepidante eum recepit dea Pasithea sinu.
Ita de quiete molli rapida sine rabie
Simul ipsa pectore Attis sua facta recoluit,
Liquidaque mente uidit sine quis ubique foret,
Animo aestuante rusum reditum ad uada tetulit.
Ibi maria uasta uisens lacrimantibus oculis
Patriam adlocuta maesta est ita uoce miseriter:

'Patria o mei creatrix, patria o mea genetrix,
Ego quam miser relinquens, dominos ut erifugae
Famuli solent, ad Idae tetuli nemora pedem,
Vt apud niuem et ferarum gelida stabula forem
Et earum omnia adirem furibunda latibula,
Vbinam aut quibus locis te positam, patria, reor?
Cupit ipsa pupula ad te sibi derigere aciem,
Rabie fera carens dum breue tempus animus est.
Egone a mea remota haec ferar in nemora domo?
Patria, bonis, amicis, genitoribus abero?
Abero foro, palaestra, stadio, et gymnasiis?
Miser ah miser, querendum est etiam atque etiam, anime.

Once again the tambourines growl, send the cymbals into a fit,
All are off for green Mount Ida, with a giddiness in their feet;
In a frenzy, madly gasping, Attis, reeling and out of breath,
Tambourine her leman, bolts through the obscurities in the wood,
As a heifer, young, unbroken, from intolerance of the yoke,
On her heels the light-foot gaggle, femininity of the feres;
So they came, depleted creatures, to the dwelling of Cybele,
Dropped to earth in sudden slumber, too exhausted even to eat,
Such a lassitude possessed them, eyelids drooping languorously,
All their savagery of spirit evanescing in bland repose.

But: when golden-featured Sol rose, all effulgence, and with his gaze
Had surveyed the luminous heaven, solid earth, untamable sea,
Had repelled night's tenebrosity with his clippity-clopping steeds,
Then the god, old Sleep, abandoned Attis wakening with a jolt
(And returned to bed, old Sleep did, to his palpitant Pasithee);
So from mild repose enjoying a remission of pulsing rage,
Attis, in a flash, took notice what was missing and where she was;
With her soul on fire that instant, she went barreling to the shore,
Stared there on the waste of waters through a mistiness of her tears,
To her homeland cried, forlorn one, in extremity of despair:

"Native land, my procreatrix, land engendering all I am,
Land I fled from, to my sorrow, much as runaway servants do
From their lord, then off to Ida, off to the backwoods, sticks and stones,
Here to sort with floe and snowdrift, shaggy denizens in their dens,
Here to haunt in my dementia every hollow in which they lurk,
Where now on the wide horizon lies the country of my desire?—
Homeland which my eyes are straining in anxiety to behold
While, this little while, my reason's perturbation is at a lull.
I—be harried far from homeland, from my world to away in woods?
From my lares and penates, mother, father, and every friend?
Bustling malls! the turf for wrestling! and the stadium! and the gym!
What am I to say but *misery?* moaning it over and over again.
In what role, what form or figure, wasn't I fated to be cast?

Quod enim genus figurae est ego non quod obierim?
Ego mulier, ego adulescens, ego ephebus, ego puer,
Ego gymnasi fui flos, ego eram decus olei:
Mihi ianuae frequentes, mihi limina tepida,
Mihi floridis corollis redimita domus erat,
Linquendum ubi esset orto mihi sole cubiculum.
Ego nunc deum ministra et Cybeles famula ferar?
Ego maenas, ego mei pars, ego uir sterilis ero?
Ego uiridis algida Idae niue amicta loca colam?
Ego uitam agam sub altis Phrygiae columinibus,
Vbi cerua siluicultrix, ubi aper nemoriuagus?
Iam iam dolet quod egi, iam iamque paenitet.'

Roseis ut huic labellis sonitus citus abiit
Geminas deorum ad aures noua nuntia referens,
Ibi iuncta iuga resoluens Cybele leonibus
Laeuumque pecoris hostem stimulans ita loquitur,
'Agedum' inquit, 'age ferox i, fac ut hunc furor agitet,
Fac uti furoris ictu reditum in nemora ferat,
Mea libere nimis qui fugere imperia cupit.
Age caede terga cauda, tua uerbera patere,
Fac cuncta mugienti fremitu loca retonent,
Rutilam ferox torosa ceruice quate iubam.'
Ait haec minax Cybelle religatque iuga manu.
Ferus ipse sese adhortans rabidum incitat animo,
Vadit, fremit, refringit uirgulta pede uago.
At ubi umida albicantis loca litoris adiit
Tenerumque uidit Attin prope marmora pelagi,
Facit impetum: ille demens fugit in
    nemora fera:

Ibi semper omne uitae spatium famula fuit.

Dea magna, dea Cybelle, dea domina Dindymi,
Procul a mea tuus sit furor omnis, era, domo:
Alios age incitatos, alios age rabidos.

Woman now . . . once man and handsome . . . youngster once . . . once
   even a tad;
I—the idol of gymnasia! I—a glory in gloss of oil!
On my porch the assembled lovers, warming the marble where they lolled,
And the floral greetings! wreathing every pillar about the place,
When at dawn I left my sanctum and went striding away for fair.
I—a temple wench forever? Still at Cybele's beck and call?
I—a Maenad? half-me only? man in figure and never a man?
I—confined to Ida's verdure—what there is of it under the snow?
I—to drag out life forever beneath Phrygia's beetling peaks?—
Woods with the elk for population, brush for the rummaging of boars.
Now I pay for all my folly; now I'm sorry I carried on."

As the speedy sound-waves rippled from the tremor of rosy lips,
Bringing news that raised their eyebrows, the forever attentive gods,
Cybele unyoked the lions that had been drowsing at her side,
Chose the left one, death on oxen, got his attention with a kick,
"Now go get him! Be your meanest, frighten him out of his blessed mind,
Frighten him into holy terror, drive him driveling into the woods.
So he thought to escape my mandate! Liberation he had in view!
We'll see. Flail your tail about you, knout of it swashing flank to flank,
Turn the region topsy-turvy with reverberant roar on roar,
With the earthquake of your shoulders fanning a wildfire in your mane."
So, with mind all menace, Cybele then let go of the rein in her fist.
Meanness in his genes, the lion worked himself into a foaming rage,
Flashed and thundered, split to kindling tracts of forest wherever he went,
Till, come rampant on damp beaches, whitecaps luminous on the strand,
He, in sight of Attis quivering by marmoreal fonts of sea,
Charged! Half out of his mind, poor Attis made a run for it toward
   the woods.

Made his bed for good, did Attis. Serving now as a nervous nun.

O divine and mighty, Cybele! Dindymon's lady—dame and doom!
Spare my home your visitation; I've no relish to be possessed.
Spur the others to fey elation; no mad dogs in the house for me.

LXX

Nulli se dicit mulier mea nubere malle
   quam mihi, non si se Iuppiter ipse petat.
dicit: sed mulier cupido quod dicit amanti,
   in uento et rapida scribere oportet aqua.

LXX

My girl says she'll take no one else as a lover.
    No one else—she says—even if Jove were to coax.
Says! but the words they say, those girls, to their panting lovers,
    Write on the giddy wind. Write on the stream as it flows.

LXXV

Huc est mens deducta tua mea, Lesbia, culpa
   atque ita se officio perdidit ipsa suo,
ut iam nec bene uelle queat tibi, si optima fias,
   nec desistere amare, omnia si facias.

LXXV

Now my mind's been brought to such a state—and it's your fault,
    Lesbia!—been so skewed by its devotion to you,
I couldn't like you again, if you turned truest of women;
    Yet couldn't fall out of love, not for the worst you could do.

LXXXV

Odi et amo. quare id faciam, fortasse requiris?
nescio, sed fieri sentio et excrucior.

LXXXV

Her that I love, I hate! "How's that, do you know?" they wonder.
Know! What's "know"? I *feel*. Ask any crucified man.

Horace

I, IX

Vides ut alta stet nive candidum
Soracte, nec iam sustineant onus
    silvae laborantes, geluque
        flumina constiterint acuto.
dissolve frigus ligna super foco
large reponens atque benignius
    deprome quadrimum Sabina,
        o Thaliarche, merum diota:
permitte divis cetera, qui simul
stravere ventos aequore fervido
    deproeliantis, nec cupressi
        nec veteres agitantur orni.
quid sit futurum cras fuge quaerere et
quem Fors dierum cumque dabit lucro
    appone, nec dulcis amores
        sperne puer neque tu choreas,
donec virenti canities abest
morosa. nunc et campus et areae
    lenesque sub noctem susurri
        composita repetantur hora,
nunc et latentis proditor intimo
gratus puellae risus ab angulo
    pignusque dereptum lacertis
        aut digito male pertinaci.

Horace

I, IX

You see how, white with snows to the north of us,
Soracte looms; how snow's over everything:
 the burdened pines no longer buoyant,
   streams at a stand in the winter weather.
So, rout the cold! Load logs on the andirons
as good hosts should do. Logs! And no rationing
 your wine, young fellow there! Your Sabine,
   hustle it out from the crusty wine-jars.
Then let the heavens see to the rest of it.
When once they've lulled the winds at their weltering
 on whitened surf, no cypress quivers,
   never a breath in the ancient alder.
What comes tomorrow, never you mind about.
Each day on waking reckon, "Another!" and
 chalk up your one more gain. Don't spurn the
   pleasure of love in your time for dancing,
while youth's in bloom, while moody decrepitude's
remote. Now haunt the malls and the stadium.
 When little whispers stir in starlight,
   make very sure you arrange to be there,
where—who's in hiding?—giveaway laughter from
the dark, a girl's laugh, muffled . . . lovely . . .
 her bracelet tussled for in fun, or
   ring from a teasingly tightened finger.

Tu ne quaesieris, scire nefas, quem mihi, quem tibi
finem di dederint, Leuconoe, nec Babylonios
temptaris numeros. ut melius, quidquid erit, pati,
seu pluris hiemes seu tribuit Iuppiter ultimam,
quae nunc oppositis debilitat pumicibus mare
Tyrrhenum: sapias, vina liques, et spatio brevi
spem longam reseces. dum loquimur, fugerit invida
aetas: carpe diem, quam mimimum credula postero.

Don't ask—knowing's taboo—what's in the cards, darling, for you, for me,
what end heaven intends. Meddle with palm, planet, séance, tea leaves?
—rubbish! Shun the occult. Better by far take in your stride what comes.
Long life?—possible. Or—? Maybe the gods mean it your last, this grim
winter shaking the shore, booming the surf, wearying wave and rock.
Well then! Learn to be wise; out with the wine. Knowing the time so short,
no grand hopes, do you hear? Now, as we talk, huffishly time goes by.
So take hold of the day. Hugging it close. Nothing beyond is yours.

Parcius iunctas quatiunt fenestras
iactibus crebris iuvenes protervi,
nec tibi somnos adimunt, amatque
    ianua limen,
quae prius multum facilis movebat
cardines; audis minus et minus iam
'me tuo longas pereunte noctes,
    Lydia, dormis?'
invicem moechos anus arrogantis
flebis in solo levis angiportu,
Thracio bacchante magis sub inter-
    lunia vento,
cum tibi flagrans amor et libido,
quae solet matres furiare equorum,
saeviet circa iecum ulcerosum,
    non sine questu
laeta quod pubes hedera virenti
gaudeat pulla magis atque myrto,
aridas frondis hiemis sodali
    dedicet Hebro.

I, xxv

Ribald romeos less and less berattle
your shut window with impulsive pebbles.
Sleep—who cares?—the clock around. The door's stuck
    stiff in its framework,
which once, oh how promptly it popped open
easy hinges. And so rarely heard now
"Night after night I'm dying for you, darling!
    You—you just lie there."
Tit for tat. For insolent old lechers
you will weep soon on the lonely curbing
while, above, the dark of the moon excites the
    wind from the mountain.
Then, deep down, searing desire (libido
that deranges, too, old rutting horses)
in your riddled abdomen is raging
    not without heartache
that the young boys take their solace rather
in the greener ivy, the green myrtle;
and such old winter-bitten sticks and stems they
    figure the hell with.

Vlla si iuris tibi peierati
poena, Barine, nocuisset umquam,
dente si nigro fieres vel uno
    turpior ungui,
crederem. sed tu, simul obligasti
perfidum votis caput, enitescis
pulchrior multo iuvenumque prodis
    publica cura.
expedit matris cineres opertos
fallere et toto taciturna noctis
signa cum caelo gelidaque divos
    morte carentis.
ridet hoc, inquam, Venus ipsa, rident
simplices Nymphae, ferus et Cupido,
semper ardentis acuens sagittas
    cote cruenta.
adde quod pubes tibi crescit omnis,
servitus crescit nova, nec priores
impiae tectum dominae relinquunt,
    saepe minati.
te suis matres metuunt iuvencis,
te senes parci, miseraeque nuper
virgines nuptae, tua ne retardet
    aura maritos.

If for all the promises you regard so lightly
one, *one* penalty ever held, Varina,
should one tooth darken, even a torn toenail
    leave you less smooth, dear,
yes, I'd trust you. But when you can swear with
"God strike me dead!" and falsify it, Lord you're
lovelier yet, as you parade. The whole male
    populace wants you.
You swear by your poor mother's corpse and
right away two-time; swear by every sign, by
heaven itself, and by the very gods, those
    durable persons.
This, I assume, amuses even Venus,
amuses nymphs (good simple souls) and callous
Cupid, forever honing up hot steel on
    his bloody whetstone.
What's more, all the adolescents love you;
droves of new callers come; their predecessors
never stamp from the house of the proud lady
    much as they vow to.
Mothers worry for their husky youngsters;
dad for bank accounts; nice girls at the altar
(poor things) brood, for fear they'll soon be groaning
    "Where is that husband?"